Bloom's Modern Critical Views

Bloom's Modern Critical Views

AFRICAN-AMERICAN POETS

Volume 1: 1700s–1940s
New Edition

Edited and with an introduction by
Harold Bloom
Sterling Professor of the Humanities
Yale University

BLOOM'S
LITERARY CRITICISM
An imprint of Infobase Publishing

Bloom's Modern Critical Views: African-American Poets, Volume 1—New Edition
Copyright © 2009 by Infobase Publishing
Introduction © 2009 by Harold Bloom

Bloom's Literary Criticism
An imprint of Infobase Publishing
132 West 31st Street
New York NY 10001

Library of Congress Cataloging-in-Publication Data
African-American poets : volume 1: 1700s–1940s / edited and with an introduction by Harold Bloom. — New ed.
    p. cm. — (Bloom's modern critical views)
  Includes bibliographical references and index.
  ISBN 978-1-60413-400-1
 1. American poetry—African American authors—History and criticism.
2. African Americans—Intellectual life.   3. African Americans in literature.
I. Bloom, Harold.   II. Title.   III. Series.
  PS310.N4A355 2009
  811.009'896073—dc22   2008054305

Contributing editor: Portia Weiskel
Cover designed by Takeshi Takahashi

Printed in the United States of America
IBT IBT 10 9 8 7 6 5 4 3 2 1

This book is printed on acid-free paper.

Contents

Editor's Note

My introduction appreciates the eloquence of our earlier major African-American poets: Paul Laurence Dunbar, Claude McKay, Jean Toomer, Sterling Brown, Langston Hughes, and Countee Cullen.

The apprentice phase of Robert Hayden is studied by Pontheolla T. Williams, while B. J. Bolden considers the onset of Gwendolyn Brooks.

Toomer and McKay, both outsiders to the Harlem Renaissance, are seen in the context of literary modernism by Wolfgang Karrer, after which James Smethurst chronicles the political development of Langston Hughes.

Dunbar's and James Weldon Johnson's experiments in dialect are surveyed by Caroline Gebhard, while Frances Smith Foster reviews the history of collaborative efforts by African-American poets.

Bardic tradition, from Phillis Wheatley to Frances Harper, is outlined by Keith D. Leonard, after which Paula Bernat Bennett details the revision of Dunbar by Lizelia Moorer, Maggie Johnson, and the Thompson sisters.

Lena Ahlin's subject is the poets of the Harlem Renaissance and their relationship to a beautiful icon, Josephine Baker, while Emily Bernard narrates the Black Arts Movement's rebellion against "whiteness" in the Harlem Renaissance.

James Smethurst juxtaposes Cullen and Hughes, after which this volume ends with an appreciation of Wheatley by April C.E. Langley.

HAROLD BLOOM

Introduction

1

Paul Laurence Dunbar was the first major African-American poet and, in my judgment, remains one of the truly authentic poets of his American generation, which included Edwin Arlington Robinson, Trumbull Stickney, Edgar Lee Masters, James Weldon Johnson, and the earlier work of Robert Frost. Dead at thirty-five (tuberculosis augmented by alcoholism), Dunbar essentially wrote in the skeptical strain of Shelley, except in dialect poems. He inherited from Shelley an agonistic spirit, expressed strongly in "The Mystery," one of his undervalued poems, where he deliberately echoes "To a Skylark": "I fain would look before / and after, but can neither do." Caught in an unhappy present for a black poet, Dunbar concludes "The Mystery" with memorable eloquence:

> I question of th'eternal bending skies
> That seem to neighbor with the novice earth;
> But they roll on and daily shut their eyes
> On me, as I one day shall do on them,
> And tell me not the secret that I ask.

The secret is the mystery of being an eternal novice, a kind of Promethean complaint, which leads to what may be Dunbar's best poem, "Ere Sleep Comes Down to Soothe the Weary Eyes." The fifth of the six stanzas is an epitome of how intensely Dunbar can transcend his situation and its limitations:

> Ere sleep comes down to soothe the weary eyes,
> How questioneth the soul that other soul,—

1

The inner sense which neither cheats nor lies,
But self exposes unto self, a scroll
Full writ with all life's acts unwise or wise,
In characters indelible and known;
So, trembling with the shock of sad surprise,
The soul doth view its awful self alone,
Ere sleep comes down to soothe the weary eyes.

"That other soul" or "awful self" is what the early African-American Baptists called "the little me inside the big me," a spark or breath that is no part of nature or history. After eleven repetitions of: "Ere sleep comes down to soothe the weary eyes," we are startled by the poem's closing line, where "seal" replaces "soothe." In his perpetual struggle between bitterness and the Shelleyan wisdom of casting out personal remorse, Dunbar most frequently yields to a bitterness that transcends his personal sorrows.

One of the lucid voicings of that bitterness is Dunbar's memorial sonnet to Robert Gould Shaw, the Harvard College colonel who commanded the black 54th Massachusetts Regiment in its suicidal attack on Fort Wagner (near Charleston) in July 1863. The sonnet's sestet laments the sacrifice of Shaw and his African-American recruits, in a skepticism still relevant today:

Far better the slow blaze of Learning's light,
The cool and quiet of her dearer fane,
Than this hot terror of a hopeless fight,
This cold endurance of the final pain,—
Since thou and those who with thee died for right
Have died, the Present teaches, but in vain!

Dunbar's emblematic poem remains "Sympathy," popularized by Maya Angelou's autobiographical appropriation of "I know why the caged bird sings!" Though Dunbar's High Romantic lyricism has long been unfashionable, his achievement in it remains considerable.

2

The Jamaican Claude McKay, who went from Marxism to Roman Catholicism, was a fierce spirit, whose sonnets have a formalist, baroque intensity that is also now undervalued, as here in "Saint Isaac's Church, Petrograd":

Bow down my soul in worship very low
And in the holy silences be lost.

Bow down before the marble man of woe,
Bow down before the singing angel host.

What jewelled glory fills my spirit's eye!
What golden grandeur moves the depths of me!
The soaring arches lift me up on high
Taking my breath with their rare symmetry.

Bow down my soul and let the wondrous light
Of Beauty bathe thee from her lofty throne
Bow down before the wonder of man's might.
Bow down in worship, humble and alone;
Bow lowly down before the sacred sight
Of man's divinity alive in stone.

This is still the admirer of Leon Trotsky, but the poem's complexity arises out of McKay's repressed awareness that something in his spirit is moving toward conversion. The sestet retreats from the octave's spirituality and overtly hymns an aesthetic humanism. And yet "The marble man of woe," a representation of the Russian Christ, is not wholly consonant with "man's divinity alive in stone."

The most rugged of McKay's poems is "The Desolate City," a Romantic lament for the lost innocence of the spirit and another indication of this poet's road to Rome. It may be that McKay, poetically speaking, was born at the wrong time, but too late rather than too early. For all his political anger, which has an authority difficult to withstand, he would have been culturally at home in the Catholicism of Gerard Manley Hopkins and Francis Thompson, a generation earlier than his own.

3

Jean Toomer's remarkable *Cane* (1923), a subtly interwoven medley of prose poem and verse, was never matched by him again in the more than forty years remaining. *The Blue Meridian* (1929) fades away in contrast with Hart Crane's *The Bridge* (1930), though Toomer and Crane were friends, and some mutual influence was involved. Toomer's immersion in quack spiritualities was fatal both to his work and his sense of identity. And yet, in his brief flowering, he became the authentic poet of what would have to be called black pastoral, as in his marvelous "November Cotton Flower":

Boll-weevil's coming, and the winter's cold,
Made cotton-stalks look rusty, seasons old,

And cotton, scarce as any southern snow,
Was vanishing; the branch, so pinched and slow,
Failed in its function as the autumn rake;
Drouth fighting soil had caused the soil to take
All water from the streams; dead birds were found
In wells a hundred feet below the ground—
Such was the season when the flower bloomed.
Old folks were startled, and it soon assumed
Significance. Superstition saw
Something it had never seen before:
Brown eyes that loved without a trace of fear,
Beauty so sudden for that time of year.

This extraordinary lyric is both beautifully wrought and humanly profound. The late blooming of the flower becomes emblematic of a freedom from psychic death, the freedom to love.

4

Sterling Brown, at his frequent best, was able to assimilate the strong influences of A.E. Housman, Thomas Hardy, and Robert Frost and to fuse them in a mode of his own. I should say "modes," for this eclectic poet had several voices, very much his own. The Frostian "Idyll" juxtaposes a sheltered woodland cranny with an intrusive hawk and sees the deep peace return after the hawk's kill, giving the reader the burden of the final irony: "The stream purred listlessly along, / And all grew quite as peaceful as before."

In another mode developed from Hardy, Brown gives us the poignant "Rain," a remarkable transformation of the sonnet form:

Outside the cold, cold night; the dripping rain . . .
The water gurgles loosely in the eaves,
The savage lashes stripe the rattling pane
And beat a tattoo on November leaves.
The lamp wick gutters, and the last log steams
Upon the ash-filled hearth. Chill grows the room.
The ancient clock ticks creakily and seems
A fitting portent of the gathering gloom.

This is a night we planned. This place is where
One day, we would be happy; where the light
Should tint your shoulders and your wild flung hair.—

Whence we would—oh, we planned a merry morrow—
Recklessly part ways with the old hag, Sorrow . . .

Outside dripping rain; the cold, cold night.

After that wonderfully gloomy octave, there is the fine poetic shock of "This is a night we planned." The speaker is solitary, erotic loss is overwhelming, and yet everything proceeds by indirection. Thomas Hardy, with his acute sense of life's ironies, might have admired Sterling Brown's "Rain," which precedes Robert Penn Warren in reviving Hardy's spirit.

5

The historical and cultural importance of Langston Hughes is unassailable. Though a number of African-American poets have developed their art more fully (Robert Hayden, Jay Wright, and Thylias Moss among them), Hughes wrote a populist poetry (like Carl Sandburg's) to serve the needs of a wider audience. Hughes's acknowledged mentors—Sandburg and Paul Laurence Dunbar—had a generous social vision and a particular sense of the place of poetry in that vision. Something authentic and powerful almost always struggles to break through into adequate form in Hughes's poetry. The struggle makes him perhaps more of a process poet than a finished craftsman, but the process is large and central and of value in itself.

"The Weary Blues," a pioneer effort to fuse formal poetry and oral tradition, seems to carry some reference to Hughes's personal isolation: "I got the Weary Blues/And I can't be satisfied." Whatever his sexual orientation (and it remains ambiguous), Hughes chose personal solitude, which is frequently the burden of his lyrics.

"The Negro Speaks of Rivers," possibly Hughes's most famous poem, has a fairly subtle undersong. The "ancient, dusky rivers," as deep as the black soul, become all but identical with the speaker, and yet they are "older than the flow of human blood in human veins." The repetition of "human" marks an origin before our universal condition, of whatever race. What is best (by implication) and oldest in the poet goes back before the Creation-Fall of Christianity and hints at Hermetic or Gnostic myth. Hughes, a secular poet, possessed a thwarted religious sensibility, which found expression in his love for, and identification with, his people. That identification tended to exclude Christianity, most memorably in the bitter "Song for a Dark Girl" where: "I asked the white Lord Jesus / What was the use of prayer." The "Song"'s conclusion seems to me Hughes's most eloquent lyric moment: "Love is a naked shadow / On a gnarled and naked tree." Realistically, as a representation of a lynching, that is vivid enough, but again there may well be an undersong, prompted by the poetic will that Rampersad has explicated so usefully. Hughes intimates another Gnostic myth, which is that only a shadow, and not the man Jesus, died upon the cross. A naked cross may be an empty one, and the Gnostics insisted that the authentic Jesus mocked at his supposed immolation. Hughes was a very complex person, split between a sophisticated consciousness and a fierce determination to create a popular and simplified poetic art. His own spirituality may have been more esoteric than we imagine.

6

I have a particular fondness for Countee Cullen, as I do for Edwin Arlington Robinson, who was a benign influence on Cullen's art, showing him how to be at once Keatsian and oneself. Like Robinson and Keats, Cullen was a highly self-conscious artist who knew that moral concerns could sink a poem without trace. Answering those who would make him only a "protest poet," Cullen eloquently prophesied for the best African-American poets after him in his "To Certain Critics":

> No radical option narrows grief,
> Pain is no patriot,
> And sorrow plaits her dismal leaf
> For all as lief as not.

That wry pun upon "leaf" and "lief" is wonderfully typical of Countee Cullen and is part of his legacy.

PONTHEOLLA T. WILLIAMS

Robert Hayden:
The Apprenticeship:
Heart-Shape in the Dust *(1940)*

Critical notice of *Heart-Shape in the Dust*, at the time of its appearance, did not exceed a few paragraphs in primarily non-literary magazines, and none of the reviewers came to grips with Hayden's concerns in any but vague and unsupported terms. "A new and vigorous talent . . . promising . . . only other challengers Sterling Brown and Langston Hughes," wrote William Harrison in his favorable *Opportunity* review.[1] He notes the enthusiastic reception that a London audience gave to a reading of "Gabriel," one of Hayden's first Afro-American history poems, but he leaves the reader to speculate whether the response was to the work or the oral interpretation. He lists three poems he considers "best" and praises Hayden's command of moods, language, and originality of expression.

James W. Ivy's short, generally unenthusiastic review in *Crisis* credits Hayden with having lyrical ability and a sensitivity to the wrongs done his race, but he attacks many of the poems as banal and lacking in real poetic fire.[2] He considers "Autumnal" best, calls five other poems noteworthy, and concludes that Hayden is a poet worth watching. Both reviews are characterized by reservations, but both recognize some potential.

Recent criticism of *Heart-Shape in the Dust* is limited to the generally superficial remarks of anthology introductions, which place the work in the lyric tradition and mention the author as a proletarian writer of the thirties.[3]

From *Robert Hayden: A Critical Analysis of His Poetry*, pp. 37–51, 222–223. © 1987 by the Board of Trustees of the University of Illinois.

7

The volume is out of print now, and Hayden did not include any of the poems in subsequent collections, not even in his *Selected Poems*.

Heart-Shape in the Dust contains forty-six poems; eleven are unrevised reprints from his 1938 prize-winning Hopwood Collection, which had also been published in various magazines.[4] While the volume is an apprentice's experimentation with modes and idioms, is often stylistically derivative, and makes use of topical Marxist themes, it points, in its feeling for Afro-American history, its feeling for subjects that are not cast in terms of race, and in its sense of the general literary tradition, toward the central qualities of his mature work.

While the major thematic concern in *Heart-Shape in the Dust* is the social condition of blacks during the Great Depression, Hayden's interest in Afro-American history surfaces in several places. One can see how these two themes interact and are unified by comparing statements in poems which deal with the purpose of the black poet. In "To a Young Negro Poet" (p. 14), which uses the simple images and declarative sentences characteristic of his early style, he says:

> Make me a song, O dark singer,
> Brimming with the laughter of honest men
> And the beauty and laughter of valiant women;
> A song with the heart-beat
> Of inarticulate millions in it.

Those "inarticulate millions" are, of course, America's neglected, scorned, and undereducated blacks. And in "Dedication" (p. 15), he says that to be that "heart-beat" the poet must

> Clasp their hands, O poet, touch their hands
>   and know the ultimate meaning of your own.
> Pray that a new prayer shall be given unto them
>   and a new fulfillment; let their prayers
> Lie like a lover on your heart. Wrestle with them
>   as with angels and learn their gathering strength.

The sensual imagery ("clasp," "touch," "Lie like a lover on your heart," and "wrestle") exhorts the poet to intimate knowledge of the race based on emotional involvement with its people. The role of the black poet, however, extends beyond that of song maker and spokesman for "inarticulate millions." In "What Is Precious Is Never to Forget" (p. 52), the poet becomes the keeper of racial history—a history which must be understood if there is to be strength to bear the present and hope for the future—and his role is to speak *to* those millions:

> This is the spirit's true armament,
> Heart's true program of defence—
>
> That we remember the traveled roads of our history,
> That in the stream of heroic yesterdays
> We find those spas which shall renew our strength.

He remembers those "traveled roads" in "Gabriel" (pp. 23–24). It is the only poem in *Heart-Shape in the Dust* on a specific black historical subject, but it is the first of several poems Hayden was to write about major black cultural heroes, such as Cinquez, Harriet Tubman, Nat Turner, Frederick Douglass, and Malcolm X.[5]

The poem treats the last minutes of Gabriel Prosser, a slave who was hanged in 1800 for leading an uprising in Virginia.[6] It is a dialogue, in ballad form, between the speaker of the poem and the hero, who is about to be executed, but the applications to the time Hayden wrote the piece are obvious. The speaker asks Gabriel to reveal the future, and he foresees

> a thousand,
> Thousand slaves
> Rising up
> From forgotten graves.

In light of communist influence, it is not difficult to see those many slaves as spirits infusing their descendants with determination to strike a blow in the cause of freedom. Certainly these lines are revolutionary:

> The blow I struck
> Was not in vain,
> The blow I struck
> Shall be struck again.

Whether or not Hayden's treatment of his topic was indeed a response to the party line, the ballad meets certain requirements of a communist strategy which held that American blacks constitute a separate nation, complete with cultural heroes.

Hayden's early social concerns, in any case, are focused primarily on the spectre of lynching, which is either the subject or the subject of key allusions in over one-fourth of the poems in the book. In all of this group he treats lynching in symbolic relationship to God, man, and government. He probes the consciousness of those who often had the closest tie to the victim: the women, whether black or white.

For example, in "BROWN GIRL'S SACRAMENT," part 1 of "Religioso" (pp. 39–40), he evokes the bereavement of the lynching victim's beloved, and in part 2 he treats the grief of the victim's mother. In the girl's vision, her lover's death blends with the crucifixion of Christ, and the mother's lament evokes the image of Mary mourning for the crucified Jesus. The crucifixion motif, popular with members of the Wright generation and, still earlier, with Countee Cullen and Langston Hughes, suggests the inhumanity of the act of lynching and the universality of the suffering of women.

Two poems treat the white woman as the real or alleged victim of rape, a crime for which, in southern custom, the penalty was lynching. In "Southern Moonlight" (p. 16), Hayden examines the strength of sexual desire in an interracial relationship by showing the inadequacy of social taboos as a restraint on the human will. Indeed, it is the white lover who sings in incantation to the moon:

> That none may see—
> Oh, moon, moon, hide your light—
> That he is black
> And I
>
>   am white.

The second poem, "Diana" (p. 43), exposes the danger inherent in such an interracial relationship. When Diana is discovered with her black lover, she screams in panic, thus insuring his ritualistic death, for the "keepers of the white rose" must

> Expunge with fire
> the tainting hands
> of the black man-beast,
> the sexual eyes
> of the satyr.

She, too, however, is a victim, for she is the real creature of desire. In the first place, she is driven by the lure of the black-stud myth to deliberately seduce her lover while she bathes "naked / amid [the] oleanders" (lines 6–7). Again, she exercises the queen-like privileges of her "whiter womanhood."

It is a role Hayden makes clear in the subtitle to the poem: "An exercise in southern mythology." It is a mythology kept operative by the "lords of purity"—a phrase that evokes what W. J. Cash calls Southern New Chivalry.[7] As a violated woman, as well as a racial symbol, she must be avenged. The interpretation of her scream as the anguish of the rape victim rather than as a reaction to the horror of discovery, and the ugly myths about the black man—he is "man-beast," a "satyr" with "sexual eyes"—set the ritual in operation for the "keepers of the white rose" who "Flay, rend, burn." What makes her a victim, of course, is that, seduced by myth to work seduction, her position and her fears compel her to act out her role as victim, thus violating humanity as she herself was not, indeed, violated.

While a poem like "Diana," which is a humanistic consideration of moral relationships, may well stir moral indignation, "Speech" (p. 27) treats lynching in terms of the labor movement. Here the poet sees it as a tool for stirring up racial animosity among the proletariat. He indicts as one and the same "the hand / Holding the blowtorch / To the dark anguish-twisted body" and "the hand / Giving the high-sign / To fire on the white pickets" (lines 5–8). In this context lynching is a means of preventing the workers of the world from uniting; the old ritual provides a convenient pretext for the modern entrepreneur.

Whatever the specific cause of a lynching, the practice becomes for Hayden a symbol of the situation of blacks in America. On one level there is the simple, stark horror. In part 7 of "These Are My People" (pp. 56–63), in lines that recall the chanting of the witches in *Macbeth*—perhaps to emphasize the ritualistic motivation of the lynch mob—he creates a vivid picture of violence and madness:

> Fire and rope
> and stone and goad,
> a black body dragged
> down a southern road.
> Moon and stars
> in the southern skies,
> and the light gouged out
> of the black boy's eyes.
> The wind dream-talking
> on a southern hill,
> and the lynch-lust voices
> crying: kill kill kill.
>   (p. 61)

In part 8 he treats the Scottsboro Case, which leads to the view of martyrdom as America's macabre reward for the labors of black people:

> O black man ploughing
> the American earth,
> gathering a harvest
> of blood and dearth.
>   (P. 62)

In "Coleman," subtitled "Negro veteran murdered by the Black Legion"
(p. 45), Hayden condemns America for accommodating such "tolerated weeds
of murder" (line 11). The poem, which is based on a real crime,[8] sees lynching
as a ritual aimed at genocide—if not physical, then certainly spiritual. The
lynching, Hayden asserts, is a symbolic act whereby "Through one they strike
at the heart of our world" (line 10).

In "The Negro to America" (p. 26), he epitomizes the paradox, or contradiction, of the black experience in a democracy by pointing to lynching as
the negation of the fundamental right to due process of law:

> You are not free
> So long as there's
> A mortgage on
> My liberty;
> So long as I die
> On the Klansman's tree,
> You are not
> Democracy.

Lynching, which went on well into the twentieth century, was primarily a
southern phenomenon; yet it was foremost in the minds of the Afro-American masses everywhere.

During the Depression, which is the period Hayden treats in *Heart-
Shape in the Dust*, the self-consciousness was also shaped and defined by the
economic landscape, in which, as Seymour Gross says, the black man was "the
most dislocated and deprived figure."[9] "Sunflowers: Beaubien Street" (p. 12)
is perhaps Hayden's most successful depiction of the black slum-dweller's
ability to overcome his degradation and allay what he suffered from dislocation and deprivation. The Beaubien Street setting is biographically authentic,
for the street was actually a part of his old neighborhood, where sunflowers
seemed to grow anywhere with little or no care.[10] Hayden develops them into
a major symbol which represents the black people who lived there.

Dual themes operate throughout this important poem. One is revealed in the Afro-Americans' sense of displacement from, and longing for, the South—their "cruel, sweet" memories of the South they loved, yet prayed to escape; the other is displayed in images of the despair and poverty they experienced in the North, yet tried to allay by planting sunflowers.

1   The Negroes here, dark votaries of the sun,
2   Have planted sunflowers round door and wall,
3   Hot-smelling, vivid as an August noon.
4   Thickets of yellow fire, they hold in thrall
5   The cruel, sweet remembrance of Down Home.

6   O sun-whirled, tropic tambourines
7   That play sad juba songs in dooryard loam,
8   Recalling chain-gang heat and shimmering pines;
9   O sunward cry of dark ones mute within
10   The crumbling shacks: bright image of their will
11   To reach through prayer, through long belief the sun
12   Fixed in heavens like Ezekiel's Wheel.

13   Here phonographs of poverty repeat
14   An endless blues-chorale of torsioning despair—
15   And yet these dark ones find mere living sweet
16   And set this solid brightness on the bitter air.

In the first stanza the sun is a vital force in the lives of the "dark votaries." They cultivate the sunflower which both evokes the "cruel, sweet" remembrance of "Down Home" and protects them from the pain of remembering. The smell, heat, and color of the South are evoked in the synaesthetic imagery of lines 3 and 4, especially in the words "Hot-smelling" and "yellow fire."

Stanza 2 develops specific dimensions of the tension involved in the oxymoron, "cruel, sweet remembrance." In lines 6 and 7 the "sweet" memory of the South they knew flows into the older memory of Africa. From this perspective, "juba" is particularly evocative since it is both the name of a river in Africa and a dance popular with the slaves. On the other hand, the "cruel" is defined in evocation of "chain-gang" labor that is not eased by climatic conditions and, perhaps, the equally oppressive turpentine camps typical of certain sections in the South, where it becomes so hot the pines seem to shimmer in the sun. The sunflower image functions as a symbol of the "bright image of their will," a will that undergirds the transplanted African's hard-won Christian faith. Indeed, in lines that reveal a poignant element of the black man's acculturation in America, visual and spiritual values of the sunflower-sun symbol join with "Ezekiel's Wheel," a symbol of God's message of hope to Ezekiel and his people, a symbol that transcends place.

The last stanza shifts the focus from the South back to Beaubien Street. In contrast to the domesticity, warmth, and hope which dominates the sunflower imagery of the first stanzas, that of the third stanza is steeped in the atmosphere of the blues. Through alliteration, consonance, assonance, and onomatopoeia, Hayden makes effective use of verse texture to support the sense that the stanza conveys. The alliterative consonants and the assonant vowels together with the onomatopoeic "blues-chorale" and "torsioning despair" serve to evoke the sometimes harsh, choked-up frustration and wailing despair that characterize the blues. The blues ambience achieved here speaks of the unremitting personal agony in the slum dwellers' collective lives. They have not, in arriving at Beaubien Street, reached the "sun." It is only their hope, symbolized by the sunflowers, that enables them to endure—and even find "living sweet." To borrow Ralph Ellison's phrase, the poem owes its success to its realization of "both the agony of life and the possibility of conquering it through sheer toughness of [the] spirit."[11]

The Beaubien Street lyric is Hayden's first published poem that utilizes the sunflower image, which was to grow in importance as a symbol of the Afro-American lower classes with whom he became preoccupied. Also, the poem is one of two in the *Heart-Shape* volume that initiates a sharp imagistic pattern and is hence a departure from the direct narration characteristic of the other poems in the book.

The "dislocation" and "deprivation" theme is the subject of other poems in the volume—poems which seem to be the target of Harrison's gentle criticism that the book has "faint echoes of past and contemporary masters."[12] In "Shine, Mister?" (p. 42) and in "Bacchanale" (p. 44), the "faint echo" seems to emanate from the poetry of Langston Hughes. Failing to find work, the character in "Shine, Mister?" shines shoes, sings the "no-job blues," and schemes to leave town. The unemployed worker in "Bacchanale" drinks gin because the "factory closed this mawnin" and he "drawed that last full pay." Both men are reminiscent of Hughes's singer in "Evening Air Blues," who comes "No'th to find work, but who [chaws] de mornin air" for breakfast and decides to "do a little dancin / Just to drive [his] blues away."[13] In both of the Hayden poems, the diction is closer to Hughes's model than to the more naturalistic diction he developed later, for example, in "The Dream."[14] In his later work, he adopts an idiom that suggests the flavor of southern speech in general, rather than a too literal imitation of black speech. This contrast of Hayden's blues lyrics to those of Hughes, however, should not be stressed too greatly. Lacking Hughes's ability to orchestrate authentically the musicality and the mood of the blues, Hayden fails to exhibit Hughes's virtuosity, which is the point that justifies the Harrison criticism. At least in his early work, he takes too many liberties with the form.

As we have seen, Hayden exhibits a great sensitivity to the oppression of his people and their struggle to overcome it. It is not surprising, therefore, to find in *Heart-Shape in the Dust* two poems which clearly express a suicidal view of things, and perhaps even a death wish. In "Monody" (p. 33), a rhymed lyric of two quatrains, the speaker expresses his despair over continuing what he feels to be a hopeless struggle:

> Better the heart should yield and fall, have done
> With these ignoble battles never to be won;
> Better the heart should be at rest that goes
> In bannered march around unyielding Jerichos.

The "unyielding Jerichos" are, of course, those of the familiar Afro-American spiritual, "Joshua Fit de Battle of Jericho."[15] Popular with the slaves because of the message of hope it carries, and feared by the masters because of its threat to them,[16] the spiritual is one in which slaves compared their predicament in America with that of the dispossessed Israelites. While the speaker in "Monody" is cognizant of the parallels between unemployed American blacks and the Israelites, he does not foresee crumbling walls and prefers death to empty dreams.

In "Sonnet to E." (p. 31), the second death-wish poem, the speaker is obsessed with the "starless times when [he] . . . longed to join the alien hosts of death."

> 1   Beloved, there have been starless times when I
> 2   Have longed to join the alien hosts of death,
> 3   Have named death father, friend, and victory
> 4   More sweet than any triumph of the breath.
> 5   In hours extreme with weeping and despair
> 6   That turned my valor's blunted sword to rust
> 7   And tore the pennons of my strength from air
> 8   To lie in crumpled heart-shape in the dust—
> 9   Oh, in such hours death has seemed a kind
> 10   And balsam-handed lord . . . But not again,
> 11   By any gentle mask death has designed,
> 12   Shall I be fooled; I see his cunning plain,
> 13   Since love with generous wisdom tutors me
> 14   To see what hitherto I could not see.

The speaker is apparently overwhelmed by the same spirit of hopelessness which overcame him in "Monody," and the military imagery of lines 6 and 7 suggests that he is here engaged in similar battles.

The "crumpled heart-shape in the dust" is an allusion to the fourth stanza of Elinor Wylie's poem "Hospes Comesque Coparis" (Guest and Companion of [my] Body).[17] The fourth stanza of the Wylie poem states her aspirations before her death, namely, to be remembered by a flowering of creativity. Hayden's use of the word "crumpled" before the quotation, however, serves as an ironic implication of the speaker's emasculation. Likewise, the lexical ambiguity of the word "pennons," line 7, which may mean either *flags* or *wings*, adds to the reader's perception of his incapacity. If the word means *pinion*, it suggests that the speaker has been stopped in flight like a bird with a broken wing, that he has fallen to earth "crumpled." On the other hand, if the word means *flag* or *banner*, given the military allusions in the poem, it may mean his courage has been so subdued he feels his fight useless and prefers the sweetness of death to the ignominy of defeat. While the speaker repents his suicidal thought in lines 9 and 10, he immediately recalls his objection to it in lines 10 and 12.

Lines 13 and 14 assert the poet's resolve to achieve a broader understanding of those forces—forces that had caused him to take a militant stance and had so "blunted [his] valor" that he fell "crumpled," and momentarily regarded death as a release. Clearly, it is "E." (his beloved Erma) who brings about his rejection of death and his broader understanding.

One may read the sonnet as a love poem, structured along the lines of Shakespeare's "When in disgrace with fortune and men's eyes," where the thought of the "dear friend" dispels gloom. It is a typical Elizabethan device to speak of vast important things then shift the focus so that the beloved object stands out against them and reduces them to relative insignificance. In this poem, despite the noble battle itself and despite the speaker's reaction to apparent defeat, the beloved is finally seen as more important than all of it. Thus the death wish serves, ultimately, in her praise.

Heart-Shape in the Dust is by no means restricted to racial themes and subjects. While the fact of Hayden's racial identity and the fancies of Communist party strategy combined to infuse his art with an unmistakable ethnic flavor, at the same time his concerns were broadly humanistic and cosmopolitan, and these too found expression in his early work.

From 1933 onward, Hitler's assumption of power, the rise of Japanese militarism, and Mussolini's successful African campaign struck reflective men with apprehension. Year by year the brutal drama moved from one scene to another—Manchuria, Ethiopia, Spain, Shanghai, Austria, Czechoslovakia. The importance of these events soon became obvious in American letters.

According to Robert Spiller, such world catastrophes changed the national attitude from isolationism to internationalism,[18] and Hayden's views coincided with this attitude.

It was the Spanish Civil War that captured the tardy interest of "reflective men," who should have been alerted by the earlier Italian invasion of Ethiopia.[19] According to Jerre Mangione, prominent members of the Federal Writers Project adopted the cause of the Loyalists against Franco, with strong participation provided by members in the New York, California, and Chicago Projects.[20] About this period Hayden met Langston Hughes, who was covering the activities of Afro-American volunteers in the International Brigades in Spain as a war correspondent for the Baltimore *Afro-American*.[21] This milieu of political concern, together with his longstanding interest in the Spanish language and culture, aroused the spirit of internationalism in Robert Hayden.

The philosophic focus of Hayden's World War II poems derives from the grim irony apparent in news headlines which juxtapose the season of rebirth with sterility and death. The first poem, entitled "Words This Spring" (p. 17), uses such a headline as its epigraph: "It is believed that the war will really get under way with a big offensive in the spring." Imagery in the first stanza evokes the human suffering which modern warfare imposes on its victims:

> The metal rumor of the skies
> Signals a fatal spring,
> Sets streamlined terrors burgeoning.
> Spring's schedules bring
> No pastoral silences, no wreathing cries
> Of birds—but steel and dum-dum agonies.

In the second stanza, however, the allusion to Robert Herrick's "Corinna's Going A-Maying" introduces an ironic *carpe diem* theme. The allusion, of course, is meant to be grotesque in that it further points up the subversion of the natural order:

> And when a-maying fair Corinna goes,
> She picks her way among the dead—
> Finds instead
> Of posies in the grass, a stark death's head.
> She wears a gas-mask, fair Corinna does,
> And thinks of spring's first air-raid while
> > seeking spring's first rose.

"The Mountains" (p. 25), too, is concerned with man and nature, but the emphasis is shifted away from the irony involved in the death-dealing confrontations of a military spring. Whereas in "Words This Spring" Hayden stresses the disruption of nature by uncontrollable forces entirely of man's making, in "The Mountains" he depicts nature as itself an uncontrollable force over which man establishes at best an uncertain dominion. Thus, even in the midst of his preoccupation with very real concerns, both domestic and international, Hayden can, even at this early stage in his poetic development, give artistic attention to questions which affect man in a generic sense and are philosophical and timeless, rather than merely topical, and couched in the language and allusion of the general poetic tradition rather than the black and Marxist tradition many were trying to create.

> There were mountains in that place:
> They hemmed us round,
> A dusk-green storm,
> Motionless, without sound.
>
> At night we felt
> The blacked-out ranges near—
> A winged shadow, vast,
> Upon the atmosphere.
>
> Once in the imminent dark
> We heard the crash of ledges
> And knew time danced
> Upon the mountains' edges.
>
> The mountain mornings
> Arched over us,
> Intense, bronze-green,
> And perilous;
>
> And we were drowned
> And sucked down under
> Unfalling waves
> Of rock-leashed thunder.

These impressions emanate from a speaker who is accompanied in the mountains by a silent companion for an evening, night, and morning. The poem merits discussion because it evinces both a knowledge of and an ironic stance toward certain Romantic conventions—a stance that characterizes much of his later work. The choice of language clearly suggests that nature is an intimidating force, divided from men.

In stanza 1 the pair are imprisoned—"hemmed in"—by the power that is represented by the mountains. In stanza 2 they feel the mountains as a dominating "winged shadow." They experience a threatening darkness, listen to the "crash of ledges," and realize their own frailty and transience in stanza 3. The coming of daylight in stanza 4 serves only to clarify and delineate more sharply that which they sensed the night before—that is, they are "arched over," not just "hemmed . . . round." In the last stanza they are symbolically "drowned / And sucked down under" (lines 17–18), entombed, overcome by their fear of the natural world whose forces are beyond their control.

The poem recalls both Wordsworth's "The Simplon Pass" and Shelley's "Mont Blanc." The central point in each poem is man in relation to nature—man's response to natural objects, mountains. However confusedly and imitatively, according to F. R. Leavis, who compared "Mont Blanc" with "The Simplon Pass,"[22] in reference to the mountain's awesome contrasts, Shelley makes the point that "the everlasting universe of things / Flows through the mind" (lines 1–2). Extending the metaphor, he raises the issue of power as manifested by the Arve River, fed by Mont Blanc, and makes the point that nature's indiscriminate power can be harnessed by the enlightened human will for constructive human ends. In "The Simplon Pass," Wordsworth details dreadful contrasts—"the tumult" and "peace," "darkness" and "light"—that he encounters in the mountain pass. Unlike Shelley in "Mont Blanc," Hayden does not attempt to show the ascendancy of man's mind in its power to control the forces of nature. Nor does he make the attempt to show, as Wordsworth does, that his speaker's sense of the "perilous," of being "sucked down under," his dread of the "blackness of night," the "brightness of day" are, as Wordsworth puts it, "workings of one mind"—"features of the same face" (lines 16–17).[23] However, in conveying nature's intimidating force and its essential separateness from man, Hayden's stand is ironic and twentieth-century.

While *Heart-Shape in the Dust* is not a great work, and while its major concerns are topical and heavily influenced by the racial, social, political, and international currents of the day, it does reveal Robert Hayden as a poet determined to draw on those sources relevant to his artistic vision, whatever they might be. It is the work of a man passionately involved in the history and fate not only of his own people, but of all people. The new symbols, such as the sunflower, stir and challenge his poetic imagination throughout. "Sunflowers: Beaubien Street" and "Gabriel" are especially significant in this connection. He is willing to make his point in the dialect of the Afro-American, but even at this early stage, he is clearly aiming at an art free of the topical concerns in current fashion or his own ethnic identity. Thus he is not totally controlled by the Marxist world view and obviously sees art itself as very important. Those "echoes" that Harrison hears contain the voices of Shakespeare, Shelley, and Keats, as well as Hughes. While they are obviously, and often blatantly, imitative, they hint at Hayden's eventual synthesis of his own concerns with the poetic tradition.

NOTES

1. William Harrison, "A New Negro Voice," *Opportunity* 19, no. 3 (March, 1941): 91.

2. James W. Ivy, "Concerning a Poet and a Critic," *Crisis* 48, no. 4 (April, 1941): 128.

3. Arthur P. Davis, *From the Dark Tower: Afro-American Writers—1900 to 1960*, pp. 174–80; Turner, *Black American Literature: Poetry*, p. 6; Arthur P. Davis and Saunders Redding, eds., *Cavalcade: Negro American Writing from 1760 to the Present*, p. 385.

4. See the Chronological Bibliography of Hayden's work at the end of this volume.

5. Hayden's *Selected Poems* contains poems about Cinquez ("Middle Passage," pp. 65–70), and Harriet Tubman ("Runagate Runagate," pp. 75–77) as well as "The Ballad of Nat Turner," pp. 72–73, and "Frederick Douglass," p. 78. Hayden's *Words in the Mourning Time* contains "El-Hajj Malik El-Shabazz," which is about Malcolm X. All these poems also appear in *Angle of Ascent* and *Collected Poems*.

6. Thomas Wentworth Higginson, "Gabriel's Defeat," *Atlantic Monthly* 10 (September, 1862): pp. 338–41.

7. W. J. Cash, *The Mind of the South*, pp. 84–86, 115–17, 128. Cash bases the centrality of the white woman in gyneolatry on (1) the fear conquered people entertain of their women being raped, (2) southern white woman being identified with the South itself—the belief in her enormous remoteness from the black man, and (3) the fact that the abolition of slavery opened up in the minds of all white southerners a vista at the end of which was the right of their sons in the legitimate line to be born to a pure white heritage.

8. Hayden, interview, July 4, 1973.

9. Seymour Gross and John Edward Hardy, *Images of the Negro in American Literature*, p. 16.

10. Hayden, interview, August 14, 1973.

11. Ralph Ellison, "Richard Wright's Blues," *Black Expression*, ed. Addison Gayle, Jr., pp. 311–25.

12. Harrison, "A New Negro Voice": 91.

13. Langston Hughes, "Evening Air Blues," in Emanuel and Gross, *Dark Symphony*, p. 207. See also Hughes, *Shakespeare in Harlem*, p. 40, especially "Out of Work."

14. Hayden, "The Dream," *Words in the Mourning Time*, pp. 12–13, *Angle of Ascent*, pp. 36–37, *Collected Poems*, pp. 66–67. Intending only to approximate what they perceived to be black idiom, both poets use phonological spelling—that is, omission of /g/s, simplification of consonant clusters, loss of /r/ sounds in final position, and the redundant use of the pronoun *me* to establish possession.

15. Langston Hughes and Arna Bontemps, eds., *Book of Negro Folklore*, p. 300.

16. Sterling Brown, *Negro Poetry and Drama and the Negro in American Fiction: Studies in American Life*, pp. 18–19.

17. Elinor Wylie, "Hospes Comesque Coparis," *Collected Poems of Elinor Wylie*, p. 124; see also p. viii for the poet's own explanation. The stanza follows:

> And the small soul's dissolving ghost
> Must leave a heart-shape in the dust
> Before it is inspired and lost
> In God: I hope it must.

Wylie based her lyric on the Latin original, which, according to Burton Stevenson (*The Home Book of Quotations*), is taken from the life of Emperor Hadrian: "Gentle little soul, hastening away, my body's guest and comrade, wither goest thou now, pale, fearful, pensive, not jesting as of old?" The title of Wylie's poem was translated by Howard D. Langford.

18. Spiller, *Literary History of the United States*, pp. 1253–62.

19. One of the first of these "reflective men," of course, was Ernest Hemingway, who became journalistically involved on behalf of the Spanish Loyalists in 1936. See Sculley Bradley and others, *The American Tradition in Literature* 2:1453–55.

20. Mangione, *The Dream and the Deal*, pp. 128–31, 176–78.

21. Milton Meltzer, *Langston Hughes, A Biography*, pp. 207–17.

22. F. R. Leavis, "Shelley," *English Romantic Poets: Modern Essays in Criticism*, ed. M. H. Abrams, pp. 345–65.

23. William Wordsworth, "The Simplon Pass," in *The Poetical Works of Wordsworth*, pp. 109–10; Percy Bysshe Shelley, "Mont Blanc," *The Complete Works of Shelley*, Cambridge ed. (Boston: Houghton Mifflin Co., 1901), pp. 347–49.

B.J. BOLDEN

Gwendolyn Brooks:
The 1940s: A Milieu for Integrationist Poetics

Gwendolyn Brooks, like many women poets, often wrote under challenging, and sometimes adverse conditions, considering the oppositional demands of artistry and domesticity. Given that as a point of discussion, *Annie Allen* raises certain questions.[1] Why did Brooks opt to approach the story of women—motherhood, daughterhood, womanhood—from such a complex technical perspective? Who constructed the artistic proving ground that demanded such a grueling exercise in prosody, language, and imagery? What were the rewards? What, in essence, were the conditions, social and literary, contributing to her need to create a framework of a classical mock-epic as the vessel for a colloquial tale?

The social and literary climate of Brooks' second book of poetry, *Annie Allen* (1949), was strategically impacted by the new spirit of optimism emanating from the postwar period of the 1940s. In "New Poets," Margaret Walker gives a brief but succinct overview of the historical setting in which Black writers came to "unusual prominence as poets" (345). The strong note of social protest, brought about by racial oppression and war, was especially evident in the poetry published between 1935 and 1945: Brooks' *A Street in Bronzeville* (1945), Robert Hayden's *Heart-Shape in the Dust* (1940), Margaret Walker's *For My People* (1942), and Melvin Tolson's *Rendezvous with America* (1944).[2] But as the social and economic status of Black Americans

From *Urban Rage in Bronzeville: Social Commentary in the Poetry of Gwendolyn Brooks, 1945–1960*, pp. 59–71, 178–182. © 1999 by Barbara Jean Bolden.

23

reflected some small measure of the prosperity generated by the New Deal and World War II, protest poetry began to level off in the late 1940s as a reflection of that optimism (Walker 348).

In an interview with Ida Lewis, Brooks comments on how she viewed the Black world in the 1940s and 50s: "I thought that integration was the solution. All we had to do was keep on appealing to the whites to help us, and they would" (*RPO* 175). Likewise, there was no question in her mind as to the identity of the target audience for her poetry: "It was whites who were reading and listening to us" (*RPO* 176). The "us" Brooks refers to in a 1940s context would have included her literary peers, Hayden, Walker, and Tolson. In her essay, "Poets Who are Negroes," Brooks clarifies the literary gauntlet that had been thrust in front of the Black writer:

> no real artist is going to be content with offering raw materials. The Negro poet's most urgent duty, at present, is to polish his technique, his way of presenting his truths and his beauties, that these may be more insinuating, and therefore, more overwhelming. (312)

A. P. Davis examines the period of transition in America that informed the works of Black writers in the 1940s in his essay "Integration and Race Literature." The "spiritual climate" of the country was pro-integration, and early attempts were visible in the armed forces, Southern graduate and professional educational institutions, and in extended voting rights (607). Davis notes that in the days of rampant discrimination and segregation, the 1920s and 30s, Black writers, fueled by the hostile efforts of their "common enemy" to resist all efforts at integration, "capitalized on oppression" in their creative endeavors of the 1940s (607). In *Black Writers of America*, Richard Barksdale and Keneth Kinnamon identify "the Black writer's need to write out of the context of the Black experience," and note that "Richard Wright's experience as a Black creative artist in America revealed that Black literary expression was inextricably linked to Black political, social, and economic experience" (654). The new mood of integration, while still controversial in many quarters of American life, gained a sufficient foothold, sending writers who had previously relied on the voice of protest in their literature to search for new thematic and aesthetic ground.[3]

Following the example of Harvard scholar Alain Locke, who provided critical direction to the writers of the Harlem Renaissance, a fresh school of Black scholars surfaced in the 1940s and 50s to formulate new critical theories, quite at variance with the old ones.[4] Barksdale and Kinnamon perceptively assert that based upon their training in Southern Black colleges, these energetic and articulate young critics used "objective precision," as opposed to the "hortatory eloquence" of Locke in the formulation of their critical opinions and undauntingly "applied the critical standards of the white literary establishment" (654). The "incisive criticism" of these literary "mainstreamers," especially J. Saunders Redding, Hugh Gloster, and Nick Aaron Ford, was a definitive statement of their contention that the goal of the Black writer should be "full integration into the mainstream of American life" (655).

In his essay, "Race and the Negro Writer," Gloster affirms his position as a staunch idealist for integration by outlining the ways in which an effusive use of "racial subject matter has handicapped the Negro writer" (369). He sees the Black writer as falling literary prey to the menace of "certain critics and publishers" who would "lure him into the deadly trap of cultural segregation by advising him that the Black ghetto is his proper milieu and that he will write best when he is most Negroid" (369). For Gloster, the alternative is a "gradual emancipation . . . from the fetters of racial chauvinism and cultural isolation" made possible by what he sees as a climate of democracy in America's literary melting pot (370).

Gloster offers an optimistic prognosis for Black writers to assimilate into mainstream white society by correcting the negative trend of culturally segregated writing that he feels has sorely "retarded" their artistic growth. He suggests that Black writers strive to lift their work to the "universal plane" by transcending the color line as Wright did in *Native Son* and create a literature that celebrates "all mankind" (370).[5] In his quest to nudge the Black writer from a posture of "ethnic individuality" to his own lofty ideal of a "universal point of view" (371), Gloster closes his essay with the bugle call of patriotism for the Black writer to become an American writer:

> The Negro writer is also an American writer, a man of letters as free as any of his national confreres to tap the rich literary resources of our land and its people. To accept the principle that racial experience is the only natural province of the Negro writer is to approve an artistic double standard that is just as confining and demoralizing in American literature as is segregation in American life. (371)

Gloster's critical posture favoring integration was not unusual at a time when Black writers hoped that America would become a united nation, rather than remain a divided one. In the same issue of *Phylon*, J. Saunders Redding, in the densely worded, but optimistic essay, "The Negro Writer—Shadow and Substance," shares a vision of hope for integration and encouraged Black writers to take advantage of "the social and intellectual and spiritual climate of Roosevelt's New Deal and of the world's second war," as an impetus for a change in outlook (372). Like Gloster, Redding earmarks a universality in writing about the human—not the Black—condition, yet asserts that the highest goal a Black writer can attain is an obscure "realistic idealism and a sort of scientific humanism" (372). Oddly, though Redding calls for Black writers to liberate themselves from their "racial chains" because they are "in no fundamental way different and particular," conversely, he ends his essay with a call to them to observe their "special category of race-experience" to uncover "a mine of creative material" (373).

Nick Aaron Ford issued the most balanced and polished statement on the debate, in direct refutation of the pure integrationist theories posited by Gloster and Redding. Different in tone and perspective, Ford's essay, "A Blueprint for Negro Authors," is stark in its simplicity: "despite one hundred and ninety years of effort, no American Negro poet has achieved a status comparable to such first-rate poets as Robert Frost or Edwin Arlington Robinson" (374). Having first issued the explicit challenge of achieving technical excellence in literature, Ford offers the "harassed author" clearly enumerated guidelines to attain a "master of craftsmanship" (374). Ford's basic premise is that although Black artists must not be compelled to forfeit their racial consciousness, they must subordinate any tendency to usurp art with pure propaganda. But, rather than displaying unqualified support for the tenet of "art for art's sake," Ford requires that social propaganda, as indicative of the time, not be ignored, but skillfully woven into the fabric of artistic patterns, as a "legitimate ingredient of serious literature" (376).

The weakness of Ford's essay is that, though he draws attention to the dearth of excellence in Black poetry, his real interest, or perhaps expertise, is situated in the technical aspects of fiction writing for examples of what he views as "chief weaknesses ... in the area of craftsmanship and design" (374). Yet his crucial point is crystal clear; Black writers, both poets and fiction writers, must excel in the quest for technical proficiency by cloaking the ever-present message of social commentary within the folds of craftsmanship. Ford's primary criteria for alleviating what he views as an artistic deficiency are the creative characterization, inventiveness of conversation, and construction of setting and mood apparent in the fictional works of Richard Wright and Willard Motley, without forfeiting cultural nuances and racial themes.[6]

In a tone of subtly veiled sarcasm, Ford brusquely dismisses the notion that Black writers should avoid racial themes and material, "and leave to white authors the exploitation of subject matter dealing with Negro life" (375). To challenge that view, he suggests: "I cannot believe that a Negro, sensitive, as all artists must be, can feel and understand anything in America as minutely and as truthfully as he can the effects of race" (375). But the reality of the influence of integration efforts facing the conscious artist was clear; as A. P. Davis writes in his essay: "protest writing has become the first casualty of the new racial climate" (608). Black fiction writers like Zora Neale Hurston, Richard Wright, Ann Petry, and Chester Himes, who had successfully published early works out of a clear racial milieu, dutifully responded to the literary dictum to elevate their works to a universal plane, representing the essence of all humanity, by issuing later works that were clearly explorations in white themes and characterizations.[7] These "universal" works did not receive the critical acclaim alluded to by the new school of critical forecasters, nor did they move the redefined Black writers into the full status of white Americans. Instead, much of the literature, focusing on the obstacles common to all humanity, died a quiet death of literary exclusion.

Despite Ford's oversight in the poetic genre, the literary and critical mandate he established for Black fiction writers, albeit unwittingly, reached the ears of the poets, whose artistic response was to create poetry with a global perspective. The tone of racial indignation that clings to Hayden's *Heart-Shape in the Dust* (1940), in poems like "Gabriel (Hanged for leading a slaved-revolt)" and "We Are the Hunted," was dramatically altered in the ornate diction and lavish imagery of lines from "A Ballad of Remembrance": "the sallow / vendeuse / of prepared tarnishes and jokes of nacre and / ormolu," as testament to his growing poetic maturity and freedom from racial mandates by the time he published *The Lion and the Archer* (1948). Tolson moved from the jarring protest of poems like "Rendezvous with America" and "Dark Symphony" in *Rendezvous with America* (1944), to a sophisticated metrical diversity in his ode, *Libretto for the Republic of Liberia* (1953) that subverted and neutralized his tone of protest. Likewise, Gwendolyn Brooks made a radical departure from the overt focus on the poverty and oppression gripping the lives of Black people in *A Street in Bronzeville* (1945) to a heightened metrical sophistication, an experimental approach to language, and an allusive use of imagery that camouflaged her social commentary about the lives of Black women in *Annie Allen* (1949).

The literary explorations of Brooks, Hayden, and Tolson support the contention that Black writers did strive to manipulate their poetics into an acceptable mode that would be well received by their white literary peers and audiences. The efforts of Black writers to join the white literary mainstream is evidenced by the words of Davis: "In an all-out effort to make integration become a reality, the Negro writer will tend to play down the remaining harshness in Negro American living and to emphasize the progress towards equality" (611). And in a failed prophecy, Redding's vision of assimilation of the Black writer by white culture signals the ultimate hope of integration: "the Black writer had found a white audience."[8] Although later found to be in err, the Zeitgeist of the time supported the general critical consensus that Black

writers could actually assimilate into American literary life with no remaining traces of their distinctive cultural identity. But Barksdale and Kinnamon
counter the optimistic perception of America's integrationist practices: "For,
in the 1940s, despite the legal gains made on all fronts to win hitherto with-
held political and social rights, America was still, literarily speaking, almost
entirely lily-white" (654).

That Black writers not only heard the bell toll for proposed integration in
America, but responded to its inviting ring, is evident and worthy of examination in the technical expertise exhibited in the subsequent works of Hayden,
Tolson, and Brooks. Similarly, each of the poets wielded the razor-sharp points
of his or her poetic quill to carve a distinctive niche in the white mainstream
poetics of America. Though immediately responding to the ongoing critical
dictate to assimilate into the mainstream of Western cultural tradition, the
noted poets, in varying degrees, were also struggling against the vise of concrete
racial definitions that had long threatened artistic individuality.[9]

Hayden, especially, swam against the tide of rhetoric directed at the question of racial identification, related to whether or not a Black artist must be
labeled a "Black poet," as illuminated in Langston Hughes' 1926 essay, "The
Negro Artist and the Racial Mountain." Hughes saw a growing tendency for
white indoctrination in the artistic expressions of Black poets and confronted
it by challenging them to define themselves by the richness of their own cultural heritage: "We younger Negro artists who create now intend to express
our individual dark-skinned selves without fear or shame" (180). He attempted
to combat a growing "urge toward whiteness" and "an aping of things white" in
some Black artists by offering his own self-definition of being a "Black poet"
who used the nuances of Black life as inspirations for writing:

> Most of my own poems are racial in theme and treatment, derived
> from the life I know. . . . So I am ashamed for the black poet who
> says, 'I want to be a poet, not a Negro poet,' as though his own
> racial world were not as interesting as any other world. (180)

Paradoxically, while the reality of the anthology Hayden edited, *Kaleidoscope: An Anthology of Negro Poets* (1967), admits to a need for an identifiable
collection of Black literature "shaped over three centuries by social, moral,
and literary forces essentially American," in its introduction, Hayden argues
against such racial classifications. His resistance to being labeled a "Negro
poet," as polar opposite to Hughes, is clear in his statement:

> But the effect of such labeling is to place any Negro author in a
> kind of literary ghetto where the standards applied to him, since

he, being a 'spokesman for his race,' is not considered primarily a writer but a species of race-relations man, the leader of a cause, the voice of protest. (xx)[10]

The pressures of a social climate fueled by the dual and often conflicting demands of artistic autonomy and race consciousness facing Brooks, Hayden, and Tolson in the integration age of the 1940s nearly mirror those of the Harlem Renaissance poets Hughes, Claude McKay, and Countee Cullen. And in the 1940s, Hayden's struggle for racial and artistic autonomy mimicked the racial ambivalence of Cullen.[11] Where Brooks and Tolson also faced the dictate to write universally in language that could speak to all humanity, while proving that they could attain the same level of craftsmanship of the Modernist school, neither of them grappled with the issue of racial identification that was to be a lifelong battleground for Hayden.[12] In an interview with John O'Brien, Hayden vehemently argued his case against "strict definitions of what a poet is or should be" and instead, insisted that the poet forge his own artistic path maintaining the integrity and artistic freedom he felt was due him as an artist (115). Even given his mandate for recognition free of racial labeling, Hayden wrote an exquisitely textured poetics that celebrated the history of stoicism in Black Americans who conquered the life-threatening odds of slavery time and time again. The finely chiseled voice in the accentual sonnet "Frederick Douglass," the renegade rhythms of a slave escape in "Runagate Runagate," and the catharsis of blues rhythms in his tribute to blueswoman Bessie Smith, in "Homage to the Empress of the Blues," tell of Hayden's intimate connection to Black life, if not to cultural self-identification.

Unlike Hayden, the pro-integrationist demand for a muted cultural identity left Tolson unperturbed; Tolson had no qualms about being called a "Negro poet," and at a conference of Black writers proudly announced: "I'm a black poet, an African-American poet, a Negro poet. I'm no accident—and I don't give a tinker's damn what you think."[13] Tolson developed his own literary armor for fighting the contention that Negro poets could not master white literary forms, yet must conquer those forms to be invited into mainstream America. Turning his attention from the struggle with racial identification to the proving ground of poetic excellence, he produced a poetics born of a cosmopolitan imagination, an ironic sense of humor, and a linguistic versatility.

In *Melvin B. Tolson*, Joy Flasch discusses the complexity of Tolson's work and the minuscule critical attention he received, like Hayden and Brooks, for poetry that defies easy explications (Flasch ii). Although Tolson had written three books by the 1940s, his second, *Libretto for the Republic of Liberia* written in 1947, was initially rejected by publishers and did not gain publication until 1953 (74). The work for which he is best known, *Harlem Gallery: Book I, The Curator*, was originally written in 1932, but was also rejected by publishers until its 1965 publication (ii). As testimony to the acknowledged stature of Tolson's work, he was able to engage eminent critics to write the introductions, but ultimately, it was that same influential status of the critics writing the introductions, not Tolson's poetry, that became his early calling card of literary acceptability (74, 134).

In 1947, Tolson was commissioned to write the *Libretto for the Republic of Liberia*, in celebration of the centennial of the founding of that African Republic. In the preface, critic Allen Tate effectively unlocked the door to white literary circles when he approved Tolson's "rich and complex language" by writing, "for the first time … a Negro poet has assimilated completely the full poetic language of his time and, by implication, the language of the Anglo-American poetic tradition" (ii). Though Tate, an influential leader of the New Poetry party, initially refused Tolson's request that he write the preface on the grounds of a too propagandistic tone in the book, he eventually complied when Tolson revised the eight-part poem by substituting the musical symbols of the diatonic scale and a broad scope of literary and historical allusions to assuage the offensive tone of propaganda and rescue his creation from the "provincial mediocrity" that Tate applied to the works of other Negro poets (Flasch 74). In lines from "RE," symptomatic of the extraordinary breadth of historic, classic, and poetic knowledge Tolson exhibited in the entire ode, Tolson had proven his artistic worth: "Europe bartered Africa crucifixes for red ivory, / Gewgaws for black pearls, *pierres d'aigris* for green gold" (Lines 68–9).

Similarly, critic Karl Shapiro established lifetime criteria for critical sparring with the mixed assessment that Tolson's *Harlem Gallery* was a "gift of tongues," "a work so fantastically stylized," with a "baroque surface," and topped off that critique with the definitive statement of Modernist obscurity: "Tolson writes and thinks in Negro" (12). Although lines from the opening segment of "ALPHA," "The Harlem Gallery, an Afric pepper bird, / awakes me at a people's dusk of dawn," and later references to *The Lord of the Flies*, "Byzantine" paintings, and "Tintoretto's *Paradise*," decry Shapiro's easy generalization, the major challenge to his statement is that in style, Tolson is akin to the school of Modernist poets, but in content, quite different. Tolson's use of metaphors, symbols, and juxtaposed ideas are similar to Eliot's work, but at that juncture, Tolson veers off into a different milieu. His work is derived from the Black community and is a celebration of its blackness; yet the Black community is not the audience to whom Tolson's work is directed, nor is it predominantly their language he is using. Flasch succinctly defines *Harlem Gallery* as "sociological commentary, an intellectual triple somersault" with the "vast mosaic" of Tolson's exaggerated use of mythological illusions, imagery from European literature and art, and extreme word-play, suggesting a lure for a white scholarly audience (99).[14]

The vibrations from the literary testing ground of the 1940s shook the early works of both Hayden and Tolson, yet altered their approaches to poetry in significantly different ways. Hayden was impelled by his natural affinity for historical research to absorb himself in a meticulous and scholarly study of Black history that enabled him to approach his poetic craft from an engrossing and contemplative stance. The result is an unrelenting collage of poetic voices that whisper the brutalities of Black history in the secure wrappings of technical expertise, expressive language, and historical grounding. Tolson's subsequent works reflect his incredible intellectual spunk, penchant for syntactical inversions, and subversive use of linguistic hyperbole to encompass his continuing but opaque message of social protest.

And finally, the same call for poetic craftsmanship over social commentary that was met by her Black literary peers, Hayden and Tolson, as an impetus for integration, was also heard by Brooks. She embarked upon a quest for new experimental ways of writing that would satisfy dual objectives. First, Brooks sought a poetics that would engage both Black and white critics, win acceptance from her white audience, and earn for her the reward of a secure position in the white mainstream school of arts and letters. Second, she needed to use her own source of inspiration, ordinary life around her, to tell her own poetic story. Brooks succeeded in her dual objectives. She did engage the critics, Black, white, male, and female; attract a white audience; and earn a reward for technical expertise—the Pulitzer Prize for Poetry in 1950. Her poetic tale is the embellished bildungsroman (a novel about the moral and psychological growth of the main character) mock-epic of a young, Black, ghetto girl, *Annie Allen*, whose response to the racism and sexism confronting her life is ensconced in complex syntax, classical imagery, and a well-finessed obscurity.

NOTES

1. Gwendolyn Brooks, *Annie Allen* (1949), rpt. in *Blacks* (Chicago: Third World P, 1987) 77–140.

2. Although Margaret Walker had received the Yale Series of Younger Poets Award in 1942 for her poems of social protest, *For My People* (New Haven: Yale UP, 1942), she would be unencumbered by the gauntlet of creating poetics amenable to a white audience; her next published work would be the historical novel, *Jubilee* (New York: Bantam, 1966).

3. A. P. Davis, "Integration and Race Literature," *Black Voices: An Anthology of Afro-American Literature*, ed. Abraham Chapman (New York: Mentor, 1968) 606–611. The essay was originally delivered at The First Conference of Negro Writers in

March 1959 and published in *The American Negro Writer and His Roots* (New York: American Society of African Culture, 1960) 34–40. Davis is candid in his asser- tion that only "surface integration and token integration" exist for the Black writer: "we do not have actual integration anywhere" (607). However, he is optimistic that although these writers currently "will have to live between two worlds," the hope for integration looms on the horizon because of the positive "spiritual climate" (607).

4. Alain Locke, "The New Negro," ed. *The New Negro: An Interpretation* (1925; New York: Arno, 1968).

5. The examples provided by Gloster of works with universal themes are Richard Wright, *Native Son* (New York: Harper, 1940); Willard Motley, *Knock on Any Door* (New York: D. Appleton-Century, 1947); Ann Petry, *The Street* (Boston: Beacon, 1946) and *A Country Place* (1947); Zora Neale Hurston, *Seraph On the Suwanee* (1948; New York: Harper, 1991); Gwendolyn Brooks, *Annie Allen* (New York: Harper, 1949); and the works of Frank Yerby.

6. Wright, *Native Son*, and Motley, *Knock on Any Door*. Ford also alludes to Frank Yerby, William Attaway, Ann Petry, Arna Bontemps, William Gardner Smith, and J. Saunders Redding, though he does not provide specific titles (374).

7. In a perceptive analysis, in contrast to Gloster, Ford targets several of the same authors to illustrate the inferiority of works that evade the racial orientation of the author. He sees Petry's *A Country Place* as "greatly inferior" because the author spent her energy "conjuring up vicarious experiences of a white society with which she was not minutely familiar"; Hurston's *Seraph* as "almost unbelievably inferior" to *Their Eyes Were Watching God* and *Mules and Men*, "her two novels of Negro life"; and Yerby's *The Golden Hawk* and *Pride's Castle*, "which completely ignore the racial angle," and inferior to the "greater artistic perfection" of his earlier two works, *The Foxes of Harrow* and *The Vixens*, which both "have a background of Negro life and action" (375).

8. J. Saunders Redding, "American Negro Literature," *The American Scholar*, XVIII (1949): 137–148.

9. M. Walker, "New Poets," *Phylon* XI (1950): 345–354. Walker discusses how white critics seemed to "beg the question of the Negro's humanity, perhaps as an answer to the white patron's attitude that Negroes are only children anyway" (346). Arna Bontemps, "Negro Poets, Then and Now," *Phylon* XI (1950): 355–360. Bontemps articulates the feeling of "injustice" some poets felt when critics insis- tently labeled them "Negro poets": "As was the case with Countee Cullen, one gets the impression that Hayden is bothered by this Negro thing. He would like to be considered simply as a poet" (356–7).

10. Don L. Lee (Haki R. Madhubuti), "On *Kaleidoscope* and Robert Hayden," *Negro Digest* (Jan. 1968): 51–52, 90–94. Lee questions Hayden's editorship of a Negro Anthology given Hayden's resistance to being labeled a "Negro poet": "If one doesn't wish to be judged or recognized as a 'negro' poet, why advertise as such?" (51).

11. Hughes asserted his race consciousness by announcing that he was a "Black poet" and embarking upon a highly acclaimed career of writing vignettes about the ordinary folk of Harlem in *The Weary Blues* (1926) and *Fine Clothes to the Jew* (1927). The Jamaican poet Claude McKay nimbly negotiated the proving ground of using traditional poetic forms by making a remarkable alliance between the sonnet form and the wrath of his racial discontent with America, in poems like "America" and "If We Must Die." But the poet who was most at variance with his need for expres- sion as a poet, without being confined to the characterizations of being a "Black

poet," was Cullen. Educated at Harvard University, Cullen was at odds with the disparity he sensed between racial identifications, his love of Keatsian verse, and his own fluidity in classical forms. He announced "I want to be known as a poet, not a Negro poet," to avoid the implied restriction of writing to racial themes and having his work judged solely on the merits of its expression of the Black struggle for equality. Though race consciousness is clear in the titles of his early works, *Color* (1925), *Copper Sun* (1927), *Ballad of a Brown Girl* (1928), and the anthology he edited, *Caroling Dusk* (1927), Cullen flinched at the idea of being labeled a "Negro poet," even in face of themes and imagery that often bespoke of his cultural heritage. See Jean Wagner, *Black Poets of the United States* (Urbana: U of Illinois P, 1973) for detailed information on the poets.

12. David Llorens, "Seeking a New Image: Writers Converge at Fisk University," *Negro Digest* (June 1966): 54–68. The conference was the site of Hayden's public disagreement with other Black writers over his stance (62). In Rosey E. Pool, *Beyond the Blues* (London: Hand and Flower, 1962), Hayden discusses when he wrote "propaganda rather than poetry" (24–25).

13. Llorens, *Negro Digest*, Tolson made his well-known comment at the same 1966 writer's conference attended by Hayden, n12.

14. Lee, *Kaleidoscope*, abruptly dismisses the technical proficiency of Tolson's work: "Melvin B. Tolson is represented with some of his less obscure poetry which still exhibits his range and his capacity to lose the people that may read him" (91). Paul Breman, "Poetry into the Sixties," *The Black American Writer*, Volume II: "poetry and drama", ed. C. W. E. Bigsby (Baltimore: Penguin, 1969) 99–109. Breman creates a trope from Shapiro's use of the word 'Negro' as a description for Tolson's language: " . . . Tolson postured for a white audience, and with an ill-concealed grin and a wicked sense of humour gave it just what it wanted: an entertaining darkey using almost comically big words as the best WASP tradition demands of its educated house-niggers" (101).

WOLFGANG KARRER

Black Modernism? The Early Poetry of Jean Toomer and Claude McKay

I f we take Pierre Bourdieu's theory of cultural fields seriously—and I mean to do so in what follows—then modernism occupies a particular position in the literary field of the twenties, and—here Bourdieu's theory somehow has limitations of its own—this position is taken in different national fields at the same time (29–73). What complicates the matter is that modernism in the United States brings together authors from different ethnic subcultures in the same field: Jewish American, Anglo-American, African American, to name the most important groups. The critical and social separation of these groups has resulted in different categorizations for modernism and the Harlem Renaissance. And only recently these differences are breaking down.

Why do we think about Toomer and McKay in terms of the Harlem Renaissance and not in terms of international modernism? Why do we say black modernism but not white modernism? Do we have to downplay Gurdjieff or Marx to highlight spirituals or Booker T. Washington? If Gertrude Stein, Sherwood Anderson, or Tristan Tzara indulge in modernist primitivism, how do their approaches to African or African American art and music differ from that of Toomer?

I shall elaborate on my reading, starting with George Hutchinson. He considers modernism a cultural field where black and white artists struggle for positions, in Europe as well as in the United States, where "writing

---

From *Jean Toomer and the Harlem Renaissance*, pp. 128–141. © 2001 by Rutgers, the State University of New Jersey and by individual contributors.

35

black" or "writing white" means what others call a "racial formation" (Omi and Winant) and where black artists and writers struggle in this formation under a distinct disadvantage.

I shall try to show how Toomer and McKay broke into literary publishing and how the retrospective grouping with the New Negro group around Alain Locke and the Harlem Renaissance distorts and simplifies their early trajectories in the literary field (Bourdieu, 276 n. 44).

To briefly recall earlier argumentations revolving around these two writers: The failure/success debate of the Harlem Renaissance and the debate whether McKay used outmoded forms like the sonnet or blackened these forms (Baker, 85) mask ideological debates about a racial formation. The cubism debate about the poems in *Cane* implies an affiliation of Toomer outside Harlem (Bush and Mitchell). I shall try to show that McKay and Toomer take far more complex positions even in their early poetry and that their ambiguities on race are reactions to various pressures from an early modernist field.

Modernism

American poetry between 1900 and 1920 was at a low point. It was the age of fiction, and the early modernist poets worked against overwhelming forces in the literary market. The romantic tradition had largely exhausted itself, and realism of the domestic and local-color varieties dominated the poetic field. Titles such as *Kentucky Poems*, *North of Boston*, *Spoon River Anthology* or *The House of a Hundred Lights*, *The Book of Joyous Children*, *The Mother and the Father* by writers such as Cawein, Frost, and Masters (Ludwig and Nault, 129–149) told the readers what to expect. These titles used keywords establishing poetic claims in a literary field that was largely dominated by the novel. At the same time, other poets tried to discover new forms through various revivals of older times. Their attempt is comparable to that of the historical novel. The sheer number of classicist, Gothic, and Renaissance titles that came out during these twenty years is simply surprising. To name just a few: *Pan: A Choric Idyl*; *Artemis to Acteon*; *Personae*; *Helen of Troy*; *Hymen*; or, on the Gothic side: *Sword Blades and Poppy Seeds*; *Merlin*; *Lancelot*; *Black Armour*; or, more relevant to our authors, the Renaissance: *Medley and Palestrine*; *Sonnets and Poems*; *Canzoni*; *Renascence*; *The Sonnets and Ballads of Cavalcanti*. The Gothic was a worn-out romantic tradition, as were titles dealing with simple nature: birds, flowers, or sunsets. Early modernists like Ezra Pound or Hilda Doolittle worked themselves out of an imitative classicist or Renaissance tradition into modernism. All these returns were in themselves a type of "renaissancism": to bring about a new flowering of poetry through the mastering of older forms and their modern deformation.

African American poetry between 1900 and 1920 remained fixed in local color or domestic conventions. Dunbar tried to repeat his success in *Lyrics of Lowly Life* (1896) in *Lyrics of Love and Laughter* (1903) and *Lyrics of Sunshine and Shadow* (1905); Braithwaite copied him in *Lyrics of Life and Love* (1904) and added a domestic variant with *The House of Falling Leaves* (1908). The innovations came from Du Bois: in *The Souls of Black Folk* (1903) and *Darkwater* (1920) he not only mixed poetry and prose but related them in new and intricate patterns.

These were the options around 1920 for McKay and Toomer: they could align themselves with the romantic school by using Gothic or nature titles; they could remain with domestic or local color realism, or they could participate in the classical or Renaissance revival. McKay chose local color in both his collections: *Spring in New Hampshire* (1920) sounds like Robert Frost, and *North of Boston* and *Harlem Shadows* (1922) sound like a combination of the local-color school, as in Sandburg's *Chicago Poems*, with Dunbar: "Shadows" or "Dark" are signifying titles in the African American tradition. *Cane* simply subverts the romantic paradigm: cane is hardly a romantic plant, it is a word with many meanings, subtly implying an agricultural region and slavery, among other things.

There were other choices besides poetry and affiliation with certain poetic traditions. Modernism in Europe was not simply neoclassicist as in the case of Hilda Doolittle or T. S. Eliot or neo-Renaissance as the early Pound. Modernism included primitivism and exoticism. Especially artists and writers in Paris, Berlin, and London, the centers of colonial power, were inspired by colonial exhibits, mainly from Africa. African arts and literature inspired a large number of German and French avant-garde writers to return to simpler, more expressive forms called "primitive." Joachim Schultz has compiled a dictionary of primitivist terms and techniques widely used by European avant-garde artists who dealt in primitivism or exoticism. Some of them are relevant to McKay and Toomer, although we do not know exactly how much they recognized European primitivism or their American equivalents like Lindsay's *The Congo* (1915). Here are some of the terms listed and analyzed in Schultz's dictionary: animal, banjo, dance, dark, fetish, jazz, jungle, laughter, mask, naive, negro, night, religion, woman. These symbols also appear in modern art, as in Picasso's *Demoiselles d'Avignon* (1906). Gottfried Benn writes *Negerbraut* (1912), Sigmund Freud writes *Totem and Tabu* in the same year, Apollinaire's *Zone* appears in 1913, Carl Einstein publishes *Negerplastik* in 1915, Cabaret Voltaire in Zurich organizes *danses nègres* in 1917, and the following year Tzara composes *Note sur la poésie nègre* (Schultz, 17).

The techniques to express primitive force were sound poems, a nonsense analogue to African poetry, and the so-called telegram style: the reduction of syntax to formulaic expressions linked without conjunctions or punctuation. Toomer experimented with both, sound poems and telegram style, McKay did not. McKay's elaborate syntax in his sonnets must be read as a firm rejection of primitivism. Both, Toomer and McKay, must have been aware of the primitivist and exoticist tendencies of modernism, as they were available in the United States as well through the Boas school of anthropology. Black modernism had to react to such pressures, but it was not simply a question of the taint of white modernism by primitivism and exoticism (Hutchinson, 19–20). Nor could it simply reject modernism as too bohemian or avantgarde as Du Bois demanded (167).

Field and Trajectory

There were other, even more pressing, things to consider: where to get published. Before 1924, young black poets had a choice between the *Crisis*, liberal white periodicals like the *Nation* or the *New Republic*, or radical socialist bohemia, represented by the *Masses* and its successors, the *Liberator* and the *Modern Quarterly*. A fourth choice was Randolph's *Messenger* or Mencken's *American Mercury* (Hutchinson, 289), both printing iconoclastic satire. The choice was a political one between conservative and liberal or left positions that were either moderate or radical. The founding of *Opportunity* in 1924 added a more conservative platform for young writers. Other options lay outside New York and did not significantly affect the Harlem Renaissance.

McKay enters the literary field through a white patron in Jamaica who introduces his dialect poems as "the charmingly naive love-songs" representing "the thoughts and feelings of a Jamaican peasant of pure black blood" (Cooper, 5, 9). His unpublished sonnet on Booker T. Washington of 1916 shows already a clear break with the dialect tradition, masking resistance very much like some of Dunbar's earlier poems. It is interesting to compare McKay's Washington poem with Dunbar's sonnet on Frederick Douglass. Both are cast in the heroic mold, poetic monuments to black political leaders. A year later McKay publishes "The Harlem Dancer" in *Seven Arts*, a modernist socialist periodical. The editor and founder, James Oppenheim, objects to the outmoded form of the sonnet. McKay insists and complains to Joel Spingarn of the National Association for the Advancement of Colored People (NAACP). In 1918, McKay joins the Wobblies (Industrial Workers of the World) and the working class. He finds it hard to publish his radical sonnets—editors like Oppenheim demand more racial subjects—and he submits "Harlem Shadows" and four other poems with an introduction entitled "A Negro Poet Writes" to Frank Harris's *Pearson's Magazine*. In 1919 he meets Max Eastman, who publishes his work in the *Liberator*. After the London interlude, where he publishes in the *Worker's Dreadnought* and the *Cambridge*

Magazine and, with help from *Cambridge*, brings out his first collection, *Spring in New Hampshire*, he returns to New York, where he joins the *Liberator* as coeditor and helps Toomer to publish some of his first poems. With the help of Joel Spingarn McKay manages to get another poetry collection published at Harcourt and Brace. It is the first important poetry collection by an African American since Dunbar's *Complete Poems* in 1913 and Fenton Johnson's *Songs of the Soil* in 1916. It brings conservative acclaim and is later considered to be a milestone for the Harlem Renaissance (Tillery, 29–64).

McKay's trajectory in the literary field is clearly left-wing. It avoids and disagrees with the uplift ideology of the *Crisis* and the NAACP until 1924; on the other hand, it resists the pressure of modernist editors like Oppenheim or Eastman to write in a more contemporary form. McKay seems to have experimented with free verse, but he never published any poems in free verse. Ironically, the *Crisis* and its literary editor, Jessie Fauset, tried to dissuade their poets from free verse. McKay was caught in a dilemma: on the one hand his poems were kept in Hoover's FBI files as incriminating evidence, and on the other hand his poems were criticized for their formal conservatism.

Today, we often get to read McKay through his *Selected Poems* of 1953. For *Harlem Shadows* (1922) and *Spring in New Hampshire* (1920) you have to go to the rare-book department in big libraries. Accounts of their contents are contradictory or vague, sometimes plainly wrong. *Harlem Shadows* contains seventy-four poems, no less, and is not a reprint of *Spring in New Hampshire*. *Selected Poems* eliminates most of the political poems, and *Harlem Shadows* selects only twenty-three poems from *Spring in New Hampshire*. Both collections omit many of the radical poems that were published in the *Liberator*.

McKay's preface to *Harlem Shadows*, "Author's Word," following the introduction by Max Eastman, reveals some of the pressures of the literary field McKay feels himself exposed to. After mentioning his British schooling and dialect poems in Jamaica and the native song tradition of rhyme and metrical stanzas he declares:

> Consequently, although very conscious of the new criticisms and trends in poetry, to which I am keenly responsive and receptive, I have adhered to such of the older traditions as I find adequate for my most lawless and revolutionary passions and modes. I have not used patterns, images and words that would stamp me a classicist nor a modernist. . . . I have never studied poetics, but the forms I have used I am convinced are the ones I can work in with the highest degree of spontaneity and freedom. I have chosen my melodies and rhythms by instinct, and I have favored words and figures which flow smoothly and harmoniously into my compositions. And in

all my moods I have striven to achieve directness, truthfulness and naturalness of expression instead of enameled originality. I have not hesitated to use words which are old, and in some circles considered poetically overworked and dead, when I thought I could make them glow alive by new manipulation. (xx)

This is a clearly premodernist position: feelings are poured into forms, and "smoothly" and "harmoniously" are hardly modernist concepts. Only the possible discord between traditional form and revolutionary passions point at the strain of this position. The representation of the revolutionary passion in *Harlem Shadows* is even more equivocal. Disguise would be the word. After the Palmer raids, euphemistically called the "Red Scare," of 1919 and the consequent anticommunism and racism of the early twenties and because he accepted help from the NAACP to find a publisher, McKay had to defend himself as a conservative in form, nor as a radical in thought. Many of his more outspoken poems from the *Liberator* and other radical periodicals are included neither in *Harlem Shadows* not in the *Selected Poems* of 1953. Here are some of the titles: "The Dominant White," "A Capitalist at Dinner," "The Little Peoples," "Samson," "To Ethiopia," "Birds of Prey," and "To the Entrenched Classes." They have never been republished. McKay either thought of them as unworthy of being published in a collection or too topical, or he feared they would endanger the support for or the reception of his first American collection.

McKay's role as a "progressive" intellectual in Alain Locke's essay "The New Negro" (Gates and McKay, 960) is clearly to the left of James Weldon Johnson, and McKay's dire predictions of the decline of the United States hardly agreed with the boosterism of Harlem as the new Mecca. Locke, who refused to print the poem "Mulatto" by McKay, could call such a position only "defiance" or "cynicism." McKay had aligned himself with the *Crisis* in the conflict with the National Urban League and *Opportunity* about who would be included in the Harlem Renaissance (Hutchinson, 127).

Although the title *Harlem Shadows* seems to promise local color and regionalism, the title poem focuses on Harlem prostitutes and exploitation, and the exoticism of the "Harlem Dancer" is demonstrably absent or exists only in the consumer's eye. McKay's Harlem is working-class and beset by discrimination and exploitation. In Cooper's words, "He conveyed a startling bitter, and essentially modern, message of despair, alienation, and rebellion" (8). This view was hardly that of Alain Locke or the Urban League.

Toomer's trajectory was different in spite of some surprising similarities. It was Waldo Frank who accepted "Harlem Dancer" for *Seven Arts*, and it was Waldo Frank who helped Toomer to get into print (Gates and McKay,

982). Toomer went through a phase of socialism between 1918 and 1920; he repeatedly tried to teach it to others. His first project after *Cane* was to write a collection of short stories on the communist influence on African Americans in Washington (Turner). But other than McKay he had little first-hand working-class experience, and his relations to literary periodicals were remote. Like McKay, Toomer was largely self-taught in literature, but he had an extended academic exposure to socialism, sociology, and psychology, and his literary studies were in modernist writers such as Sherwood Anderson, Waldo Frank, and the imagists. Internal evidence even points at Gertrude Stein for some of the prose experiments in *Cane* (Jones, 44). Toomer had already collected a trunk full of literary experiments before he returned from Georgia to begin the sketches that would ultimately become *Cane* (Turner, xv). It is significant that he reported his project to the *Liberator* while he published the first sketches in various periodicals. Of the poems, McKay, who was the editor, accepted "Georgia Dusk." *The Crisis* published "Song of the Son," *Nomad* printed "November Cotton Flower," and a New Orleans magazine published "Harvest Song" (Jones and Latimer, 258). Toomer's trajectory was clearly more modernist than socialist. The poems reflected various stages of formal experiments but hardly foreshadowed the complex achievement of *Cane*. It was hard work unifying these pieces, as Toomer reports in his letter:

> I've had the impulse to collect my sketches and poems under the title perhaps of *Cane*. Such pieces as K. C. A. ["Karintha," "Carma," "Avey"] and Kabnis (revised) coming under the subhead of Cane Stalks and Chorouses [*sic*]. Poems under leaves and Syrup Songs. Vignettes under leaf traceries in Washington. (Rusch, 11)

A little later he writes:

> Having as Sub-heads Cane Stalks and Chorouses [*sic*] (Karintha, Fern, etc. and two longer pieces), leaves (poems), and Leaf Traciers [*sic*] in Washington, under which I shall group such Things as For M. W. and other sharp, brief vignettes . . . (12)

And again:

> I see the importance of form. The tree as a symbol comes to mind. A tree in summer. Trunk, branches, structure. Leaves the fillers-out, one might almost say the padding. The sap is carried in the trunk etc. From it the leaves get their sustenance, and from their arrangement comes their meaning, or at least leaves upon the ground do not

make a tree. Etc. This symbol is wanting, of course, because a tree is stationary, because it has no progressions, no dynamic movements. A machine has these, but a machine is all form, it has no leaves. Its very abstraction is now the death of it. Perhaps it is the purpose of our age to fecundate it? But its flower, unlike growing things, will bud within the human spirit.... (22)

The stance here is clearly modernist. The organic analogy seems to belie this at first. The longer prose sketches are the trunks of *Cane*, the poems between the sketches their leaves, the short poetic lines inserted in the sketches (mainly at the beginning and end of each sketch) are the traceries of the leaves. But the rather regular, almost mechanic, alternation of poems and vignettes with sketches (two poems between each sketch and the next; two vignettes at the beginning and the end) point to another symbol: the machine. Both symbols overlap: *Cane* is organic and mechanical. More precisely, *Cane* is the interaction between both: "From their arrangement comes their meaning." This modernist principle of spatializing meaning as collage or montage determines not only the poems in *Cane* but also determines its double structure. *Cane* is not only "about" cane, it is not only built like a cane plant: it is meant to fecundate the machine that replaces it. The revolution is a spiritual one, and it happens in the mind of the readers of the new machine age. *Cane* is also a spiritual growth in the mind of the reader. Although this comes close to the circle concept that Toomer adopted later, it is not the same. The circle is mystic and comes from Gurdjieff and spiritism; cane comes from Georgia and a history of slaveholding. *Cane* thus contains pieces from different periods of experimentation, and the poems in particular reflect the temporary ideological orientations behind these experiments. To assume one spiritual entity behind *Cane*, as Toomer did later in his mandala quote (Rusch, 26–27), is to reduce *Cane* to Toomer's development behind the sketches. In this development "Bona and Paul" comes first—it dates back to his Chicago days—and "Harvest Song" last—it appeared in *Double Dealer* in December 1922. Instead of constructing a cyclic movement for *Cane*, as various critics have done, one comes closer to *Cane*'s conception by sticking to the principles of trunk-leaves-traceries and meaning-from-arrangement.

Poems such as "Her Lips Are Copper Wire," "Evening Song," and "Storm Ending" are imagist experiments from the trunk: they were written before Georgia, and whatever new meaning they acquire in *Cane* comes from their arrangement between the sketches and interaction with each other. They clearly belong to Toomer's aesthetic period (Jones, 3–20). The Georgia poems, some of which were published before *Cane*, belong to Toomer's ancestral-consciousness period and date roughly from September 1921 to

December 1923 (Jones and Latimer, xiv). Of the poems first published in *Cane*, only "Cotton Song" and "Prayer" show a clearly spiritist vocabulary. The bulk of the leaves in *Cane* falls between the two phases, marking the earliest and latest texts assembled in *Cane*. A convincing case has been made for a cubist technique in some of them (Bush and Mitchell). But imagism, impressionism, and primitivism have also left their traces. Ideologically, aestheticism, the cultural nationalism of "Song of the Son," and the European spiritism of the later poems hardly make for a single spiritual entity behind the work. As I will try to show by examining one of the poems in *Cane*, we are on safer and more historic ground if we follow modernist principles of collage and apply the plant/machine analogy.

The Field in the Poems

I shall take Toomer's poem "Conversion" as an example and compare it later to "The Little Peoples" by McKay:

> African Guardian of Souls,
> Drunk with rum,
> Feasting on a strange cassava,
> Yielding to new words and a weak palabra
> Of a white-faced sardonic god—
> Grins, cries
> Amen,
> Shouts hosanna. (26)

The first thing that strikes the ear are the half rhymes in an otherwise unrhymed poem: *cassava, palabra, hosanna*. On second thought one realizes that they come from three different cultures—Native American *cassava* from Yucatan, Spanish *palabra* (word), and Hebrew *amen* (so be it) and *hosanna* (help me)—and reflect three stages of colonial experience: "strange cassava" indicates an African who is accustomed to other types of manioca and who has been exposed to Spanish and English Christianization. Another look reveals proud capitals for "African Guardian of Souls" and a lower-cased "g" for "god." The African God Legba seems to have lost his strength by yielding to drink and Christianity. Religious conversion seems to have weakened the god, but why "sardonic," and what does "weak palabra" mean?

Readers of *Cane* know that poems like "Conversion" grow out of the stories like leaves out of tree trunks. Bell proposes that "Conversion" heightens King Barlo's parable in "Esther" (326), but if the African Guardian of Souls weakens under Christianity, does the poem not undermine King Barlo's parable of black power? The Christian term that makes Esther shrink from physical contact with Barlo is "sin": "conception with a drunken man must be mighty sin" (25). Is Barlo an African Guardian of Souls weakened by alcohol, and does Esther fail to see him as such?

The alcohol in the poem is rum, and rum is made from sugar cane. It is echoed in the parallel poem "Portrait in Georgia," which springs from "Blood-Burning Moon": "Breath—the last sweet scent of cane" (27). Breath here stands for rum. Syrup, sweetness, and rum stand for the product of cane, beginning with the motto of the text: "Oracular / Redolent of fermenting syrup." In other words, our reading of *Cane* is intended to be an intoxicating experience. Here is an ambivalence. A second word that ramifies throughout the text is "soul." It carries Christian, African American, and—by way of "Cotton Song" and "Prayer"—also spiritist connotations inspired by Gurdjieff. The African sense of "Guardian of Souls" has been converted to the Christian one. Is the African American concept of "soul" still present in the poem? Do *amen* and *hosanna* still mean "so be it" and "help me" or do they simply signify assimilation?

The word clusters in *Cane* are not restricted to one trunk or sketch as Rice has shown ("Repeated Images"; "Incomplete Circle"); they reach much further. "Conversion" develops its full power only if we read it as a companion piece to "Kabnis," which summarizes many of the foregoing patterns, very much as "The Dead" does for *Dubliners* or "Departure" for *Winesburg, Ohio*. After a night of drinking—whiskey, not rum—Kabnis lies prostrate before Father John in the hole; his long monologue can be understood as a cry for help. Father John obliges with a cryptic remark about the lies in the Bible. Kabnis who does not understand, calls him an "old black fakir" (116), the very words used to describe King Barlo when he tries to be a guardian of African American souls (20). Carrie doubles the ironies by answering Kabnis with: "Brother Ralph, is that your best Amen?" (116)

If we use "Conversion" as a key to "Kabnis," or rather if we construct meaning out of the arrangement of the two in the canebrake that is *Cane*, Brother John emerges as another African Guardian of Souls, and his rejection of Christianity does not reach Kabnis because of alcohol and the latter's concept of sin. "Sin" again is a keyword in "Kabnis," and Ralph Kabnis half believes in it (106). There is little doubt that the new word and weak *palabra* that the Spanish and English colonizers brought to Native and African Americans alike was "sin," or *pecado*. The preachers and teachers in "Kabnis" are weakened African guardians. "Conversion" is not a primitivist but a colonial parable of the weakening of the African American spirit through Christianization. Drinking mostly becomes an escape from sin or from fear of lynching in "Kabnis." In spite of all the degradation in the hole under Halsey's store, Stella and Cora emerge after a night of "weak" (108) and drunken sex as "two princesses in Africa going through the early-morning ablutions of their pagan prayers" (112).

In other words, African religion and vitality suffer under Christian colonization, and the ancient gods have become weak preachers and leaders of the African American communities. Certainly Kabnis is no spiritual leader for the black Georgia community; his soul is branded with the fear of lynching and cut off from the African spirit embodied in Father John. Lewis, who serves as a kind of foil to weak Kabnis, could become a leader, but he is too secretive. For a moment there seems to be a chance for a union with Carrie, but again she is stopped by the notion of sin: "The sin-bogies of respectable Southern folks clamor at her" (102), and the union between North and South, between Lewis and Carrie fails: "He wants to take her North with him. What for?" (102). All we learn about Lewis is that he takes notes about lynchings in Sempter, and the case that is mentioned—a particularly gruesome case of a murder of a mother and the child in her womb—frightens and horrifies Ralph Kabnis; it is also a case that Claude McKay wrote a famous sonnet about, "The Lynching" (1920). Both Toomer and McKay took the account from an NAACP documentation on lynching in the South, and Lewis may either represent an NAACP worker or a socialist. Both would explain his secretiveness. Whatever his politics, his union with the South fails, just as that of Kabnis does. One can only speculate that the union of Kabnis's soul with the intellect of Lewis, the strength of Halsey in addition to the vitality of Father John, which survives in Carrie, Stella, and Cora, will bring about the dawn that at the end seems to replace the eternal dusk in the South. Here, too, the meaning would arise out of the interplay between the characters. Otherwise the birth song of the newly risen sun would meet only barren streets and sleepy windows that cannot be fecundated.

My second example, McKay's "The Little Peoples," was published in the *Liberator* in July 1919 and never reprinted. It is a protest against the failure of the Paris Peace Conference to take action in the decolonization of Africa:

> The little peoples of the troubled earth,
> The little nations that are weak and white;—
> For them the glory of another birth,
> For them the lifting of the veil of night.
> The big men of the world in concert met,
> Have sent forth in their power a new decree:
> Upon the old harsh wrongs the sun must set,
> Henceforth the little peoples must be free!
> But, we, the blacks, less than the trampled dust,
> Who walk the new ways with the old dim eyes,—

We to the ancient gods of greed and lust
Must still he offered up as sacrifice:
Oh, we who deign to live but will not dare,
The white world's burden must forever bear! (Donohue, 166)

This is a kind of poetic editorial, anger poured into the traditional form of a Petrarchan sonnet turning the thought with line nine. But the love sonnet becomes a hate sonnet; McKay inverts the form. Not just the form; McKay systematically inverts colonial diction and metaphors to serve his sarcastic indictment: Kipling's "White Man's Burden" becomes the white world perceived as a burden to the rest of the world, and the Austrian-Hungarian Hapsburg empire upon which "the sun never sets" becomes "upon the old harsh wrongs the sun must set." The setting of the sun seems to be the end of this empire. Quoting Du Bois—"the lifting of the veil of night"—not only extends decolonization to Georgia and *The Souls of Black Folk*, it also creates an ironic contrast between the imperial sunset and the veil of night. Political decolonization does not necessarily mean freedom from double consciousness. Neither does it guarantee a renaissance or "the glory of another birth." In a fourth sarcastic inversion, pointing at Africa and modernist primitivism, McKay identifies European and U.S. imperialism with human sacrifice: it sacrifices its colonial subjects to the ancient gods of greed and lust. Finally, the sarcastic contrast of little peoples with great men points at numbers: the Paris conference decides the fate of millions of people. And that undercuts the seeming resignation in the second-to-last line. International solidarity and daring—implied by the Georgia parallel—would be able to throw off the white world's burden. Echoes of the October Revolution? The "we" in the poem clearly sides with the so-called little peoples, probably another allusion to a contemporary phrase. (Today, "Kosovo" would be much clearer.)

McKay here parodies conventional form and diction to achieve a double vision: we are invited to read "weak and white" as "strong and black" to see the Paris conference as a primitive ritual of human sacrifice. The Africanism in the poem is quite different from King Barlo's vision of black power, but still relates to it.

The Cane Field

Toomer works with a modernist aesthetic of collage that owes as much to the mixture of prose and poems in the work of Du Bois as to similar experiments in those of Sherwood Anderson, Ernest Hemingway, and William Carlos Williams between 1919 and 1923. Toomer plays with modernist ideas of Africanism, primitivism, and exoticism, but he carefully balances them with issues of cultural nationalism, such as the question of Northern leadership for the South and of internal cultural colonization. He even questions the political role of the black middle class both in the North and South and thus adds class-related problems to cultural nationalism. Some of the sketches and poems in *Cane* reveal contradictory positions, others create ambivalences. The forces active in the literary field—the aesthetic avant-garde, the socialist party, and the official position of the NAACP—are reflected in the tensions and contradictions in *Cane*. Toomer's hope to bring them together in the organic image of the sugar cane fertilizing the machine or in the spiritist image of the circle remains just that—a hope. *Cane* remains oracular, and it does not predict a role of leadership of the "Talented Tenth" or Harlem for the South. Nowhere does the union of male leadership and female vitality create offspring that will lead into a new future. As in *The Waste Land*, written in 1922, the voice of the wind and the spirituals carried by it remain unheard.

McKay suffers less from uncertainty and doubt. The question of leadership is not relevant to his poems; he writes from a working-class and socialist position. His poetry is either private or public, and in the public poems he is simply a spokesman for an international movement of socialists. He does not write primarily as an American, and he does not meditate on Harlem's role of leadership for the South. To him, the United States is an imperial power, and its patterns of racial discrimination can only be challenged by an international process of decolonization. He has little patience with the cultural nationalism of the Harlem intellectuals (Hutchinson, 157) and the struggles between the NAACP and the National Urban League to publish and define the "New Negro." He is careful to distinguish himself through allusions and omissions from the *Crisis* and later from the *Opportunity* poets. His Harlem is proletarian, the center of imperial power, and no Mecca for Southern or Caribbean migrants. Like Toomer's Washington, McKay's Harlem does not have much to offer to the rural masses. They also have to beware of not being sacrificed to the ancient gods of lust and greed, even in Harlem. Primitivism is a mask for colonialism. The sonnet may be another mask—but for rebellion. McKay would later find a subtler voice in the modern prose of *Home to Harlem* and *Banjo*.

Both Toomer and McKay remained outsiders to the Harlem Renaissance. Their early poetry shows the different pressures of a literary field that had not yet stabilized around Harlem. Both modernism and socialism had only a fleeting or marginal influence on developments after 1924. Local-color realism and protest sonnets would continue to be written after that date, but new beginnings were made with Zora Neale Hurston's inversion of gender relations in the local-color tradition, the urban naturalism of Richard Wright, and the vernacular free-verse form of Langston Hughes. Toomer and McKay,

in different ways, contested the racial formation of cultural nationalism that
was to become the Harlem Renaissance, and both were retrospectively hailed
as its forerunners or highlights, a position they had hardly asked for. Their
texts ironically question—either by conversion or inversion—Harlem's claim
in the twenties to be the cultural leader for the overwhelming majority of
African Americans still living in the South.

WORKS CITED

Baker, Houston A., Jr. *Modernism and the Harlem Renaissance*. Chicago: University of Chicago
    Press, 1987.
Bell, Bernard. "A Key to the Poems in *Cane*." In *Jean Toomer: A Critical Evaluation*, ed. Ther-
    man B. O'Daniel, 321–328. Washington, D.C.: Howard University Press, 1988.
Bourdieu, Pierre. *The Field of Cultural Production: Essays on Art and Literature*. Ed. Randal
    Johnson. London: Polity Press, 1993.
Bush, Ann Marie, and Louis D. Mitchell. "Jean Toomer: A Cubist Poet." *BALF* 17, 3 (1983):
    106–108.
Cooper, Wayne F., ed. *The Dialect Poems of Claude McKay*. 2 vols. in 1. Plainview, N.Y.: Books
    for Librarians Press, 1972.
Donohue, Charles Terrance. "The Making of a Black Poet: A Critical Biography of Claude
    McKay for the Years 1889–1922." Ph.D. diss., Temple University, 1972.
Gates, Henry Louis, Jr., and Nellie Y. McKay, eds. *The Norton Anthology of African American
    Literature*. New York: Norton, 1997.
Hutchinson, George B. *The Harlem Renaissance in Black and White*. Cambridge, Mass.:
    Belknap Press of Harvard University Press, 1993.
Jones, Robert B. *Jean Toomer and the Prison House of Thought: A Phenomenology of the Spirit*.
    Amherst: University of Massachusetts Press, 1993.
Jones, Robert B., and M. Toomer Latimer, eds. *The Collected Poems of Jean Toomer*. Chapel
    Hill: University of North Carolina Press, 1988.
Ludwig. Richard M., and Clifford A. Nault. *Annals of American Literature, 1602–1983*. New
    York: Oxford University Press, 1986.
McKay, Claude. *Harlem Shadows*. New York: Harcourt Brace, 1922.
Omi, Michael, and Howard Winant. *Racial Formation in the United States: From the 1960s to
    the 1980s*. New York: Routledge, 1986.
Rice, Herbert W. "Repeated Images in Part One of *Cane*." *BALF* 17, 3 (1983): 100–104.
———. "An Incomplete Circle: Repeated Images in Part II of *Cane*." *CLA Journal* 29, 4
    (1985–1986): 442–461.
Rusch, Frederik L., ed. *A Jean Toomer Reader: Selected Unpublished Writings*. New York:
    Oxford University Press, 1993.
Schultz, Joachim. *Wild, Irre und Rein: Wörterbuch zum Primitivismus der literarischen Avant-
    garden in Deutschland und Frankreich zwischen 1900 und 1940*. Gießen, Germany:
    Anabas, 1995.
Tillery, Tyrone. *Claude McKay: A Black Poet's Struggle for Identity*. Amherst: University of
    Massachusetts Press, 1992.
Toomer, Jean. *Cane*. 1923. Reprint, New York: Liveright, 1975.
Turner, Darwin T. Introduction to *Cane*, by Jean Toomer. New York: Liveright, 1975.

JAMES SMETHURST

The Adventures of a Social Poet: Langston Hughes from the Popular Front to Black Power

One of the peculiar things about critical assessments of Langston Hughes's career is the still pronounced tendency to think of Hughes as primarily a Harlem Renaissance writer. In recent years there have been critical efforts to rethink Hughes's post–Harlem Renaissance work, particularly that of his "revolutionary" period in the 1930s and his work during the civil rights and Black Power eras. However, critics still quite commonly regard the "red" poetry as second-rate didactic efforts lacking the lyricism and nuance of voice found in other periods of Hughes's work and dismiss the early Black Power–period poems as weak and opportunistic efforts to repackage Hughes's work in order to find a niche in changing times (Ford; Sundquist; Vendler). What is peculiar about these assessments is that the later Hughes resonates with popular African American audiences so strongly, the fame of such early poems as "The Negro Speaks of Rivers" and "Mother to Son" notwithstanding. It is largely the later poetry, drama, fiction, and sketches, the "Simple" stories, such poems as "Harlem," "Theme for English B," and "Let America Be America," such plays as *Black Nativity* and *Simply Heavenly*, that have made Hughes among the most beloved writers for a general black readership—and for many post–World War II black artists and intellectuals. In fact, one might say that the work of Hughes not only appealed to a general black audience but in no small part created

From *A Historical Guide to Langston Hughes*, pp. 141–168. © 2004 by Oxford University Press, Inc.

that audience for a serious, often formally difficult, vernacular-based and politically radical African American literature that engaged the forms and resources of popular culture.

Hughes's work at the beginning of the 1930s was in three distinctive registers aimed at three relatively discrete audiences. This division of Hughes's work into three basic modes can be seen as a reflection of the relative weakness of the Left within the broader African American community in the early 1930s at the same time that the political, cultural, and economic impact of the Great Depression and a new Communist Party engagement with "Negro Liberation" drew African American intellectuals and artists further into the circles of the communist Left. One register might be thought of as the emphatically "literary" in a modernist vein. The primary audience for this work was the relatively small, interracial (though largely white) group(s) of readers who habitually read "serious" modern literature. Hughes's writing in this mode included not only the lyrics collected in *Dear Lovely Death* (1932) but also his early short stories, which were largely modeled on the short fiction of D. H. Lawrence. These lyrics and stories are suffused with feelings of alienation, fragmented identity, and failed attempts to constitute or reconstitute family and community. Perhaps the most representative stories in this regard are those based on Hughes's experiences as merchant seaman in the early 1920s. As with Melville's Ishmael, the African American narrator who has shipped out on a freighter bound for West Africa with a polyglot crew of "Greeks, West Indian Negroes, Irish, Portuguese, and Americans" finds an "America" in which normative bonds of race, nationality, and ethnicity are at times temporarily transcended, redrawn, and reconfirmed—tellingly, the Americans, black and white, are not always clearly marked by race. An African American narrator frequently searches for an organic connection to an African heritage but finds himself strangely rejected and assigned to another community in which he is an outsider when the indigenous people see him indistinguishable from his "white" (and "brown") mates. At the same time, "American" customs are sometimes upheld in a context that totally changes their meaning, as in "The Little Virgin." In that story, Mike, an older sailor from Newark, New Jersey, strikes an African prostitute for spilling his beer in a waterfront bar in Senegal. A younger sailor, "The Little Virgin," who is a sort of protégé of the older man, deranged by loneliness and a loss of community, attacks Mike. The story ends with "The Little Virgin" deliriously chanting over and over, "He oughtn't to hit a woman." The African American narrator's understated outrage over the injustice of colonialism, racism, sexual exploitation, and the miserable treatment of merchant seaman mixes with a confusion of racial, gender, class, and national lines that results from his own implicit alienation and lack of community. Hughes would take up this irony again later in a far more humorous vein in the 1946 story "Who's Passing for Who."

Another mode of Hughes's writing was what might be thought of as African American uplift. This mode consisted largely of dramatic monologues, such as "The Negro Mother," "The Colored Soldier," and "The Black Clown," collected as *The Negro Mother and Other Dramatic Recitations* (1932), that served as much of the basis for Hughes's early reading tours across the South. These readings, largely at African American educational institutions, were predominantly attended by "middle-class" African American audiences (Rampersad 1986, 223–34). This material consisted largely of formally conservative poems of black pride and perseverance leavened by the occasional humorous piece, such as "Broke." Interestingly, "Broke" draws on the conventions of African American vaudeville that had their origins in black or "Ethiopian" minstrelsy:

> Aw-oo! Yonder comes a woman I used to know way down
> South. (Ain't seen her in six years! Used to go with her, too!)
> She would be alright if she wasn't so bow-legged, and cross-eyed,
> And didn't have such a big mouth.
> Howdy-do, daughter! Caledonia, how are you? (*CP*, 150)

Drawing on the resources of minstrel-derived comic theater seems at odds with several of the "serious" uplift poems, such as "The Black Clown" and "The Big-Timer," in which minstrel images serve as metonymies for black false consciousness. In some respects, this contradiction mirrors traditional African American divides of secular and sacred, of uplift and popular entertainment. Few other black writers, with the exception of Helene Johnson, were willing to take on the representation of this divide without devaluing one side or the other. One could see the coexistence of "Broke" with the uplift poems as a gesture by Hughes toward the split of Paul Laurence Dunbar in "We Wear the Mask" and elsewhere. It also anticipates Hughes's future attempts to put different African American voices, different discourses really, in conversation with each other.

The final sort of work Hughes wrote in the early 1930s was his "revolutionary" poetry, prose, and drama. Hughes's revolutionary writing includes the many poems that he published in such journals associated with the communist Left as *New Masses*, the *Daily Worker*, and the *Harlem Liberator*. In fact, Hughes's work probably appeared more frequently in the communist Left press than that of any other writer. Of course, Hughes had published poetry in leftist journals since the mid-1920s. However, the combination of the economic crisis of the Great Depression, which struck the black community particularly hard, and the single-minded devotion to the causes of "Negro Liberation" and anticolonialism on the part of the Communist Party of the United States of America drew Hughes into a much closer relationship with the communist Left in the early 1930s. He served as president of the League of Struggle for Negro Rights and participated prominently in the Left-led struggle to save the nine Scottsboro defendants from execution, as well as in other Left-initiated campaigns.

One of Hughes's most widely circulated radical pieces of the period was his jazz-inflected semiverse play "Scottsboro Limited." This play was performed in a variety of locations around the country by leftist theater groups as part of the campaign to save the Scottsboro defendants. It ended with black and white workers joining the newly revolutionary Scottsboro defendants, each now the "new red Negro," in smashing the electric chair—and, by extension, racist and capitalist oppression. While Hughes's shorter revolutionary lyrics of the 1930s seem to draw away from the vernacular language- and music-based pieces of the 1920s, "Scottsboro Limited" is a testament to Hughes's embryonic attempts to imagine an African American popular radical art that would appeal to a broad black audience beyond a relatively small cadre of organized radicals.

Hughes's project of creating a popular radical art that would appeal to a wide African American (as well as non-African American) audience found new opportunities with the rise of the Popular Front era in the mid-1930s. A full description of the features and events of the Popular Front are beyond the scope of this essay. However, some general comments on the Popular Front and on Popular Front aesthetics and literary practices are in order. As to periodization, while the official era of the Popular Front as a policy of broad-based antifascist coalition building by the Communist International might be marked from the Seventh Comintern Congress, in 1935, to the Hitler–Stalin Pact, in 1939, the Popular Front approach dominated the communist Left, particularly in what was known as the "cultural work," until at least 1948. One of the most notable, and most noted, features of Popular Front aesthetics is a conscious mixing of genres and media—of "high" and "low," of "popular" and "literary," of Whitman and Eliot, of folk culture and mass culture, of literary and nonliterary documents.

Another important of feature of much Popular Front art was an interest in race and ethnicity and the relation of racial identity and ethnic identity to an American identity. Some commentators have considered the Popular Front to be a retreat from earlier communist concerns with ethnic and national identity, particularly with the African American "nation," promoting instead a sentimental and blandly assimilationist multiculturalism. While there is some evidence for this argument, when one considers the poetry of Sterling Brown, Frank Marshall Davis, Langston Hughes, Waring Cuney, and Margaret Walker in the second half of the 1930s, narratives such as Donato DiPietro's *Christ in Concrete*, Jerre Mangione's *Mount Allegro*, Daniel Fuchs's Williamsburg trilogy, Carlos Bulosan's *America Is in the Heart*, H. T. Tsiang's *And China Has Hands*, Richard Wright's *Native Son*, the famous "Spirituals to Swing" concerts of 1939, and paintings by Jacob Lawrence, Ben Shahn, Aaron Douglas, and Jack Levine, to name but a few of many, many examples, it is clear that race and ethnicity remained overriding concerns during the Popular Front. It is true that these concerns were often as much about transformation, interaction, and hybridity as they were about tradition, distinction, and separate development. This interest in race, ethnicity, and nationality within artistic, literary or quasi-literary works of the Popular Front was frequently linked to a strong sense of community and region and the relationship of place, particularly (though not exclusively) the urban neighborhood, to American identity.

While the poetics of the Popular Front shaped (and were shaped by) Hughes's poetry, especially in such poems as "Broadcast on Ethiopia," "Air Raid over Harlem," and "Seven Moments of Love," as well as his "poetry-play" (and musical) "Don't You Want to Be Free?" the foremost examples of Hughes's Popular Front approach (and perhaps the premier literary achievement of the Popular Front) are his "Simple" stories. Of course, the composition and publication of these stories spanned several literary/political/historical periods, from the late Popular Front to the McCarthy era to the civil rights period to the early stirring of the Black Power/Black Arts era. The "Simple" stories (named after their protagonist, Jesse B. Semple, aka "Simple") first emerged as part of Hughes's "From Here to Yonder" *Chicago Defender* column in 1943 and continued to appear until 1965. While the home paper of the stories was the *Defender* (and, at the very end of the series' life, the *New York Post*), the stories were syndicated to a wide range of papers, including such nationalist journals as *Muhammad Speaks*.

These stories were shaped by the cultural conversations of World War II and Cold War America, particularly among African Americans, and how in turn they attempted to push the boundaries of acceptable political and aesthetic discourse in the Cold War era or at least to retain some shred of Popular Front poetics and politics. Hughes is adamant about avoiding political and artistic marginalization in the Simple stories, as in much of his work, both in terms of the African American community and American society generally. Instead, Hughes is determined to place, or re-place, the African American speaker, and his or her voice, at the center of some of our society's primary defining stories.

These stories were molded by late Popular Front aesthetics (of which, as noted, Hughes was one of the chief creators) of the World War II era but were adapted brilliantly to the Cold War. World War II provided African Americans unprecedented opportunities to break through the legal and extralegal barriers of Jim Crow segregation, particularly in the areas of housing and employment. These opportunities occurred for what might be thought of as ideological as well as practical reasons—not that you can completely separate the two. On a practical level, the vastly increased demand for labor in the war industries, which included everything from meat packing to making bombs, and the vastly decreased availability of white male workers, many of whom enlisted or were drafted into the military, opened up to African Americans jobs that had previously been thought of as "white." This, along with a continued decline in the tenant farmer system in southern agriculture, accelerated the migration of African Americans to urban centers, such as Chicago, Detroit, Baltimore, St. Louis, Memphis, Birmingham, Los Angeles, and, of course, New York.

On an ideological level, the system of Jim Crow and the American ideology of white superiority were obviously uncomfortably close to the tenets of Nazi Germany and to notions of Aryan superiority. The civil rights movements, significantly led by communists, socialists, Trotskyists, and other sorts of leftists during World War II, spent much time emphasizing to great effect the contradiction inherent in supporting white supremacy while fighting Nazism. Also, a certain ideological space for the fight against racism was created by actual and feared antiwhite propaganda appeals by the Japanese to African Americans, whom the U.S. government feared might see the early victories of Japan over the United States, Britain, France, and the Netherlands as victories over the ideology of white superiority.

In short, a combination of guilt, fear, and contradiction allowed civil rights organizations to argue effectively against racism to an extent not seen since the end of Reconstruction. This is not to say that it was easy or that Jim Crow did not remain the law of much of the land, including much of the North, only that it was possible for movements, such as the labor and civil rights leader A. Philip Randolph's March on Washington movement in 1942, to make large demands on a national and local level and to achieve significant results, such as Roosevelt's executive order banning discrimination in federal employment and the establishment of the Fair Employment Practices Commission.

It is worth noting that this sort of thing had happened before, if not to this extent. During World War I, labor shortages also opened up new jobs to African Americans, prompting the beginning of what we now call the "Great Migration" of African Americans from the South to the North. And, while in that conflict the United States was not at war with an explicitly racist enemy, it did mobilize for the war with a rhetoric of democracy that civil rights leaders, such as W. E. B. Du Bois, felt provided an opportunity for African Americans to argue against institutionalized racism. However, in what might be thought of as the racial reconversion process after the war, such hopes were dashed to a large extent. Many African Americans lost their wartime jobs once the First World War was over. The Ku Klux Klan grew into a national organization with millions of members in the late 1910s and 1920s. And, even before the war ended, a wave of racist violence began, ranging from lynchings, often of black soldiers in uniform, to race riots in East St. Louis, Chicago, Omaha, Knoxville, and many other American cities, where white mobs attacked black neighborhoods. The often frankly stated purpose of the violence was to remind African Americans of "their place," whether in terms of jobs, housing, public accommodations, or general demeanor. This violence was carried out with a minimum of federal interference despite the activities of civil rights organizations, such as the "silent parade" of 1917, in which ten thousand African Americans marched down New York's Fifth Avenue to protest lynchings and assaults on black communities such as the East St. Louis riot of 1917.

What made the post–World War II era different from the period after World War I was the interrelated phenomena of the Cold War and decolonization in Asia, Africa, the Caribbean, and Latin America. The post–World War II period was characterized by competition and conflict between what might be thought of as a capitalist bloc of nations led by the United States and a communist bloc of nations led by the Soviet Union, or, as it was often put in the United States, democracy versus communism. The period of the late 1940s, 1950s, and early 1960s was also marked by a huge upsurge in anticolonial struggles, both violent, as in China, Algeria, Cuba, the Philippines, Malaya, Kenya, and Indochina, and relatively peaceful, as in India, Ghana, South Africa (until the 1960s), and Guyana. These anticolonial struggles complicated the Cold War for the United States in that the bloc of nations led by the United States included the leading colonial powers—Britain, France, the Netherlands, Portugal, Belgium, and the United States itself. The situation was further complicated by the fact that many anticolonial struggles were led by communists and/or other sorts of leftists who were relatively open to Communism. While the United States on occasion directly supported the old colonial powers, as in Indochina and in the Portuguese colonies in Africa, more and more the United States's policy vis-à-vis decolonization tended to be the support of anticommunist alternatives to Left-led anticolonial movements. The result was that the battle for the hearts and minds of what we sometimes refer to as the Third World (a term that has its origins in the era of Cold War decolonization) became a crucial aspect of the Cold War and American international policies.

American racism and the institutions of Jim Crow became hugely important factors in this struggle for hearts and minds. In the first place, while not exactly the same as U.S. racism, the ideological underpinning of colonialism rested to a large extent on notions of white supremacy. As a result, the peoples of European and American colonies and neo-colonies were extremely interested in and identified with the conditions and struggles of black people in the United States where the fight against white supremacy had been sharper and antiracism more clearly articulated than in any other country. And, of course, these same peoples remained very suspicious of U.S. claims for American-style democracy while the glaring contradictions of Jim Crow remained. Left-led movements and the bloc of communist nations were not slow in pointing these contradictions out. For example, when the militant Florida NAACP leader Harry Moore was assassinated by the Ku Klux Klan in 1951, the Soviet ambassador to the United Nations denounced Moore's murder on the floor of the UN General Assembly. Similarly, Soviet premier Nikita Khrushchev repeatedly raised the issue of racial discrimination in the United States with Vice President Richard Nixon in their famous 1959 "Kitchen Debates." And, African Americans here in the United States also noted the contradictions between U.S. rhetoric abroad and the U.S. reality for African Americans at home—as seen in various of Hughes's works, such as the early Cold War–era story "When a Man Sees Red," in which the narrator, Simple, imagines himself denouncing the John Martin Wood, the Georgia congressman and open Ku Klux Klan member who chaired the House Un-American Activities Committee and who conflated African American equality and communism (*RS* 84–86).

Thus, it is not surprising that many of the actions of various branches of the federal government, such as the U.S. Supreme Court's decision in *Brown vs. the Board of Education*, specifically cited the Cold War as a justification for the ending or restricting of various aspects of Jim Crow segregation. This is not to say here that the federal government was completely sympathetic to the civil rights movement—or that these victories did not require tremendous struggle, organization, courage, and sacrifice on the part of the civil rights activists, only that the Cold War provided African Americans with new leverage to fight against Jim Crow, and prevented, at least partially, the sort of racial reconversion that followed World War I. And, in much the same way that the earlier struggles of African Americans influenced contemporary anticolonial movements, the liberation movements in Asia, Africa, and Latin America galvanized African Americans. At the same time, the rapid changes worldwide brought on by the anticolonial movement around the world inspired a sense of impatience in many more activist African Americans who found the rate of change in the United States much too slow by comparison.

The late 1940s and early 1950s witnessed high-profile federal interrogation and/or persecution of many of the African Americans who were, or had
been, most prominently linked to the Communist Party, such as the leading
black Communists Benjamin Davis and Henry Winston, W. E. B. Du Bois,
the singer and actor Paul Robeson, and Hughes himself. In addition to high-
profile trials, hearings, jailings, deprivation of citizens' right to travel, and so
on, the period also featured lower-profile (and sometimes covert) disruptions
of the lives of various black artists and intellectuals deemed "disloyal." At the
same time, Left-led black organizations, such as the Southern Negro Youth
Congress, the National Negro Labor Council, the Civil Rights Congress, and
the Southern Conference for Human Welfare, were denounced as "communist fronts," isolated, and destroyed.

Of course, the Communist Party created plenty of its own problems during the period and was torn apart by Khrushchev's 1956 revelations about the
extent of Stalin's murderous activities and the Soviet-led invasion of Hungary.
But it is worth recalling how limited political discourse in the United States
was once the domestic Cold War really intensified around 1947. Thus, you
had an ironic situation in which the Cold War, with its international competition with communism, provided new opportunities to challenge Jim Crow
practically and ideologically, as in the campaign that resulted in President
Truman's 1948 order abolishing segregation in the armed forces, while at the
same time the actual organizations and individuals that had led the struggle
for African American equality during the 1930s and 1940s were destroyed,
discredited, isolated, or forced to bend over backward to prove their anticommunist purity, as in the case of the NAACP, which supported the government
persecution of W. E. B. Du Bois. On an ideological level, an anticommunist
consensus of liberals and conservatives is declared; individualism becomes
emphasized, and forms of group identification, especially of class and race, are
considered passé, if not downright un-American; the notion of ideological
struggle in which Marxism, communism, and socialism are legitimate positions is attacked, and even the word "ideology" itself becomes suspect.

Thus, the "Simple" stories grew out of the late Popular Front moment
and Popular Front hybrid, multigeneric, multimedia aesthetics but were used
by Hughes to engage the cultural moment of the Cold War. For example,
the story "Temptation," Simple's working-class, African American revisionist take on *Genesis*, first appeared in book form in the 1950 collection *Simple
Speaks His Mind*. A partial list of the texts, movements, institutions, figures,
and events that this short and seemingly "Simple" piece references the Bible,
African American folk religion, popular American religious culture, Milton's
Paradise Lost, an array of African American religious figures from fifty years of
Harlem history, African American nationalism (particularly Marcus Garvey's

Universal Negro Improvement Association and its religious arm, the African Orthodox Church), the Cold War and the arms race, the antinuclear weapons gospel song "Atom and Evil" by the Golden Gate Quartet, Bing Crosby, the 1936 film *The Green Pastures*, African American variety-show comedy (with the generally unnamed narrator as the straight man), the African American rhetorical practices of capping (or ritualized insult) and toasting (a form of rhymed and often bawdy narrative oratory), and what might be thought of as the ur-text of American racism from which black people as full humans are absent. Perhaps the most frequent "high culture" reference is to the most iconic canonical English writer, Shakespeare, recalled by Simple's nutty and often free-associative rants, which frequently make disturbing sense (as in the jump from apple to atom), more sense generally in the context of political and cultural politics during the high Cold War than the pronouncements of the more "reasonable" narrator. The most overt invocation appears in the narrator's typically stiff world-as-stage comment at the end of the story: "I trust you will not let your rather late arrival on our contemporary stage distort your perspective." (Simple tersely and with perfect timing answers, "No") (*TBOS* 28). This obvious reference to Shakespeare and Hamlet's famous speech recalls also the clown-gravediggers of *Hamlet* and their comments on Adam, thereby connecting Simple with the Shakespearean fool who speaks truth, albeit often obliquely—a useful ability in the Cold War era.

The issue of audience, imagined and real, is crucial to our understanding of what Hughes is doing in the Simple stories. To start with the stories in their original context of the *Chicago Defender*, one needs to note that the *Defender* and the more reputable journals of the African American press and their readers were not necessarily in sympathy with the street culture embodied by Jesse Semple, who is definitely one of what Amiri Baraka, in his play *Dutchman*, called "all these blues people" (Baraka 98). For example, other than accepting ads for new record releases, the *Defender* was notably unengaged with the blues boom of the 1920s and early 1930s. While this was somewhat less true later, the attitude of the *Defender* and many of its readers, to generalize broadly, was a lot like that of Simple's wife Joyce, who is always taking Simple to lectures, "classical" European music concerts, poetry readings, and the Episcopal church in hopes of "improving" him, without notable results.

Thus, Hughes uses Simple to make an intraracial (as opposed to interracial) argument against a Eurocentric model of cultural value that enshrines dead or near-dead white people at the expense of the culture of the majority of African Americans. This model of cultural value is bad, Hughes argues through Simple, because it ignores living African American "high" artists unless they have been certified by white taste makers—as seen in "Banquet in Honor," where an elderly African American artist takes an "elite" black gathering to task for not supporting him until he was called a genius by the *New York Times* (*TBOS* 46).

Hughes also criticizes this Eurocentric model because it excludes the vast majority of African American cultural expression and, by extension, the producers and consumers of this expression such as Simple. Such an approach is seen as elitist, pessimistic, and self-hating. Simple does not completely reject "high" culture but instead explicitly proposes a model in which African American popular expression, particularly music, is integrated, so to speak, with "high" culture. This approach is seen as far more optimistic, self-affirming and democratically inclusive of the entire African American community:

> A jazz band like Duke's or Hamp's or Basie's sure would of helped that meeting. At least on Saturday afternoon, they could have used a little music to put some pep into the proceedings. Now just say for instant, baby, they was to open with jazz and close with jam—and do the talking in between. (*TBOS* 244)

Simple's construct of the African American popular tradition is one that stretches from the "classic" blues of the 1920s, as seen in the story "Shadow of the Blues," to the big band jazz of the 1930s, as seen in "Jazz, Jive, and Jam," to the bebop of the 1940s as seen in "Bop"—from Ma Rainey to Duke Ellington to Dizzy Gillespie. As he did so often in his career, Hughes is making an argument for the fundamental continuity of African American expressive culture. Here Hughes is making not only an intraracial argument but also an interracial argument. Once again, the issue of audience, imagined and real, comes into play. While the audience for the columns in the *Defender* was almost entirely African American, the audience for the collections, especially *The Best of Simple* (1961), was another thing. In the 1940s and 1950s, various schools of white critics and listeners adopted jazz for their different cultural purposes. This period featured a "Dixieland Revival" in which versions of early New Orleans jazz were promoted as the "real" jazz; there were similar champions of Big Band jazz; finally there was a bohemian or "avant-garde" school that adopted bebop as its badge of rebellion (Gennari 1991). By featuring so prominently stories that proclaim the continuity of African American music—and, by extension, African American culture—Hughes pointedly argues against appropriations of African American culture that would remove pieces of that culture from their larger context. And, of course, the notion that African American popular culture had a place within Euro-American "high" culture—and Euro-American popular culture—was also directed as much to white audiences as black and so became a prominent part of the collections, especially *The Best of Simple*.

The arguments Hughes makes here are not simply sociological, political, or even broadly cultural but are also literary in that he is polemicizing against what might be considered the "high" neo-Modernist approach that arose in American letters during the 1950s. What this neo-Modernism consisted of, for the most part, was a stripped-down "high" modernism derived from a fairly restricted reading of European and American "high" literary modernism of the early twentieth century, such as the works of Eliot, Yeats, and the early Joyce, a neo-Modernism that was formally conservative and aspiring toward a sort of "universality" that tended to avoid or decry the concerns with popular culture, ethnicity, race, and locale that animated the Popular Front. While we most prominently associate the "high" neo-Modernist styles championed by the New Critics and the New York Intellectuals with such diverse poets as Robert Lowell, Delmore Schwartz, John Berryman, and Allen Tate and with fiction writers such as Saul Bellow, Schwartz, and Mary McCarthy, it also had a huge influence on African American letters in the work of such writers as Ellison, Robert Hayden, Gwendolyn Brooks, and Melvin Tolson. Of course, Ellison is very difficult to pigeonhole because he adopts the radical and largely abstract individualism that marks much neo-Modernist art during the 1950s while retaining the engagement with folk culture and popular culture that was a hallmark of many of the early works of the literary Left in which Ellison, as well as Hughes, participated. Hughes, instead, argued through these "Simple" stories, and in his poetry, for a style that was popular and modern, even postmodern, and that drew on the resources of mass culture.

This is not to say that the essence of Hughes's argument translates into a simplistic style for a debased audience. On a formal level, the Simple stories are quite complex. The metaphor of conversation appears so much in this essay because it arises organically from these texts, which are often literally a series of conversations, say between Simple and the narrator, which in turn often describe a dizzying spiral of interlocking conversations. Consider the levels of narration in the Simple stories for a minute. For example, in a number of stories, you have Simple's Cousin Minnie or Joyce or the "old gentleman" artist of "Banquet in Honor" speaking through Simple speaking through the narrator speaking through Langston Hughes the author whose presence as author is established by the forewords of the various collections. Such a plethora of overlapping narratorial voices reminds us that the Simple stories foreground, are in fact virtually nothing but, the overt representation and recreation of a wide range of African American speakers. These stories, as is virtually all of Hughes's work, are characterized by the representations and re-creation of diverse black voices and white voices. This much resembles the Russian literary critic Mikhail Bahktin's notion of heteroglossia in what Bahktin calls dialogic fiction, in which different voices contained within a text represent different, and often conflicting, social groups (Bahktin 1984). (One might also raise the formal principle of antiphony, or call and response, which characterizes much vernacular [or folk] African and African American culture.) Hughes allows the voices to remain in all their diversity and conflict while insisting on an ultimate community between these integral African American speaking subjects. In short, this is, as Simple says, not quite simple.

Other formal aspects of the Simple stories are worth mentioning. First, there is the obvious influence of music, not only thematically, as in the genealogy of the blues cited by the narrator and Simple in "Shadow of the Blues," but in the diction and syntax of Simple's speech. Not only does Simple quote fragments of blues, but the blues often inflect Simple's speech:

> But Zarita has ruint my life. You don't know how it feels, buddy, when somebody has gone that you never had before. I never had a woman like Joyce. I *loved* that girl. Nobody never cared for me like Joyce did. (*TBOS* 83)

Not only does this passage engage the sensibility and the thematics of the blues, but the repeated "never" gives the flavor of a three-line blues stanza.

Simple's speech is similarly inflected by folk and popular African American expressive forms, including jokes, the dozens, tall tales, badman stories, and toasts. And, of course, probably the most important influence on the form of the story is black vaudeville, with the stories resembling a comic routine in which the narrator plays the straight man to Simple's clown. (It is worth mentioning that the vaudeville-style variety show survived in the African American community until the late 1960s [at the Apollo Theater, in New York City, the Regal Theater, in Chicago, the Howard, in Washington, D.C., and so on].) While in some respects the impact of African American popular music on the form of the Simple stories is more clearly foregrounded, it is hard to overemphasize the crucial connection between the Simple stories and African American vaudeville comedy. While it is one of the most difficult formal elements to analyze, in part because it is so invisible so to speak, the translation of vaudeville comic timing and rhythm onto the page in the stories is among the most brilliant accomplishments of Hughes.

Obviously, these stories, after the manner of most newspaper columns, take on many of the topical concerns of the day and respond to immediate events. One of the uses of a character as goofy as Simple is that Simple allowed Hughes to make points that were difficult to make during the Cold War. Hughes, as readers may know, was called before Joseph McCarthy's Senate committee in 1953. Hughes, unlike Paul Robeson, and unlike Simple in "When a Man Sees Red," written before Hughes's appearance, essentially apologized for his earlier radical activities and proclaimed his patriotism—though he did not name names, as they said back then. Hughes lay very low politically for quite a while after that. This is important to our understanding of the shape and content of the *Best of Simple*, which appeared in 1961. The collection features the illustrations of Bernhard Nast, a German artist who first illustrated a German edition of the Simple stories. Nast's drawings put Simple in a depoliticized frame, emphasizing the aspects of Simple as a lover and hanger-around, rather than as a worker and commentator on race and class relations. After 1953, Hughes also toned down, though he did not eliminate, his criticism of the various communist-hunting government committees. Hughes did not include even this muted criticism in *The Best of Simple*. Neither did he comment on anticolonial struggles much in *The Best of Simple*, though he often mentioned these struggles in his *Defender* stories even after 1953.

Nonetheless, even in *The Best of Simple*, Simple makes many points, including the right to armed self-defense against racists in "A Toast to Harlem," and refers to the Cold War in such stories as "Radioactive Red Caps" and "Temptation" in ways that might have been considered subversive. After the manner of fools in Shakespeare's plays, Simple plays the clown who speaks the truth for discerning listeners (readers) to hear. That Simple speaks the truth to an often ambiguous and ambivalent narrator who is sometimes identified with Hughes further suggests the nature of Hughes's own mask during the McCarthy era.

The Cold War clearly shaped not only the subjects and the denotative meaning of the stories but also the formal choices that Hughes made—even down to the selection of stories and illustrations for *The Best of Simple*. However, while shaped by many of the same concerns and pressures as other artists, Hughes argues against much of Cold War culture. Hughes, like many artists of that era, is much concerned with the relation between individual identity and group identity. As vivid a personality as Simple is, Hughes nonetheless makes the claim in the Foreword to *The Best of Simple* that "it is impossible to live in Harlem and not know at least a hundred Simples." The point here is that Simple is both a type and an individual and that there is not necessarily a contradiction between individual identity and group identity—whether of race, class, or gender. This is obviously different from such diverse cultural products of the Cold War era as Ralph Ellison's novel *Invisible Man*, the abstract expressionist painting of Willem de Kooning, Jackson Pollock, and Franz Kline, and the films *High Noon, Invasion of the Body Snatchers*, and *Rebel Without a Cause*, to name a few of the most famous high-art and popular-culture works of the era, which emphasized a heroic but somewhat abstract individualism (as indicated semantically by the names of the most famous James Dean movie [*Rebel Without a Cause*] and the dominant movement in the visual arts [abstract expressionism]). Thus, on the level of formal construction, Hughes pushes the limits of Cold War end-of-ideology culture. In this, we have an excellent example of how formal choices have a certain cultural meaning and how particular arguments, including what constitutes literary value, cultural value, and political value, are advanced by the shifting diction, the complex layering of narration, the incorporation of the forms, subjects, and inflections of African American folk culture and popular culture, and a huge range of literary, musical, folkloric, sociological, political, and historical allusion seamlessly compressed into a "Simple" style—a style so "Simple" that it seems to be a natural expression and not the sort of literary production that, like the most critically valued postwar fiction, say *Invisible Man*, wears its literariness on its sleeve.

Hughes's poetry in the late 1940s and early 1950s, particularly *Montage of a Dream Deferred* (1951), also in many ways continues a Popular Front sensibility in a Cold War context, though it is more clearly engaged with "neo-Modernist" poetics than his short fiction. "Neo-Modernist" here refers to the powerful trend among black and white writers, such as Delmore Schwartz, John Berryman, Robert Lowell, Allen Tate, Randall Jarrell, Gwendolyn Brooks, Melvin Tolson, and Robert Hayden, to propose the "high" Modernist work of the early twentieth century, particularly the work of Eliot and Pound, and, to a lesser extent, of Stevens and Crane, as the necessary ground of any truly serious contemporary literature. Hughes is mentioned less often with this neo-Modernist aesthetic. If one looks for a "high" Modernist analog of Hughes's *Montage*, it would be found in the work of William Carlos Williams, rather than that of Eliot, Pound, Stevens, or even Hart Crane—though Crane's *The Bridge* certainly has some affinities to Hughes's poetic sequence. (Hughes's *Montage* could be productively paired with William Carlos Williams's *Paterson*, though that is beyond the scope of this essay.) Certainly, the fact that Hughes's text is rooted in African American rhetoric—song lyrics, jokes, turns of speech—and is, as announced in the prefatory note, organized formally with the "conflicting changes, sudden nuances, sharp and impudent interjections, broken rhythms" of bebop in mind—makes problematic the model of the neo-Modernist text that draws back from the vernacular-influenced diction and "social realism" that characterized much of the poetry of the 1930s and early 1940s (*CP* 387). Unlike other forms of American neo-Modernist art, abstract expressionist painting for example, Hughes's work not only retains the stance of rebellion but also makes rebelliousness and potential rebellion quite explicit, most famously in "Harlem," which both psychologically contextualizes the Harlem riots of 1935 and 1943 and also predicts future unrest.

At the same time it is necessary to point out that Hughes's choice of the word "montage" in the title of the poem signals his desire to connect his work with an earlier era of artistic modernism. Of course, Hughes's use of a montage-like technique has in its origins in his earliest work, such as the 1925 "The Cat and the Saxophone," and can be clearly seen in such poems of the 1930s as "Radio Broadcast on Ethiopia" and "Air Raid over Harlem." But Hughes took this polyvocal technique further in *Montage* than he did in any of his earlier works, with the possible exceptions of his verse plays, notably the 1938 semimusical "Don't You Want to Be Free?" And, even in these plays, the juxtaposition of the voices is less radical and the transitions between scenes is usually less abrupt than the transitions of the *Montage* sequence. Of course, one can read a number of Hughes's earlier collections, notably the 1927 *Fine Clothes to the Jew* and the 1942 *Shakespeare in Harlem*, as essentially polyvocal montages of black America, but even in those collections there is a sense that the individual poems stand on their own far more than those of *Montage*, despite the relative fame of the poem "Harlem." That Hughes included *Montage* in its entirety in his *Selected Poems*, with one significant change that will be noted later, indicates that he too saw this work as a single long poem or a poetic sequence, rather than a collection.

The use of the word "montage" in the title indicates a connection to an earlier era of modernist art, notably the overtly Left side of German expressionism and the early Soviet cinema, especially the films and criticism of Sergei Eisenstein. However, the claim that the sequence is formally influenced by bebop—a claim thematized in many of the sequence's poems—argues for a new, politically engaged African American modernism based on postwar urban African American experience and expressive culture. While the protest elements of the sequence are often quite explicit, as in "Freedom Train," which was removed from the "Montage" section of the *Selected Poems* by Hughes and placed in the "Words Like Freedom" section, more often they are explicitly implicit, or, to put it another way, anger is linked with fear and concealment so that the concealment of anger becomes the dominant theme of the sequence. Thus, the first poem of the sequence, "Dream Boogie," provides a guide to reading the rest of the text:

> Listen to it closely:
> Ain't you heard something underneath
> like a—
> *What did I say?* (*CP* 388)

There is an obvious connection with the longstanding African American notions, both in literature and in the folk culture, of the need to conceal one's true identity from white people, particularly those who can exercise direct power over one. *Montage* is in many respects a perfect poem for the Cold War era, as well as a revision of Paul Laurence Dunbar's bitter rondeau from the early Jim Crow period, "We Wear the Mask." (In fact, when one considers his later testimony before Joseph McCarthy's communist-hunting Senate Permanent Sub-Committee on Investigations, in which Hughes disavowed his earlier radical poems under aggressive questioning, it becomes almost heartbreaking) (Rampersad 1988, 209–21). In this poem are sounded the themes of discontent transvalued into "nonsense" syllables and "wild" music (*"Hey, pop! / Re-bop! / Mop!"*) in the face of a consensus compelled by force on those unwilling to accept it otherwise (*CP* 388). It both thematizes and embodies the enforcement of this consensus while making its shortcomings with respect to African Americans obvious. It maintains a link with Hughes's earlier "communist" poetry both in its representation of the Harlem community and its problems, which in many respects is quite "realistic," and in the implication of a coming explosion of the "dream deferred," which, while not perhaps quite as ideologically delineated as in his earlier work, is quite consonant with the calls for and predictions of social revolution in such works as "Air Raid over Harlem," "Scottsboro Limited," and "Don't You Want to Be Free?" In addition, one can also say that Hughes is making an argument for how such themes may be expressed in the Cold War era before the civil rights movement, when it is not only dangerous to express radical political positions directly but also difficult in that the institutions—whether *The New Masses*, which under the pressures of the period had retrenched from a weekly journal to a monthly and merged with the journal *Mainstream* in 1947, or the National Negro Congress, which folded in 1946—that had provided both forums and forms for such sentiments had collapsed or were becoming increasing isolated.

In many ways, Langston Hughes was himself a national African American literary institution during the 1950s and 1960s. His constant reading and lecture tours, his network of contacts across the United States (and the world), his syndicated "From Here to Yonder" column (though its home was in the *Chicago Defender*, the column, which often featured Hughes's "Simple" stories, appeared widely in the black press, from the most conservative to *Muhammad Speaks*), his work as editor of the poetry anthologies *Poetry of the Negro* (1949 and 1970) and *New Negro Poetry* (1964), and his prolific letter writing were among the many factors that made Hughes far more than a regional figure.

Nonetheless, despite his national status, from the late 1930s, at least, Hughes was strongly associated with Harlem as its most famous permanent literary resident in whose work the literary landscape of Harlem figured prominently. If Harlem retained its place as an iconic African American landscape that was both special and typical, it was in no small part through the poetry, columns, short stories, and plays of Hughes during the 1940s and 1950s. The "Simple" stories and the poetry sequence *Montage of a Dream Deferred* were particularly influential in maintaining Harlem as a literary site where the somewhat conflicting figurations of the neighborhood as a place of refuge, home, and prison intersect.

In many respects, it was the work of Hughes that made Harold Cruse's claims for Harlem as the necessary locus of the new black revolution in *Crisis of the Negro Intellectual* (1967) and Amiri Baraka's (and that of other proto–Black Arts intellectuals in the East) initial sense of Harlem as "home" plausible. The move of Baraka and other African American artists and intellectuals (either physically or in terms of orientation, since many, including Sun Ra and other "new thing" musicians, continued to live downtown) from Greenwich Village or the Lower East Side to Harlem gained much of its power from the work of Hughes.

Hughes was also an influential model for those artists and intellectuals who were trying to imagine and define a "Black Aesthetic." Hughes, after all, had been investigating the possibilities of a distinctly African American literary diction and literary forms for decades. As noted, Hughes had written poems, sketches, and stories that drew on the formal resources of jazz, the blues, gospel, r & b, toasting, badman stories and songs, tall tales, black vaudeville humor, the dozens and other forms of "signifying," street corner and barbershop conversations, sermons, and so on since the 1920s. For those black artists and intellectuals, particularly such East Coast intellectuals as Baraka, Touré, and Larry Neal, who imagined a continuum of African American culture from Africa to the United States present, including folk, popular, and avant-garde elements, Hughes was the great predecessor. Hughes's work had long been distinguished by his willingness to draw on folk blues, popular music, and various "art" music traditions simultaneously. This can be seen during the 1950s not only in his explicit formal and thematic references to bebop generally in *Montage of a Dream Deferred* but specifically in his great utopian poem "Projection," from *Montage*, where the speaker dreams that "Paul Robeson / will team up with Jackie Mabley" (*CP* 404).

Beyond Hughes's work as a writer and editor was the impact that he had as a tireless supporter of younger black writers, both formally and informally. On a formal level, Hughes (like his close friend Arna Bontemps) was constantly writing (often without solicitation by the artist) recommendations, letters of support, and so on, to gain grants, fellowships, and other sorts of institutional support for young black writers, such as Amiri Baraka, Ron Milner, and Conrad Kent Rivers, as well as for older writers who would play significant roles in the Black Arts Movement, such as Margaret Danner (Bontemps and Hughes 53; Rampersad 1988, 310–11). Hughes was also famous for writing letters of encouragement to young writers (and not so young writers) who published what Hughes considered to be strong work. Hughes also made an effort to appear on programs with younger and/or less-known writers and to meet with groups of these writers on his reading trips (Smith 107–11). Hughes was a particularly strong supporter and presence in New York for such proto–Black Arts institutions as the Market Place Gallery readings organized in Harlem by Raymond Patterson and the Umbra group, based primarily on the Lower East Side (Rampersad 1988, 311). On a less formal level, Hughes, as he had for decades, constantly introduced writers and intellectuals to each other, extending circles of acquaintance and interest at social gatherings in a seemingly offhand way.

Some Black Arts activists did sharply criticize Hughes and his basic commitment to integrationism, as well as his use of popular culture (O'Neal). However, it is easy to see why so many cite him as a crucial influence, as evidenced by memoirs, introductions, and dedications to volumes, poems (e.g., Larry Neal's "Don't Say Good-Bye to the Porkpie Hat" and Etheridge Knight's "For Langston Hughes"), and tributes, such as Woodie King's "On Langston Hughes," which appeared in two major Black Arts journals, *Negro Digest* (later renamed *Black World*) and *Black Theatre*. Hughes's work as a writer, columnist, and editor, his formal and informal support of younger writers, and his tireless effort to build and extend networks of black artists and intellectuals (and to connect those artists to an audience) were crucial in the emergence of the new black writing, especially in New York City. If New York was an early center of the emerging Black Arts Movement, it was in no small part because of Hughes.

Like a number of the most politically engaged older black writers and intellectuals, such as Margaret Burroughs, Margaret Walker, John O. Killens, and Melvin Tolson, Hughes maintained a stance of critical support toward the emerging Black Arts Movement in his work. Some have read Hughes's final collection, *The Panther and the Lash* (1967), as a largely unconvincing attempt to repackage himself so as to advance his career (Ford). Others have seen it, in the final analysis, as a repudiation of the new black poetry (Rampersad 1988, 412).

However, the collection, which combines new politically militant poems with older radical poems from the 1930s and 1940s, is both a critique and a gesture of support. A large part of Hughes's project in the collection was to encourage younger poets and activists while reminding them of earlier moments of African American cultural and political radicalism. In this, Hughes was like a number of older writers, such as Dudley Randall, Margaret Walker, and John

O. Killens, who became associated with the Black Arts Movement, as Hughes might have had he lived long enough.

Another aspect of it seems to be an attempt to rethink Hughes's own career, and by extension those of the radicals and former radicals of his generation, within the frame of the new militants. The ending of "Stokely Malcolm Me" may not be, as Arnold Rampersad suggests, a parodic "beat" critique of Black Power and the new black poetry:

Stokely,
did I ever live
up your
way?
???
??
?
          (*CP* 561)

While it is possible that Hughes was lampooning the Beats and the Student Non-Violent Coordinating Committee (SNCC) leader Kwame Turé (Stokely Carmichael), the shape of the poem's end mirrors the ending of Hughes's "Elderly Leaders" (first published in 1936 as "Elderly Race Leaders"), which appeared in the first section of *The Panther and the Lash*:

They clutch at the egg
Their master's
Goose laid:
$$$$$
$$$$
$$$
$$
$$
          (*CP* 194)

As Arnold Rampersad points out, the former poem was composed in the aftermath of a bitter debate around the term (and concept) of "Black Power," which had been popularized by Turé. This debate featured the forceful denunciation of the idea of Black Power by "elderly race leaders," notably Hughes's friend Roy Wilkins, of the NAACP. This criticism was met by often personally vituperative responses on the part of Black Power supporters such as Amiri Baraka, who threatened "to stick half my sandal up / his ass" (Rampersad 1988, 411). However, it is worth noting that Hughes's critique in the later poem is hardly less cutting, if less verbally violent, than Baraka's. It is telling that the dollar signs of the earlier poem are replaced by the question marks of the later work. The dollar signs are linked to the denounced race leaders of the earlier poem, while the question marks are connected to the later poem's speaker. The relation of the pronouns in the later poem are telling in this regard. If Hughes were simply critiquing Turé (you) and the Black Power advocates, and if the "I" ("me") referred to the voice of an African American everyman/woman, as often was the case in Hughes's poetry, then Hughes could suggested a distance between Black Power and "the people" by saying "Did you ever live up my way?"—much as Simple criticized "race Leaders" "I have not laid eyes on" in "Letter to Mr. Butts" (*STW* 1953).

However, instead the speaker asks if he or she ever lived "up your way." In other words, the speaker could be Hughes, or his generation of engaged artists and intellectuals, trying to remember when he lived in something like Turé's ideological neighborhood and criticized "elderly race leaders" in much the same spirit that the Black Power activists did Wilkins. In short, rather than simply critiquing Turé and his generation of militants for their extremism and lack of historical perspective, Hughes could also be chiding his generation, and himself, for their failure of political imagination (and memory) and their own lack of historical perspective. In this way, again like others of his generation who engaged Black Arts and Black Power, Hughes was genuinely a bridge between different moments of cultural activism, prodding, chiding, reminding, supporting, and honoring.

The notion of Ralph Ellison and others that Hughes in the end was a limited artist because he did not "grow" is clearly mistaken (Rampersad 1988, 286). There does seem to be a core to Hughes's work, especially after the early 1930s, that is fairly constant. That core consists of a sense of the importance of popular African American culture to the black literary artist (and a sense of the cultural continuum between different eras of black cultural expression) and a commitment to the freedom struggles of African Americans. In fact, Hughes is notable among his contemporaries not only for his distinguished efforts in so many genres over so many years but for his efforts to negotiate, renegotiate really, changing cultural and political eras while remaining basically true to his core. This project, in fact, forced Hughes's work to change while he attempted to retain links to the past. In part, that is why one Simple story, "Bop," retells the popular story of the relationship between bebop and police violence (*TBOS* 118) in one sketch and renders what is essentially a prose praise poem to Ma Rainey in another (*TBOS* 168). It is this drive to remain current while being cognizant of the past, along with a recognition of the need to rethink his core values and poetics and their relationship to the present moment, that made Hughes's work so powerful and so popular with audiences beyond what is normally thought of as the market for "serious" literature.

Works Cited

Bahktin, Mikhail. *Problems of Dostoevsky's Poetics*. Edited and translated by Caryl Emerson. Minneapolis: University of Minnesota Press, 1984.

Baraka, Amiri. *The LeRoi Jones/Amiri Baraka Reader*. Edited by William J. Harris. New York: Thunder's Mouth, 1991.

Bontemps, Arna, and Langston Hughes. *Letters, 1925–1967*. Selected and edited by Charles H. Nichols. 1980. Rpt. New York: Paragon, 1990.

Ford, Karen Jackson. "Making Poetry Pay: The Commodification of Langston Hughes." In *Marketing Modernisms: Self-Promotion, Canonization, Rereading*. Edited by Kevin J. H. Dettmar and Stephen Watt, 275–96. Ann Arbor: University of Michigan Press, 1996.

Gennari, John. "Jazz Criticism: Its Development and Ideologies." *Black American Literature Forum* 25, no. 3 (fall 1991): 449–523.

Hughes, Langston. "Don't You Want to Be Free?" *One Act Play Magazine* 2 (October 1938): 359–93.

———. *Short Stories of Langston Hughes*. Edited by Akiba Sullivan Harper. New York: Hill and Wang, 1996.

O'Neal, John. "Black Arts: Notebook." In *The Black Aesthetic*. Edited by Addison Gayle, Jr., 46–56. New York: Anchor, 1972.

Rampersad, Arnold. *The Life of Langston Hughes, Volume I: 1902–1941, I, Too, Sing America*. Oxford: Oxford University Press, 1986.

———. *The Life of Langston Hughes, Volume II: 1941–1967, I Dream a World*. Oxford: Oxford University Press, 1988.

Smith, Suzanne E. *Dancing in the Street: Motown and the Cultural Politics of Detroit*. Cambridge, Mass.: Harvard University Press, 1999.

Sundquist, Eric. "Who Was Langston Hughes?" *Commentary* 102, no. 6 (December 1996): 55–59.

Vendler, Helen. "The Unweary Blues." Review of *The Collected Poems of Langston Hughes*. *New Republic*, March 6, 1995, pp. 37–42.

CAROLINE GEBHARD

Inventing a "Negro Literature": Race, Dialect, and Gender in the Early Work of Paul Laurence Dunbar, James Weldon Johnson, and Alice Dunbar-Nelson

"There is now a negro literature," *The Tuskegee Student* declared in 1900.[1] That year, a single issue of *The Southern Workman* (November 1900) featured three black writers with national reputations: Paul Laurence Dunbar (1872–1906), Alice Dunbar (1875–1935) (later Dunbar-Nelson), and Charles W. Chesnutt (1858–1932). Dunbar's contribution, "De Critters' Dance," is a whimsical satire of religiosity. His spouse's contribution, "Esteve, the Soldier Boy," explores a major theme in her work, the murky politics of racial identity. Chesnutt's piece, "Tobe's Tribulations," contains "virtually the whole of Chesnutt's folk aesthetic."[2] By 1900 Paul Dunbar was the most famous black writer in America, yet he knew he had competition. Upon hearing Chesnutt was writing a novel, he wrote Alice, "As long as the Negro literary field held me above I could afford to take it pretty easily, but now that another Richmond has come on—a Richmond so worthy of my mettle, too,—'a horse, a horse!'"[3]

White literary America began to take notice: critic and poetaster Richard Henry Stoddard seconded the *Tuskegee Student*'s pronouncement on the new "Negro literature." Nevertheless, he claimed that "this negro literature has thus far been furnished practically exclusively by writers of the white race, almost the only exception being Mr. Paul Laurence Dunbar."[4] *The Tuskegee Student*, however, rejected his claim that blacks were not the authors of this

From *Post-Bellum, Pre-Harlem: African American Literature and Culture, 1877–1919*, pp. 162–178. © 2006 by New York University.

new literature; it pointed to the "brainy Du Bois," "Mrs. Harper" and "our own Principal Washington." Furthermore, the *Student* wrote, Daniel Murray, the assistant librarian of Congress who had assembled the black literature exhibit for the Paris Exposition of 1900, "will gladly send Mr. Stoddard a list of Negro authors."[5] The exhibit, widely covered in the press, was selected from over one thousand titles of "real literary merit" by black Americans uncovered by Murray.[6]

The conviction was widespread in African American circles that blacks had begun to make their mark in literature, notwithstanding white America's slowness in recognizing it. "It will not be easy to convince the American people that the negro has made even a beginning as an author and contributor to American literature," Fannie Barrier Williams admitted. Nevertheless, she argued that Murray's labors proved it. Although she paid tribute to a long history of black writing, Williams emphasized the literary striving of her own contemporaries. She praised work by Washington, Du Bois, Dunbar, and Chesnutt as "representative of the best things contributed to American literature by negro authors."[7]

Yet the self-conscious creation of a "Negro literature"—distinct from antebellum black writing that had been pervaded by antislavery politics and dominated by nonfictional genres—has often been thought to have begun only with the Harlem Renaissance in the 1920s.[8] The commentary of Williams and others shows, however, that in 1900 black critics recognized the birth of a new literature that reflected the postbellum aspirations and lives of black Americans and at the same time brooked no special pleading on the question of literary merit. Yet this birth was far from easy. In his essay, "Post-Bellum–Pre-Harlem," Chesnutt recollected that Thomas Dixon and Thomas Nelson Page were widely appreciated while "at that time a literary work by an American of acknowledged color was a doubtful experiment both for the writer and the publisher."[9]

What Chesnutt and his fellow writers achieved has been obscured, in part because of the low artistic valuation of the earlier period by influential critics like William Stanley Braithwaite (1878–1962). Identifying with the later "New Negro" movement, he dismissed Dunbar and earlier writers as "negligible, and of historical interest only."[10] Yet the term "New Negro" dates back to 1895, even though it is most often associated with Alain Locke's celebrated 1925 anthology.[11] Eager to claim the mantle of the "new," the heralds of the Harlem Renaissance elided the fact that twenty years before, black writers had also aspired to make a great "Negro" literature that would be "racial" yet "universal."

But what would the hallmarks of this new "Negro" literature be? How would writers themselves only one generation removed from slavery handle themes like the plantation, or should they treat such subjects at all? Should the African American writer see himself as engaged in a project of educating white audiences about black experience? And what was the place of the "New Negro" woman? Above all, what language would or should this new literature be written in—literary English or the vernacular English spoken by most blacks in America? These questions cannot be fully addressed here; however, this essay will grapple with the one that implicates them all: language. Comparing the early work of Dunbar and James Weldon Johnson sheds new light on the vexed question of black dialect, especially in view of Johnson's well-known later condemnation of this mode as limited to "only two stops: pathos and humor."[12] However, Dunbar-Nelson's early work suggests alternative choices in the linguistic palette of the new black artist. Considering these three writers together reveals how dialect and gender are intertwined in the emerging domain of "Negro literature." This approach also illuminates the role of mastery of "literary English" in its founding. Finally, framing these writers' early works as a literary field demonstrates that black literature is not the creation of a single artist nor one era alone—that the brilliant work of the Harlem Renaissance is thoroughly rooted in the post-bellum–pre-Harlem experiments of Dunbar and his fellow artists.

First, it is crucial to recall what literary success meant to the children and grandchildren of former slaves. Chesnutt put most plainly literature's advantages to literate African Americans who otherwise had little access to capital: "I want fame; I want money; I want to raise my children in a different rank of life from that I sprang from."[13] For this generation, literary achievement promised, then, "cultural capital," conferring not just material but also social benefit. John Guillory, extending Pierre Bourdieu's seminal concept, identifies several forms of "cultural capital"; the most critical here is "linguistic capital"—"the means by which one attains to a socially credentialed and therefore valued speech, otherwise known as 'Standard English.'"[14] In the literary arena, Guillory explains, "Authors confront a monumentalized textual tradition already immersed as speakers and writers in the social condition of linguistic stratification that betrays at every level the struggle among social groups over the resources of language, over cultural capital in its linguistic form."[15]

Circa 1900, African American writers, on the one hand, confronted the "monumental" tradition of English letters, and on the other, competed with other social groups, in Guillory's terms, for "the resources of language." However, as Gavin Jones observes, the hottest linguistic commodity in late-nineteenth-century America was dialect; moreover, while dialects from Maine to Louisiana could be parodied or invoked to assert the cultural superiority of the white middle class, they also registered "an anxious, constantly collapsing attempt to control the fragmentation and change that characterize any national tongue."[16] Because dialect was both wildly popular and a peculiarly charged site of cultural anxiety, African American dialects presented a critical opportunity for the black writer. Yet tapping this black linguistic resource has too often been viewed as an illegitimate form of cultural capital—crass exploitation or racist collusion. Yet the fact that white writers capitalized on "black" characters—i.e., characters who speak in dialect—did not mean that black writers of the era gave up their right to this material or believed they could not do it better. Moreover, black dialect offered the black writer "cultural capital" in another sense: it stood for the value of a cultural heritage in a society that denied that blacks had any culture of their own. Henry Louis Gates Jr. argues that dialect is the black poet's "only key" to the African past, functioning as "a verbal dialectic" between "English" and the lost African mother tongue.[17] Dunbar, Gates concludes, wrote his best poetry when he mined the resources of dialect.[18] Even Gates, though, charges Dunbar with "opportunism."[19]

But Dunbar understandably viewed black dialect as his patrimony. In it, he saw far more than a way to reach white audiences: the true inheritors of this speech—just like the best interpreters of the slave past—were African Americans like himself. The World's Columbian Exposition in 1893, where he encountered the Dahomeyans, proved pivotal. When Dunbar heard the music of this West African people at the Chicago fair, he had an epiphany: "Instantly the idea flashed into my mind: 'It is a heritage.'"[20] The black American, he wrote, should "seize upon these songs, preserve them and make them distinctively his own."[21] Although he had experimented in a variety of dialects, from then on black dialect became one of Dunbar's signature modes. Already concerned that "others" were stealing the black's true heritage, he questioned his future wife in terms that argued the "Negro" writer should claim his linguistic heritage:

> I want to know whether or not you believe in preserving by Afro-American writers those quaint old tales and songs of our fathers which have made the fame of Joel Chandler Harris, Thomas Nelson Page, Ruth McEnery Stuart and others? or whether you like so many others think we should ignore the past and all its capital literary material.[22]

However, black writers were more likely to be seen as imitative, or at least not sufficiently distinctive, by white and even some black critics when they wrote in so-called pure English. Significantly, then, Dunbar, and Chesnutt and Johnson as well, not only staked their claim to black dialect but refused to relinquish their rights to "literary" English as well. Chesnutt, for example, recalls that the framing narratives in *The Conjure Woman* "were written in the best English I could command."[23] Although Negro literature was thus from the outset a fractured linguistic field, such fracturing should not be read as a sign of schizoid cultural inferiority on the part of the artist. Too many critics have viewed this double claim as compromised ambivalence rather than artful strategy; Dickson Bruce Jr., for example, asserts that because of his "assimilationist ideals,"[24] Dunbar was torn between black dialect as a "basis for molding a distinctive black identity" and standard English poetic forms. But this is to read literary history backwards; as Gates suggests, "we tend to forget how startling was Dunbar's use of black dialect as the basis of poetic diction."[25] Later, writers did come to see black dialect as emblematic of the black artist's tragic double bind in white America. Circa 1900, however, this strategy—which also appears in W. E. B. Du Bois's writings—of valuing Negro dialect as the language of black American cultural transmission enabled writers to defy the color line by simultaneously affirming black forms and the black artist's freedom to move between language registers: while Dunbar and his fellow black writers felt they must reclaim black dialect and black themes for the black artist, they also could not afford—nor did they wish—to abandon their equal claim upon the language of American high culture.

Two early poems show Dunbar's originality in employing this double stratagem: one in literary English, the other addressing a similar theme, only this time in black dialect. The first, with the deceptively simple title "Song" (1895), was published in *Majors and Minors*.[26] Later, it was included in *African Romances*, with music by S. Coleridge-Taylor, under the title, "An African Love Song" (1897).[27] This brief lyric evokes English ballads going back to "The Nut-Brown Maid" (c. 1503). Dunbar may have had this poem in mind because of its popularity; not only was it collected as a Child Ballad, but also a number of poets of the 1890s, including his bride-to-be, made use of the image of the "lissome nut-brown maid."[28] In any case, "Song's" archaic language ("thy," "thine"), the reference to wine, and the setting all conjure up pastoral tradition dating back to the English Renaissance, which elevated the rural subject by casting him as a lovesick "swain" smitten with a country maid. Dunbar, however, boldly inserts an "African" maid into the pastoral mix, thus consciously racializing this traditional mode:

> My heart to thy heart,
> My hand to thine;
> My lip to thy lips,
> Kisses are wine

Brewed for the lover in sunshine and shade;
Let me drink deep, then, my African maid.[29]

In the second stanza, Dunbar subtly connects the quintessential emblem of perfect love, the rose, with the ardent black lover: "Lily to lily, / Rose to Rose; My love to thy love / Tenderly grows."[30] The implication is that this bloom is not only *not* inferior to the white one; in some respects, it surpasses it. That the lily implicitly stands in for the white pastoral couple of English poetry is suggested by the next lines calling for black lovers not to be separated: "Rend not the oak and the ivy in twain, / Nor the swart maid from her swarthier swain."[31] The logic of separation by race may seem troubling now, but the poem's thrust is to declare the black beloved worthy of the highest forms and symbols of romantic poetry.

To put black lovers on the same poetic ground as white ones seems hardly revolutionary now, but this was far from true then. The media was permeated by racist characterizations of black people as bestial or ridiculous: blacks were hardly serious subjects of romance or courtship. For example, *Leslie's Weekly*, a magazine akin to *Life Magazine* in capturing its time in photographic images, ran a popular series of photographs called "The Blackville Gallery." In one photo, captioned "The Blackville Wedding," a poor African American couple taking their vows is held up to ridicule: the solemnity of the occasion is burlesqued by the caption, "Honey, does you' lub yo' man?" and the prominently placed sign on the wall, "Lebe you razzer At de Do, Deakin Jonez."[32] The way the Jim Crow social contract was routinely underwritten by white derision is suggested by the popularity of this series with white readers.[33]

Still, the antiracist message of black love poems in literary English, like "Song," did not resonate with readers until the mid-twentieth century: although this poem was always included in editions of Dunbar's poetry printed during his life and in the 1913 posthumous edition, it was not otherwise reprinted until 1950.[34] However, another Dunbar love poem, "Negro Love Song," written in dialect, has been widely and continuously reprinted. First published in *Century Magazine*,[35] it later became part of the path-breaking musical *Clorindy; or, The Origin of the Cakewalk* (1898), with music by Will Marion Cook and lyrics by Dunbar, under the title, "Jump Back Honey." Its original title, "A Negro Love Song," points to Dunbar's attempt to control discourse about African Americans of the time. Words like "African" and "Negro" register the writer's desire to dignify blackness. Yet Dunbar refused to write as if formal English were the superior tongue: dialect, this poem asserts, is as capable of expressing a lyrical tenderness as the most proper English diction. The playful refrain of this poem mimics the delicate dance of Eros—a one-step-closer, one-step-backward process. The lover both asks and demands, "Love me, honey, love me true? / Love me well ez I love you?"[36] One can imagine why it was so popular when set to music: like a classic Beatles lyric, it captures both the innocence and sensuousness of the first stages of love.

> Seen my lady home las' night,
>   Jump back, honey, jump back.
> Hel' huh han' an sque'z it tight,
>   Jump back, honey, jump back.[37]

"Jump back" works as a paradoxical, braking figure of speech playing against the urgent desire the poem plots—the poet escorts his lady home, holds her hand, feels his heart beating, hesitates at her door, then puts his arm around her waist, and, finally, kisses her. The repeated refrain, "jump back," literally tells her to back off as he pulls her closer: this mock warning intensifies the erotic tension, yet suggests the playfulness of an artful lover:

> Put my ahm aroun' huh wais',
>   Jump back, honey, jump back.
> Raised huh lips an' took a tase,
>   Jump back, honey, jump back.[38]

Dunbar's masterly refrain reveals his recognition of dialect's potential to voice complex emotion: nothing about the poem capitulates to minstrel notions of black inferiority. Alice, who saw *Clorindy* on a roof-top theater in New York, told her husband, "Jump back, honey, jump back goes like a flash," adding, "The audience went wild and demanded an encore."[39]

James Weldon Johnson saw himself in 1900 as similarly engaged in bringing "a higher degree of artistry to Negro songs."[40] Reappropriating dialect for black art was central not only to Dunbar's but also to Johnson's rediscovery of what Johnson called "the importance of the American Negro's cultural background."[41] Yet because of dialect's strong association with minstrelsy, employing it was, as Kevin K. Gaines has argued, equivalent to walking a tightrope "between minstrelsy and uplift."[42] We must retrace Johnson's own fraught relationship with black dialect because despite his early experimentation with this form and his admiration of Dunbar, he later almost categorically rejected it. Yet this fact has too often been divorced from his early work, which was more deserving than anything Dunbar wrote of the criticisms he later leveled at dialect in general. Like many writers, Johnson became a harsh judge of his early efforts; moreover, the new race militancy after World War I led him, as well as many others, to turn against a mode that had begun to

seem craven in the face of white power. Ironically, even as he sought to preserve Dunbar's reputation as "the first American Negro poet of real literary
distinction,"[43] his attack on black dialect helped consign his friend in many
critics' eyes to the dust bin of minstrelsy.

It has become commonplace to attribute the dichotomy in Dunbar's
work between standard English and black dialect to the poet's own supposed racial schizophrenia.[44] Yet Johnson follows Dunbar's same practice of
grouping poems according to their language registers. In *Fifty Years and Other
Poems* (1917), he separates his poems in literary English from his "jingles
and croons," as he labeled his dialect poems. Nevertheless, few critics have
viewed this division as a sign of Johnson's own racial confusion, even though
his poetry freely employs terms that Dunbar uses far more sparingly: "pickaninny," "darkies," "mammy," and "coons." Johnson takes many more risks in
conjuring minstrel stereotypes than Dunbar. Indeed, although he culled a
group of poems from his popular turn-of-the-century stage work in *Fifty
Years*, he was already having misgivings about his dialect creations; some work
he chose not to republish at all and at least one poem, "Run Brudder Possum,"
was revised to eliminate the word "coon."[45] Indeed, Johnson's oeuvre suggests
he always viewed dialect as best suited to comedy and not appropriate for
serious poetry. For example, the subject of love elicits race-neutral language,
even on occasion imagery suggesting whiteness: "How fair and slender was
your throat, how / white the promise of your breast," the poet sings to his
"princess" in "Vashti."[46] There is nothing to compare to Dunbar's "African
maid" in *Fifty Years and Other Poems*, and Johnson's own "Negro Love Song,"
"Ma Lady's Lips Am Like De Honey," is not only derivative of Dunbar's
"Jump back, Honey," but done with a much cruder touch that pushes the
poem toward buffoonery: "Honey on her lips to waste; / 'Speck I'm gwine to
steal a taste."[47]

Still other dialect poems in this volume cross the line into full-fledged
clowning. The last of the "Jingles and Croons," "The Rivals," tells how a suitor
bests his competitor, causing him to be thrown from his mule, splitting his
store-bought pants wide open: "W'en dat darky riz, well raly, I felt kinder bad
fu' him; / He had bust dem cheap sto' britches f'om de center to de rim."[48]
Johnson's most distinctive dialect poems do mine folk material for comic
pathos. However, this side of Johnson is rarely on display; instead it is "Sence
You Went Away" (1900) that always exemplifies his dialect poetry. Significantly, this is the poem Johnson himself chose to anthologize; ironically, it is
also the poem where Dunbar's influence is at its strongest—and where the
dialect, less bound to folk type, expresses a universal emotion, loneliness.

Johnson is far more at home addressing serious race themes in high
poetic diction. The noble sentiments of his Negro national anthem, "Lift

Every Voice and Sing," are perfectly in harmony with the title poem, "Fifty Years," and poems such as "To America," "O Black and Unknown Bards," and "O Southland!" In these, the collective struggle is commemorated in formal English, as if the poetry of racial striving must be strictly segregated from the vernacular. This bifurcation is not surprising, given Johnson's conviction that "the first step" in writing poetry is mastering standard English: "The English language is the material . . . to be moulded and chiseled and polished into thought forms of beauty."[49] That Johnson means standard English is unmistakable: he also calls for poets-in-training to learn correct usage for such words as prepositions. Yet in contrast to the high oratorical style of Johnson's public race poetry—and in sharp contrast to Dunbar—the only moment where race and Eros meet in Johnson's early poetry in literary English is in "The White Witch." This poem warns black men against white women, their erotic appeal likened to a lynching, the body burning "like a living coal,"[50] the victim powerless to resist.

Johnson's own best poetry is not written in dialect; indeed, rejecting it to represent the rhetorical effects of black preachers in *God's Trombones* (1927) marked the culmination of a long artistic evolution. In his 1922 preface to *The Book of American Negro Poetry*, he defends spirituals and ragtime but is far more skeptical of the value of the black vernacular: "Naturally, not as much can be said for the words of these songs as for the music."[51] Although he credited Dunbar for being "the first to use it [Negro dialect] as a medium for the true interpretation of Negro character and psychology,"[52] he nevertheless believed dialect defunct because of its close association with minstrel and plantation traditions: black writers should transcend dialect through "a form that is freer and larger than dialect, but which will still hold the racial flavor."[53] Certainly, this is his goal in *God's Trombones*—to render black speech rhythms in more or less standard English.

Late in life he even suggested that Dunbar shared his distaste for dialect. In *Along This Way* (1933), he remembers Dunbar saying, "I have never gotten to the things I really wanted to do"; yet admitting that "Paul never told me definitely what the things were that he really wanted to do," he hazards the guess that Dunbar planned to write epics in "straight English that would relate to the Negro."[54] Despite Johnson's assertion that he and Dunbar often discussed the limitations of dialect, Dunbar's letters paint quite a different picture. To Alice, Dunbar wrote that Johnson wanted him "to join the quadruple alliance, Cole—R. Johnson, J. Johnson & me."[55] Was the young Johnson, soon to go to New York to become a professional songwriter specializing in black dialect, really such a keen critic of it circa 1900? Johnson himself confesses that it was only much later that his ideas about poetry were "thoroughly clarified."[56] It is hard not to conclude that, looking back on conversations that had taken place thirty years earlier, now convinced of a new artistic creed, Johnson would interpret Dunbar's remarks in the light of his present views. Nor should critics underestimate the literary rivalry here. Although it was important to Johnson, personally, to discard black dialect, unfortunately his bias against it has been rarely taken into account. Instead, his pronouncements about dialect have become "more or less canonical."[57]

Like Johnson, as an anthologist and polemicist during the Harlem Renaissance Dunbar-Nelson helped to define the modern canon of African American literature. In 1922 she called for a "Negro Literature for Negro Pupils," pointing to the damaging effects of being given only "a milk-white; literature to assimilate."[58] Unlike Johnson, however, she did not turn away from black dialect; rather, she worried that Dunbar would be remembered only as a dialect poet. Her first anthology, *The Dunbar Speaker and Entertainer* (1916), devotes two sections to dialect, one "humorous" and the other "serious." Nevertheless, Dunbar-Nelson's view early in her career suggests that the black woman writer in 1900 inevitably approached the issue differently than her male peers.

Circa 1900 black dialect work, like twentieth-century rap, was largely a masculine preserve. For African American male performers like Bob Cole, Rosamond Johnson, Ernest Hogan, Bert Williams, and George Walker, such work offered opportunities in all-black musical theatrical shows or in traveling vaudeville acts.[59] Poets such as Daniel Webster Davis and James D. Corrothers, who wrote primarily in dialect, also made money performing their work at readings, and again, like today's hip-hop artists, found a market for their work with black as well as white audiences. Conversely, for the kind of woman that Alice Ruth Moore was before she married Dunbar—young, aspiring to a literary career, active in the black women's club movement—public performances for money, especially dialect poems, would have called into question her refinement and taste.[60]

This gendering of black dialect is further supported by Dunbar's script for *Jes Lak White Fo'ks* (1900), an "operetta." In it, the poet puts heavy black dialect into the mouth of the patriarch, Pompous Johnsing: "But I an goin' get no bargain counter duke for my daughter, huh-uh, honey. . . . I has been engaged in diplomatic regotiations wid an Af'ican King."[61] But Dunbar makes Johnsing's daughter, Mandy, speak very proper English: "Father you're only mocking / Such levity is shocking."[62] Even Harper's "Aunt Chloe" poems featuring a former slave woman tend toward standard English, only sketchily suggesting black speech."[63] Black women writers—perhaps until Zora Neale Hurston—felt more constrained than men in the way they could develop their linguistic inheritance—their "cultural capital" from slavery. As partners in racial uplift, black women could ill afford to dispense with the prerogatives of genteel femininity. For black women, so often caricatured as hypersexual and ignorant, language associated with a lack of proper decorum or education carried a double risk.

From the outset, Dunbar-Nelson resisted the idea that black writers had to use dialect: "But if one should be like me—absolutely devoid of the ability to manage dialect—I don't see the necessity of cramming and forcing oneself into that plane because one is a Negro or a Southerner."[64] Instead, she took an individualist stand, adding, "I frankly believe in everyone following his bent. If it be so that one has a special aptitude for dialect work, why it is only right that dialect work should be made a specialty." These statements comprise her answer to Dunbar's rhetorical question about whether African American writers should draw upon the slave past.[65] Although in her reply to Dunbar, she appears to reject dialect for herself, it is not true that she could or did not write it. Instead of the "Negro dialect" associated with the plantation, however, she skillfully renders contemporary "hybrid" dialects of Creoles of color.

Dunbar-Nelson's "The Praline Woman," first published in *The Goodness of St. Rocque and Other Tales* (1899) but also included in her anthology under "serious" dialect pieces, consists almost entirely of the enterprising flow of talk by a woman who sells her pralines on Royal Street in New Orleans. Her speech is represented as a true Creole, a mix of Black English and Gallic speech patterns:

"Praline? Pralines? Ah, ma'amzelle, you buy? S'il vous plait, ma'amzelle, dey be fine, ver' fresh. Sho chile, ma bébé, ma petite she put dese up hissef. . . . You tak' none? No husban' fo' you den!"[66]

Through her monologue to prospective customers, we learn her story; we also learn that she resents patronizing comments about her speech. Recalling an Irishman's question to her—"Auntie, what fo' you talk so?"—she includes her rejoinder, "An' I jes' say back, 'What fo' you say faith an bejabers?' Non, I don' lak I'ishman, me!"[67]

Another early story making use of black Creole dialect also explores the tension between the Irish immigrants and African Americans in New Orleans. In "Mr. Baptiste," the Irish longshoremen strike to oppose the hiring of any black workers, but the blacks resist by breaking the strike. When Mr. Baptiste, an indigent, elderly Creole who discourages inquiry into his personal history, has the temerity to cheer for the blacks, he becomes the first victim of the white mob's violence. Here, too, Mr. Baptiste speaks a mixture of French- and southern black-influenced dialect: "Yaas, dose cotton-yardmans, dose 'longsho'mans, dey . . . t'row down dey tool an' say dey work no mo' wid niggers."[68] Dunbar-Nelson's early Creole stories demonstrate that America vainly tries to reduce everything to black and white, whereas the reality is often not so simple. Her Mr. Baptiste appears to be a "gigi"—a special sort of Creole of African descent who "abhors everything American" yet keeps "negroes at bay for fear of familiarity" as well as keeping "whites from knowing him too well."[69] Still, she does not permit us to judge him too harshly when his one expression of solidarity with the blacks of his native city costs him his life.

What emerges in Dunbar-Nelson's early work is an individualist and feminist ethos, leading to alternative forms of linguistic experimentation for the new Negro literature. From the beginning, she strikes a feminist note; in *Violets and Other Tales* (1895), she celebrates the independence of the working woman, frankly wondering whether women should give up their liberty for marriage.[70] She also expresses the spirit of the "brave new woman" in her deft use of what her husband-to-be called her "bowery slang," that is, the laconic, tough-talking style of the stories of Edward W. Townsend.[71] In one story, "A Carnival Jangle," a young girl is tempted during Mardi Gras to don a male mask: "'You'd better come with us, Flo, you're wasting time in that tame gang. Slip off, they'll never miss you; we'll get you a rig, and show you what life is.'"[72] For Alice Ruth Moore, "bowery slang," not black or even black Creole dialect, represented artistic and social freedom. This proto–jazz age style appealed to a young woman who liked to take walks down "Anarchy Alley."[73] However, "bowery slang" did not turn out to be the "cultural capital" she needed to launch a successful career as a mainstream writer, though she continued to publish in the black press.

The question of language—especially dialect—has continued to be central to definitions of African American literature. The question of how to tap the resources of the black vernacular without calling up pernicious stereotypes, however, is an issue that did not end with Dunbar and other writers of the post-bellum–pre-Harlem era. Later writers such as Hurston faced accusations that in representing black speech they merely reintroduced the stereotype of the "happy darky." More recently, the furor over "Ebonics" reveals how the question of black dialect remains loaded. Yet the work at the turn of the twentieth century by Dunbar, Johnson, Dunbar-Nelson, and others marks a critical chapter in the history of black cultural production in the United States. If the Renaissance of the twenties was a rebirth, the birth of "Negro literature" came more than twenty years earlier. Those writers like Braithwaite and Johnson who lived to take part in Harlem's Renaissance benefited from a long apprenticeship in mastering their craft. And those who did not—for example, Dunbar, who died in 1906, or Chesnutt, who stopped writing literature about the same time, or Pauline Hopkins, who died in obscurity—nevertheless deserve to be recognized for daring to invent the field of "Negro literature." In so doing, they showed the way for all their successors.

NOTES

1. My source for this *Tuskegee Student* editorial is Richard Henry Stoddard, "Literary Notes," *New York Mail and Express* (February 26, 1900), Paul Laurence Dunbar Papers, Manuscript (MS) 114, Box 18, Ohio Historical Society. Despite its name, the paper, edited by Emmett J. Scott, was not a student production; however, Charles Alexander, associate editor, probably wrote the literary editorials; see Booker T. Washington, vol. 4 of *The Booker T. Washington Papers*, ed. Louis R. Harlan et al. (Urbana: University of Illinois Press, 1972–89).

2. Eric J. Sundquist, *To Wake the Nations: Race in the Making of American Literature* (Cambridge, MA: Harvard University Press, 1993), 314.

3. Paul Laurence Dunbar to Alice Dunbar, 13 September 1898, in "The Letters of Paul and Alice Dunbar: A Private History," ed. Eugene Wesley Metcalf Jr. (Ph.D. diss., University of California, Irvine, 1973), 681–82; Metcalf, ed., "Letters," 683, footnotes the allusion to Shakespeare's *King Richard III* 5.4.7.

4. Stoddard, "Literary Notes," Dunbar Papers.

5. *The Tuskegee Student* (March 17, 1900), Dunbar Papers, MS 114, Box 18.

6. *Ideas* (Feb. 3, 1900), Dunbar Papers, MS 114, Box 18.

7. Fanny Barrier Williams, "The Colored Man Is Making His Mark in the Literary Field of To-day," *Chicago Times Herald* (April 29, 1900), Dunbar Papers, MS. 114, Box 18.

8. See Henry Louis Gates Jr., "The Trope of a New Negro and the Reconstruction of the Image of the Black," *Representations* 24 (Fall 1988): 143–44.

9. Charles Waddell Chesnutt, "Post-Bellum–Pre-Harlem," in *Breaking into Print*, ed. Elmo Adler (1931; repr. New York: Simon and Schuster, 1937), 53.

10. William Stanley Braithwaite, "The Negro in American Literature," in *The New Negro*, ed. Alain Locke (1925; repr. New York: Atheneum, 1968), 36.

11. See Amritjit Singh's "New Negro" in *The Oxford Companion to African American Literature*, ed. William L. Andrews et al. (New York: Oxford University Press, 1997), 536.

12. James Weldon Johnson, ed., *The Book of American Negro Poetry*, rev. ed. (New York: Harcourt, Brace, 1931), 4.

13. William L. Andrews, *The Literary Career of Charles W. Chesnutt* (Baton Rouge: Louisiana State University Press, 1980), 9–10.

14. John Guillory, *Cultural Capital: The Problem of Literary Canon Formation* (Chicago: University of Chicago Press, 1993), ix.

15. Ibid., 63.

16. Gavin Jones, *Strange Talk: The Politics of Dialect Literature in Gilded Age America* (Berkeley: University of California Press, 1999), 11.

17. Henry Louis Gates Jr., *Figures in Black: Words, Signs, and the "Racial" Self* (New York: Oxford University Press, 1987), 172.

18. Ibid., 179.

19. Henry Louis Gates Jr., *The Signifying Monkey: A Theory of African-American Literary Criticism* (New York: Oxford University Press), 1988, 176.

20. Paul Laurence Dunbar, "Negro Music," in *In His Own Voice: The Dramatic and Other Uncollected Works of Paul Laurence Dunbar*, ed. Herbert Woodward Martin and Ronald Primeau (Athens: Ohio University Press, 2002), 184. They date this important essay, which escaped previous bibliographers, 1899; however, my examination of the original in the Dunbar Papers, MS 114, Box 17, indicates that it more likely appeared in 1893 when Dunbar was writing for the *Chicago Record*.

21. Ibid., 184.

22. Dunbar to Alice Ruth Moore (17 April 1895) in Metcalf, ed., "Letters," 34.

23. Chesnutt, "Post-Bellum–Pre-Harlem," 49.

24. Dickson D. Bruce Jr., *Black American Writing from the Nadir: The Evolution of a Literary Tradition, 1877–1913* (Baton Rouge: Louisiana University Press, 1989), 71, 61.

25. Gates, *Signifying Monkey*, 176.

26. See "Song" in *The Collected Poetry of Paul Laurence Dunbar*, ed. Joanne M. Braxton (Charlottesville: University Press of Virginia, 1993), 13. The Dunbar poems here are reprinted with the permission of the University of Virginia Press.

27. Eugene Wesley Metcalf Jr., ed., *Paul Laurence Dunbar: A Bibliography* (Metuchen, NJ: Scarecrow Press, 1975), 92.

28. Alice Dunbar-Nelson, "At Bay St. Louis," in *The Works of Alice Dunbar-Nelson*, ed. Gloria T. Hull, vol. 1 (New York: Oxford University Press, 1988), 106–7.

29. Braxton, ed., *Collected Poetry*, 13.

30. Ibid., 13.

31. Ibid., 13.

32. "A Blackville Wedding," The Blackville Gallery No. 11, *Leslie's Illustrated Weekly* 86.2208 (January 6, 1898), 8–9.

33. Editorial column, "Features of *Leslie's Weekly*," *Leslie's Illustrated Weekly* 86.2210 (January 20, 1898), 34.

34. Metcalf, ed., *Dunbar: A Bibliography*, 164.

35. Paul Laurence Dunbar, "Negro Love Song," *Century Magazine* 49 (April 1895) 960.

36. Braxton, ed., *Collected Poetry*, 49.

37. Ibid., 49.

38. Ibid., 49.

39 Alice Dunbar to Dunbar [Summer 1898], in Metcalf, ed., "Letters," 601.

40. James Weldon Johnson, *Along This Way: The Autobiography of James Weldon Johnson* (1933; New York: Viking, 1973), 192.

41. Ibid., 152.

42. Kevin K. Gaines, *Uplifting the Race: Black Leadership, Politics, and Culture in the Twentieth Century* (Chapel Hill: University of North Carolina Press, 1996), 184.

43. Johnson, ed., *Book of American Negro Poetry*, rev. ed., 50.

44. See, for example, Michael Flusche, "Paul Laurence Dunbar and the Burden of Race," *Southern Humanities Review* 11.1 (Winter 1977): 49–50, and, more recently, Eleanor Alexander, *Lyrics of Sunshine and Shadow* (New York: New York University Press, 2001).

45. Bruce, *Black American Writing*, 247.

46. James Weldon Johnson, *Fifty Years and Other Poems*, with an introduction by Brander Matthews (Boston: Cornhill Company, 1917), 58.

47. Ibid., 64.

48. Ibid., 91.

49. Johnson, "Poetry Corner," in *The Selected Writings of James Weldon Johnson*, ed. Sondra Kathryn Wilson, vol. 1 (New York: Oxford University Press, 1995), 253.

50. Johnson, *Fifty Years*, 20.

51. Johnson, ed., *Book of American Negro Poetry*, 1st ed., 18.

52. Ibid., 35.

53. Ibid., 41.

54. Johnson, *Along This Way*, 161.

55. Paul Laurence Dunbar to Alice Dunbar, 31 March 1901, in Metcalf, ed., "Letters," 833.

56. Johnson, *Along This Way*, 161.

57, Johnson, ed., *Book of American Negro Poetry*, rev. ed., 3.

58. Alice Dunbar-Nelson, "Negro Literature for Negro Pupils," *The Southern Workman* (February 1922): 60.

59. See Thomas L. Morgan and William Barlow, *From Cakewalks to Concert Halls: An Illustrated History of African American Popular Music* (Washington, DC: Elliott and Clark, 1992).

60. Later Dunbar-Nelson gave many readings of her late husband's work, including his dialect poetry.

61. Martin and Primeau, eds., *In His Own Voice*, 136.

62. Ibid.

63. Melba Joyce Boyd argues that Harper's use of "aural association and syntax" instead of phonetic spelling to represent black speech is an important innovation. Andrews et al., eds., *Oxford Companion*, 32.

64. Alice Ruth Moore [Dunbar-Nelson] to Paul Laurence Dunbar, 7 May 1896, in Metcalf, ed., "Letters," 37–38.

65. In fact, she interprets his question to be essentially about dialect: "You ask my opinion about Negro dialect in literature." Ibid., 37.

66. Alice Dunbar-Nelson, "The Praline Woman," in *The Dunbar Speaker and Entertainer*, with an introduction by Akasha (Gloria) Hull (New York: G. K. Hall, 1996), 66. She made minor changes to the original; I quote the later version as reflecting her final intention.

67. Ibid., 66.

68. Alice Dunbar-Nelson, *The Goodness of St. Rocque and Other Stories*, in Hull, ed., *Works*, 1:115.

69. Alice Dunbar-Nelson, "A Creole Anomaly," *Leslie's Weekly* (15 July 1897): 43.

70. Alice Dunbar-Nelson, "The Woman," in Hull, ed., *Works*, 1:25.

71. Paul Laurence Dunbar to Alice Ruth Moore [Dunbar-Nelson], 23 March 1896, in Metcalf, ed., "Letters," 87.

72. Alice Dunbar-Nelson, "A Carnival Jangle," in Hull, ed., *Works*, 1:77–78.

73. Ibid., 56–62.

FRANCES SMITH FOSTER

Creative Collaboration:
As African American as Sweet Potato Pie

The stories of African American collaboration—particularly the coalitions of artists and activists who worked in formal organizations and in informal communities to articulate goals and to promote progress towards racial equality, spiritual maturity, social competence, and self-esteem—are less well known in our culture than those of the rugged individualists who succeeded against the odds.[1] Particularly in narratives of African American cultural history before Emancipation, the lone fugitive, the fiery rebel, the singular sojourner, or the inspired visionary dominates our attention. Our narratives of racial progress generally feature a heroic Moses while making it seem that half of his challenge was convincing those he would rescue that if they stopped acting like crabs in a barrel, they could become a people with a purpose.

The essays of this volume counter or complement dominant narratives by emphasizing collaborative efforts of African American writers, artists, and thinkers at the turn of the twentieth century: that is, between 1880 and that era most often referred to as the "Harlem Renaissance." This essay introduces or contextualizes those discussions by describing eighteenth- and nineteenth-century creative intellectual precursors. It focuses upon a few particular examples while suggesting that they represent a tradition of collaborative creative industry that is as African American as sweet potato pie.

From *Post-Bellum, Pre-Harlem: African American Literature and Culture, 1877–1919*, pp. 17–33.
© 2006 by New York University.

In our communities, as in our culinary inventions, people of African descent living in the North American colonies and in the first century or so of the United States combined the materials at hand with memories in head to feed their bodies, minds, and souls. They formed families, neighborhoods, organizations, and larger, sometimes international, networks to provide for themselves the strength of numbers and the solace of like minds and similar aesthetics. Whether in creating spirituals and work songs, newspapers and novels, churches, schools, or lodges, collaboration was a necessary and nurturing part of these enterprises.

The centers of U.S. economic and artistic dominance were generally in the urban Northeast and above the Mason-Dixon line. England and its traditions, while not the sole source from which U.S. America developed its philosophical and artistic concepts, had an unusually significant impact. Thus, it makes sense to assume, as most people do, that much of African American cultural development, including its concepts of family, friendship, and fraternity, integrates Anglophone and European elements and that its spokespersons articulate their hybridity in English. Certainly the scholarship on our organizations and cooperative enterprises focuses primarily on the events and individuals in and around the bustling corridor from New England to New York and Philadelphia. However, just as the so-called Harlem Renaissance was in fact infused, influenced, and supported by writers, artists, and intellectuals from California to Oklahoma and Florida, from Jamaica and Cuba to Mexico, Senegal, France, Germany, and beyond, so, too, one very important achievement of earlier artist/activist coalitions was the diversity and pervasiveness of their influence and effect. Perhaps, therefore, the instances of collaboration among artists and intellectuals whose energies were employed in lesser discussed areas such as the pre–Civil War South and in community building among African American Muslims or Louisiana Creoles are all the more important to recall. Thus, as a way of reminding us why discussions of the achievements of African American writers, artists, and thinkers should recognize the minority as well as the majority confederations within our common heritage, this essay begins with instances of two minority communities that must not be overlooked when the achievements of African American writers, intellectuals, and artists are tallied. The second part of this essay concentrates upon organized efforts to theorize and practice progressive racial politics using combinations of education, art, and reason. Mutual aid and literary societies and the emerging African American press provide such examples.

Among the earliest African American communities were those of African Muslim slaves. From all accounts, they were a numerical minority in this country and in the local African American populations within which they resided. However, as scholars such as Sylviane A. Diouf point out, "they preserved a distinctive lifestyle built on religious cohesiveness, cultural self-confidence, and discipline," and their memoirs form "a disproportionate number" of extant African-in-America narratives.[2] Some scholars use data, such as the places in which certain texts have been found and the kinds of paper and ink with which they were produced, to hypothesize that African American Muslims, along with African Americans of other religious and cultural traditions, participated in an international network among African Americans and people of African descent in Brazil, Italy, and other parts of the world. Their work suggests collaboration and cooperation melding art and aesthetics, artifice, and activism in ways that parallel or presage certain twentieth-century Pan-African, Caribbean, and Continental integrations and interventions by Harlem Renaissance figures such as Langston Hughes, Zora Neale Hurston, Claude McKay, Marcus Garvey, Jean Toomer, and W. E. B. Du Bois. Speculations about established antebellum international and interreligious networks are intriguing and merit more concentrated research. Still, the evidence that we already have makes it clear that African American Muslims were an important part of early African American culture, and that their writers, artists, and thinkers expressed ideas and conserved traditions essential to group survival and prosperity.

Most of the extant writings from African Muslim slave communities are in Arabic.[3] Many of them can be considered as slave narratives, for they are personal accounts of lives in slavery and attempts to free themselves from bondage. However, most narratives by Muslim slaves, in emphasis and perhaps intent, are different from the more commonly discussed antebellum fugitive narratives. For example, Muslim slave narratives tend to be much briefer and to give little attention to antislavery or abolitionist rhetoric. In this, they are more similar to those by Olaudah Equiano or Venture Smith, whose memoirs tend to be more communal, more descriptive of religious, artistic, social, and familial practices and observances. Their treatments of literacy, both in their communities and in their own lives, suggest greater sophistication than that of marveling over how they learned the English alphabet or to write their names. In fact, because they are written in Arabic and they assume literacy as a given and not something snatched by stealth, such narratives imply that some intellectual traditions survived the Middle Passage and continued despite enslavement and laws designed to eradicate them. They remind us that it was not unheard of for at least some African Americans to be literate and multilingual. In narratives by African Muslim slaves, as in narratives by many other slaves who did not choose to write in the tradition of the fugitive slave narrative genre, learning to read and to write in English were less important than other endeavors, such as acquiring a greater degree of economic or physical independence or preserving metaphysical concepts and religious practices. Texts such as those written by African American Muslims may be considered early examples of African American collaboration within African America. They seem more intended to build and to preserve community, to protect themselves and others from at least some of the disintegrative aspects of U.S. American enslavement, than to argue or plead with Euro-Americans for surcease or succor.

Among the African American Muslims who wrote and provided intellectual or spiritual guidance for their communities is Umar (Omar) ibn Said. Said spent most of his life as a slave in Fayetteville, North Carolina. The legends, myths, and controversies around him, his writings, and his relationships are myriad and difficult to resolve. Some things, however, are clear. He was a leader in his community and esteemed for his intellectual acuity. A contemporary newspaper article about him deemed him "An African Scholar." Allan D. Austin writes that African Americans generally considered him "a 'pray-god to the king,' a *marabout*, or a kind of religious counselor, to non-Muslim rulers."[4] Among his fourteen extant manuscripts are excerpts from the Koran and from traditional commentaries on the Koran, lists of family members, the Lord's prayer, and an autobiography. These topics imply concern with conservation of religious traditions, preservation of family history, and possible revisions of identity as people of African descent now living in the intersections of Christianity, Islam, and racial oppression.

Another example comes from Bilali (aka Bilali Mohamed and Ben-Ali), who lived on Sapelo Island in Georgia. An *imam* or *admaamy* of the local African Muslim community, Bilali wrote a highly unusual and controversial text generally referred to as *Ben Ali's Diary or Meditations*.[5] According to translators, a portion of the extant Bilali manuscript excerpts a tenth-century Islamic legal work that was common in the curriculum of many Muslim schools in West Africa. Excerpts of cultural history, such as this, were essential to claiming and preserving the diversity and integrity of an important aspect of African American culture. In *(Dis)Forming the American Canon*, Ronald A. T. Judy argues that Bilali's manuscript "prompts a study of the conditions of knowledge determining the field of modernity, and within that field a special order of cultural studies."[6] Judy's suggestion that Bilali's achievements in the nineteenth century can be a key influence for thinkers and scholars of the twenty-first can be applied generally to his Muslim American colleagues also.

Bilali and Umar ibn Said are but two of several early African Americans who preserved in Arabic ideals and ideas of African Americans. Their extant texts evidence a strong, if small, community of African Muslims who produced letters, autobiographies, histories, and texts that range from excerpts of the Koran and theological commentaries to strategies for political rebellion and social integrity. As Diouf summarizes, these Arabic-writing intellectu-als "used their knowledge not only to remain intellectually alert but also to defend and protect themselves, to maintain their sense of self, to reach out to their brethren, to organize uprisings, and, for some, to gain their freedom."[7] In sum, they were pre-Emancipation forerunners to those in the post-bel-lum–pre-Harlem era and later years. Like their African American sisters and brothers of other religious persuasions, like those who wrote in English, and like those whose achievements occurred decades later, they worked to pre-serve cultural values and to offer alternate modes of transcendence by, for, and of people of African descent in America.

French, too, was a lingua franca for some African Americans, and the collaborative achievements of French-speaking intellectuals form part of our legacy from African American writers, artists, and thinkers before 1880. They demonstrate a way in which some people of African descent rejected external definitions that tried to conflate and to dictate the cultural ingredients they should use. Instead of following the North Star, they sometimes sought free-dom by sailing to France. However, these communities did not so much deny their African ancestry as they affirmed the African American Francophonic or Creole culture they constructed. Consideration of their art and shared endeavors provides a different starting point for narratives of the develop-ment of the African American press as well as our understanding of Afri-can American literary production. For example, the life and early writings of Alice Dunbar-Nelson become more nuanced and less odd and the chronicle of the development of African American fiction changes.

To begin with the last point, if one accepts, as did the editors of the first edition of the *Norton Anthology of African American Literature* (1997), Victor Séjour's short story, "The Mulatto," as African American fiction, the earli-est extant short story can be dated from 1837 rather than 1852.[8] Accepting Victor Séjour as an African American seems appropriate since he was born in New Orleans, his father was a free mulatto from Santo Domingo, and his mother was a Louisiana native of African ancestry. Moreover, Séjour grew up within a larger African American community than many African Americans of the eighteenth-century colonies did. He was educated at Sainte-Barbe Academy, a school run by an African American writer, Michel Séligny. As a young man, Séjour went to France, where he found recognition as an artist and intellectual. In important ways, Séjour's journey parallels or prefigures those by other African Americans such as sculptor Edmonia Lewis in Italy, painter Henry Ossawa Tanner in France, violinist Portia Washington in Ger-many, and singer/actor Paul Robeson and writer Dorothy West in Russia.

Before leaving the United States, Victor Séjour had belonged to a dynamic literary community in New Orleans that produced in 1843 what some call the "first Negro literary magazine."⁹ *The Literary Album, Journal of Young People/L'Album Littéraire, Journal des Jeunes Gens* began as a bimonthly, bilingual (French/English) compilation of "poems, editorials, sketches and short stories," but proved so popular, write Armistead S. Pride and Clint C. Wilson II, that "it soon became a semi-monthly."¹⁰ Slaveholding New Orleans, Louisiana, was not only the birthplace of what is considered the "first" literary magazine by African Americans, but it was also home to what has been identified as "the first Black newspaper in the South," *The Union/ L'Union* (1862), and in 1864, the "first Negro daily newspaper," *The New Orleans Tribune/La Tribune de la Nouvelle-Orleans*.¹¹ While they did not represent the majority of African Americans in the South, the French and/or multilingual newspapers and literary societies were African American intellectual collaboratives that flourished during slavery. The newspapers, magazines, and literary anthologies of Francophonic African Americans were part of a southern cultural establishment that included or led to other collectives such as *The SemiWeekly Louisianian*, edited in 1870 by P. B. S. Pinchback, and the *Southwestern Christian Advocate*, which in 1892 published Octavia Victoria Rogers Albert's serialized *The House of Bondage; or Charlotte Brooks and Other Slaves*.... Multilingual and other intellectual communities off, and sometimes far distant from, the Atlantic Corridor were essential to the development of the African American press. Nor were they the only such communities. Even during the period of enslavement, in southern locations that include Charleston, South Carolina, Baltimore, Maryland, Savannah, Georgia, and Natchez, Mississippi, African Americans banded together to organize schools and societies. Founders, teachers, students, and graduates of these schools were among the early editors, journalists, and publishers of African American newspapers and periodicals. Nineteenth-century editors and publishers, writers, and readers laid the foundations upon which were built later collaboratives such as *The Colored American* (1900), *The Woman's Era* (1894), *The Crisis* (1910), *Negro World* (1918), *The Brownie's Book* (1920), and *Opportunity* (1923).

However, the best known activity among African American intellectuals and artists before the twentieth century, like that of Euro-Americans as well, occurred in and around the Atlantic Corridor from New England to Philadelphia. The data on collaborative efforts of artist/activists before the 1770s is, as of yet, still quite fragmented and inconclusive. Collaboration began, I suspect, during the Middle Passage, for it is difficult to believe that, even or especially in those most nightmarish circumstances, there were not dream weavers, griots, and storytellers who kept alive the souls within those tortured bodies. Our earliest records of African American publications include a narrative by Briton Hammon in 1760 and a poem by Jupiter Hammon in that same year, and it is probable that members of their African American communities influenced and were influenced by their thoughts. Certainly, coalitions or societies that encouraged articulate and artistic communities existed before 1760. We know, for example, that Lucy Terry Prince created the poem "Bar's Fight" about 1746. The fragment that survives is in ballad form, suggesting the work was intended as a communal offering. Historians such as Sidney Kaplan and Emma Nogrady Kaplan report that Prince and her daughter Duroxa both had reputations as poets, and her son Festus was a gifted musician.[12] In his *History of Deerfield* (1972), George Sheldon adds that the Prince household was a gathering place for African American conversation and storytelling.[13]

There is sufficient evidence from the 1770s for us to know that African Americans joined forces to articulate, to argue, and to effect social change. There were petitions such as that by "many Slaves, living in the Town of Boston, and other Towns in the Province"—sent on January 6, 1773, to Governor Hutchinson and the General Court by Peter Bestes, Sambo Freeman, Chester Joie, and Felix Holbrook "in behalf of our fellow slaves in this province and by order of their Committee"—which was published as a pamphlet in April 1773.[14] There were African American churches formed in Silver Bluff, South Carolina, that later united with congregations in Savannah, Georgia, and sent ministers to organize congregations in Jamaica and Sierra Leone.[15]

A very good example of artistic unity and collaborative support in the latter part of the eighteenth century centers around Phillis Wheatley, whose book of poetry appeared in 1773. Wheatley's circle (or circles) included Europeans, European Americans, and at least one Native American intellectual, Samson Occum; however, most relevant to this discussion is her African American collegium. Recent discoveries of letters, manuscripts, and publications by and about Wheatley suggest that Wheatley herself was at the center of an informal group who encouraged, advised, and emulated one another.[16] Such rediscoveries and reinterpretations of Wheatley's works redirect our attention from Phillis, the isolated prodigy, to Phillis, the consciously committed artist and community leader. Although casual critics generally point to Wheatley as an instinctive poet alienated from the African American community and focused more on evangelical cant than on community or intellectual matters, some evidence suggests quite the opposite. As the title of her first and only published volume of poetry declared, Wheatley wrote "On Various Subjects, Religious and Moral" (1773). Indeed, reading these poems on various subjects reveals a woman deeply concerned about issues such as art, philosophy, and political action. One need only scan the titles or read the contents of such works as "To the King's Most Excellent Majesty," "To the Right Honourable William, Earl of Dartmouth," or "To His

Excellency General Washington" to realize her interest in and readiness to address major political figures of her time. "To the University of Cambridge, in New-England," "To Maecenas," "Deism," "Atheism," "Liberty and Peace," and the newly rediscovered "Ocean" illustrate her intellectual and aesthetic priorities. In fact, in "Ocean" Wheatley uses the occasion of the ship's captain casually killing an eagle who flew too close to reflect upon the meaning of seemingly random destruction of weaker humans and animals. In so doing, Wheatley reveals herself as a philosopher, and she may also be considered one of our earliest published ecological conservationists.

Phillis Wheatley's artistic/activist efforts were consciously collaborative and often racially specific.[17] For example, her poem "To S. M., a Young *African* Poet, on Seeing His Works" not only affirms her acquaintance with the works of other African American artists but also declares her idea of reciprocal inspiration and common goals. Wheatley's Boston readers would have identified "S. M." as Scipio Moorhead, another African American artist whose artistic "genius" was acknowledged by colonial New Englanders.[18] The odds are great that especially if, as many scholars believe, Scipio Moorhead drew the frontispiece portrait of Wheatley in her book, not only did Phillis the enslaved African American poet know and support Scipio the enslaved African American painter, but she also saw their efforts as having an element of collaborative conspiracy.

In "To S. M.," the poet tells the painter that his work stimulates her imagination, that their works "conspire." She declares,

> When first thy pencil did those beauties give,
> And breathing figures learnt from thee to live,
> How did those prospects give my soul delight,
> A new creation rushing on my sight? (3–6)[19]

Later, she embraces the commonality of artistic concerns across genres by exclaiming,

> . . . may the painter's and the poet's fire,
> To aid thy pencil, and thy verse conspire! (9–10)[20]

With lines such as these, which suggest an idea of art as both aesthetic pleasure and racial affirmation, Wheatley is participating in conversations attributed to the Enlightenment in ways beyond the religious and theological. Rosemary Fithian Guruswamy's statement that "because of the double Enlightenment appeal to . . . Christianity and . . . natural law that spoke for the essentiality of freedom, African Americans were able to participate openly in a related thread about 'black uplift,'"[21] has a particular resonance when applied to Phillis Wheatley's work.

The "essentiality of freedom" and racial relevance for this particular poem begins with its title. "S. M." is deliberately and directly identified as a "young *African* artist" (emphasis in original). This invites readers to approach this writing as being about art and especially about its function and effects for African American artists and for the tradition they are creating.

A few years after the publication of Wheatley's book, another African American writer, Jupiter Hammon, suggests that Wheatley's circle encompassed more than the African Americans of Boston, Massachusetts. Jupiter Hammon wrote from Hartford, Connecticut, to "Miss Phillis Wheatly [*sic*], Ethiopian Poetess, in Boston" on behalf of himself and "a number of his friends, who desire to join with him in their best regards to Miss Wheatly [*sic*]." In the poem entitled "An Address to Miss Phillis Wheatly, Ethiopian Poetess ..." (1778), Hammon and friends first present a philosophical or theological premise that Wheatley is where and what she is because of God's "tender mercies." They advise this prominent African American woman that because she is a role model, she therefore has particular responsibilities to maintain her piety, both private and public: "That thou a pattern still might be, / To youth of Boston town" (21–22).[22] The word "still" acknowledges her current position as well as its vulnerability and the necessity that she protect and defend her exemplary status. "An Address to Miss Phillis Wheatly, Ethiopian Poetess ..." is both a tribute and a testimony from one group of African Americans in one New England colony to and about their colleague in another New England colony. It suggests, at the very least, an informal concept of community and collaboration among colonial African Americans.[23]

Despite or maybe because of their slave status, Phillis Wheatley, Scipio Moorhead, Jupiter Hammon, his friends, and others understood themselves as part of a community of African American writers, artists, and thinkers who could perhaps write things right. Theirs was undoubtedly an informal or virtual mutual aid society. By the end of the eighteenth century, among freer African Americans, such communities were more formally constituted and such collaborations were more public. The work of twentieth-century archivists and academics such as Dorothy Porter and Elizabeth McHenry suggests that formalized mutual aid societies agreed with the informal evidence from our colonial artist and authors that "stimulation of reading and spreading useful knowledge" were essential to social, political, spiritual, and moral health.[24] Whether their primary or original purpose was to offer health and death insurance, support local churches, or simply provide social contact, such societies generally encouraged the creation and expression of elocution and oratory, of reading and writing, of public articulation of ideas and ideals about personal and public concerns. Like the characters who arrange the "conversaziones" depicted in late-nineteenth-century works—such as Frances E. W. Harper's *Iola Leroy; or, Shadows Uplifted* (1892), these groups organized lectures and discussions and urged members to read and write, listen and critique for themselves and for others that which they read and heard. Documents such as bylaws, minutes, membership rolls, and program announcements make more visible ways in which African American writers, artists, and thinkers organized and collaborated not only by providing the occasions for individual members to publish their creations and argue their ideas but also by creating reading rooms, libraries, and schools. The societies did not operate in a vacuum, nor were they isolated oases existing in a desert of ignorance unaffected by and unaffecting the larger environment. The chronology of their establishments suggests that the success of some sparked the creation of others. For example, the Reading Room Society in Philadelphia began in 1828, the Clarkston Society of New York started the next year, the Theban Literary Society of Pittsburgh was founded in 1831, and the Afric-American Female Intelligence Society of Boston dates from 1832.

Reading rooms and literary and intelligence societies developed authors and audiences whose influence extended well beyond their memberships. It was the Female and Literary Society of Philadelphia that provided many of the poems, essays, and other writings published in Garrison's *Liberator* during 1831–1832, and the Afric-American Female Intelligence Society was a site of one of Maria W. Stewart's first public lectures. In much the same way as the African American women's groups gave money and spaces for Ida B. Wells to lecture and publish her work at the end of the nineteenth century, so too did many mutual aid groups, literary societies, and other community organizations support artist/activists in the beginning of that century. They not only supported artist/activists but also created them, and they created the necessary public venues for their work. The connections among W. E. B. Du Bois, James Weldon Johnson, Alain Locke, and others underlay the founding and success of journals such as *Crisis* and *Opportunity*, whose salubrious effects upon the careers of Langston Hughes, Countee Cullen, and Nella Larsen, and the existence of what is called the Harlem Renaissance, are well documented. Nearly a century earlier, similar connections were at play. The earliest extant African American newspaper, *Freedom's Journal*, is a prime example.

Freedom's Journal, first published in New York City in 1827, began with a consortium of individuals from several states. The paper officially began after a meeting at the New York City home of Boston Crummell of several prominent African Americans, including Nathaniel Paul, an Albany, New York, abolitionist minister; A.M.E. Bishop Richard Allen of Philadelphia; John

B. Russwurm, recently graduated from Bowdoin College in Maine; William Hamilton, chairman of the People of Color of New York; and the Reverend Samuel Cornish, former missionary to Maryland slaves and founding member of several abolitionist societies. About the same time, in Boston, David Walker hosted an auxiliary meeting with Thomas Paul (Nathaniel's brother), James Gould, George B. Holmes, and others. These Massachusetts leaders organized to provide financial and journalistic support for the paper. *Freedom's Journal* was, from its conception, the result of collaboration. It was intended as a national and even international forum for discussion among people of African heritage, discussion that would produce collective enlightenment and progress. Its first issue proclaimed its purpose as "the dissemination of useful knowledge among our brethren, and . . . their moral and religious improvement." Kenneth D. Nordin summarizes its basic objective as "to produce a nationally circulated newspaper which would develop a sense of fraternity, a black consciousness, as it were, among the freemen and ex-slaves living in scattered communities throughout the northern states."[25]

Like the New Negro Movement at the end of the nineteenth century, these early-nineteenth-century movers and shakers were centered in New York City and in many ways presented New York as the symbolic capital of African America. Yet they were from diverse areas, with diverse and sometimes divergent perspectives, and they intended to chronicle and to foment artistic and political change and racial self-esteem throughout the African Diaspora. Among the "authorised Agents" listed in the first edition were Ruben Ruby of Portland, Maine; George C. Willis of Providence, Rhode Island; John W. Prout of Washington, D.C.; and Theodore Wright, James Cowes, and B. F. Hughes from Princeton, New Brunswick, and Newark, New Jersey. And, as Pride and Wilson report, during the two years of its existence, the paper listed at least forty-four agents representing a dozen U.S. states and territories as well as Canada, Haiti, and England.[26]

From its inception, *Freedom's Journal* aspired to attract and affect African Americans in all the important aspects of their lives. Its motto, "Righteousness Exalteth a Nation," can be interpreted in various ways. "Righteousness" evokes "moral and religious improvement." The word "Nation" applies to the United States in which they lived and of which they demanded actions in accordance with the idealistic words of its Constitution and Declaration of Independence. "Righteousness" therefore implied that the United States should do right by itself and its citizens. But, if the opening editorial and the contents of the paper are to be taken seriously, "Nation" here also means "African America." *Freedom's Journal* was also about the building and preservation of the African American "nation." And to that end the paper promised to articulate, educate, and admonish African Americans about themselves,

present, past, and future. To that end, the paper promised that "useful knowledge of every kind, and every thing that relates to Africa, shall find a ready
admission in our columns."[27]

The paper was a wonderfully eclectic mix of material submitted by a
large number of agents, correspondents, and contributing authors along with
articles, poems, and essays reprinted from newspapers from the United States
and around the world. The first issue combined "Foreign News" and "Domestic News" with a serialization of the "Memoirs of Capt. Paul Cuffee" and
the "True Story" of the miraculous reunion in England of Mary Davis with
her kidnapped son. *Freedom's Journal* regularly published poetry and essays by
new and established writers. It sometimes mentioned significant publications
such as a history of New England Indians published by "Davis Cusick, an
Indian of the Tuscarora tribe" in Lewistown, New York. The paper promoted
the importance of earlier African American authors such as Phillis Wheatley and George Moses Horton. Contributors from Haiti and Jamaica shared
news of their communities along with reprinted items on global and economic issues such as "Chinese Fashion" and "The Egg Trade." *Freedom's Journal* noted births, deaths, and marriages, crimes and crowning achievements
of African America. To stimulate intellectual interest and provide avenues
for material success, the paper advertised businesses such as B. F. Hughes's
School for Coloured Children of Both Sexes and Charles Mortimer's Shoe
and Boot Shop. In short, *Freedom's Journal* functioned to stimulate and to
nurture, to be a renaissance of and resource for cultural, historical, political,
and economic identity and influence.

It is also important to recall that those who founded and represented
Freedom's Journal not only were collaborating on this historic achievement, but
they were also related to, or in relationships with, other individuals, groups,
and communities that supported, influenced, and were influenced by the collective actions and attitudes that *Freedom's Journal* reflected and inflected. It
worked because the founders themselves were veterans of other campaigns to
create, celebrate, and cultivate African American cultural, educational, and
political progress; and they would continue working with other groups in the
future. Richard Allen, along with Absolom Jones and others, had founded the
Free African Society in 1787 and in 1817 had incorporated what may have
been the first African American publishing company, the A.M.E. Book Concern. Allen was also a poet, essayist, and autobiographer with a long history
of collaboration with others on publications such as *Confessions of John Joyce*
(1808) and the history of the A.M.E. Church, which appeared in the first
Discipline (1817) of that denomination. David Walker, author of the *Appeal
. . . to the Coloured Citizens of the World . . .* (1829), was also a friend and mentor to Maria W. Stewart, whose essays and lectures sought to stir men and

women to higher education, greater appreciation of their African heritage and innate abilities, and stronger public agitation for equal rights. His colleague, Thomas Paul, had officiated at Maria W. Stewart's wedding. Thomas Paul was head of the African Church on Belnap and later founded Abyssinian Baptist Church in New York City. He was also a member of the Boston School Committee, husband to Catherine Paul, who operated a private school, and father to Susan, whose *Memoir of James Jackson* (1835) was exhibited in bookstores alongside volumes by Phillis Wheatley and Lydia Maria Child.[28] Boston Crummell, the father of Alexander Crummell, became the founder of the Phoenix Society of New York in 1833. On its board of directors were *Freedom's Journal* coeditor Samuel E. Cornish and Charles B. Ray, editor of one of *Freedom's Journal*'s successors, the *Colored American*. Charles B. Ray was father of Cordelia Ray, whose affiliations included the *New Era*, which under the title of *New National Era*, was edited by Frederick Douglass.

The list can go on. We would consider the work of the Annual Conventions of Free Persons of Colour and note the memberships that overlap but also extend. We could talk about the African American antislavery and vigilance groups that were part of the Underground Railroad. During the Civil War and Reconstruction, an example of African American collaborative efforts is the Contraband Relief Agency, headed by Elizabeth Keckley and strongly supported by community groups such as that from the Fifteenth Avenue Presbyterian Church. In 1881, the Bethel Literary and Historical Association was, in Jane Rhodes's words, "Washington's central gathering place for black intellectuals and public figures," and Mary Ann Shadd Cary, editor and founder of the *Provincial Freeman*, was one of the "nation's distinguished African Americans [who met] to discuss the pressing issues of race and society, as well as science and letters."[29] The Bethel Literary and Historical Association was but one of many such groups that Daniel Payne and others had founded, and it was another direct descendant of the mutual aid and literary societies that began in the eighteenth century, perhaps even on the dreadful Middle Passage. But, hopefully, the point has been made. Informal and formal organizations of artists, writers, and thinkers are intricately interwoven into the fabric of African American history. Their social, religious, economic, and political organizations and associations led to institutions, such as the African American press, which were essential to the development of African American art and literature. These organizations were not always identical in their scope, philosophies, or significance. Nor were the languages, rituals, and beliefs of their members always in harmony with them or with the communities they purported to impact. Cliques, class, and cultural differences were common. Criticism and controversy were never in short supply. There were also, of course, the lone individuals, the solitary thinkers and artists, the isolates and the iconoclasts whose achievements we now revere. But, and still, and nonetheless, collaboration, too, is as African American as sweet potato pie.

NOTES

1. This is not to suggest that collaborations among African Americans or the social networks and organizational activities of early African Americans have been entirely ignored. Many scholars, from Monroe Majors to Dorothy Porter, Benjamin Quarles, and James O. Horton, have discussed this topic. My point here is that despite a long history of alternative narratives, the dominant and more often cited images are of individual and singular success.

2. Sylviane A. Diouf, *Servants of Allah: African Muslims Enslaved in the Americas* (New York: New York University Press, 1998), 2.

3. Recent scholarship has provided translations. My comments are based upon the English translations.

4. Quoted in Diouf, *Servants of Allah*, 131.

5. Bilali's text defies easy translation, in part because the manuscript has deteriorated and ink seepage has rendered parts illegible, and in part because he used a mixture of what Sylviane A. Diouf states is "classical Arabic and Pulaar written with Arabic characters." In Diouf, *Servants of Allah*, 126–28.

6. See Ronald A. T. Judy, *(Dis)Forming the American Canon: African-Arabic Slave Narratives and the Vernacular* (Minneapolis: University of Minnesota Press, 1993), 24.

7. Diouf, *Servants of Allah*, 144.

8. Given the great amount of African Americana that has been destroyed, displaced, or appropriated, I am not convinced that proclaiming a text or author as "the earliest" or "the first" of anything means a great deal. However, when one tries to establish origins of or intertextuality among particular conventions and character types in African American fiction, establishing priority can be significant. For example, if one begins, as do many scholars, not with "The Mulatto" but with Frederick Douglass's "The Heroic Slave" (1853), African American fiction began with an integrated abolitionist story featuring a dark-skinned hero. Beginning with Séjour's story, published fiction started in French with a gothic revenge tale revolving around the psychological conflicts of a mulatto searching for the identity of his father.

9. Armistead S. Pride and Clint C. Wilson II, *History of the Black Press* (Washington, DC: Howard University Press, 1997), 73–75.

10. Ibid., 75.

11. Two very helpful discussions of such collaborations are Jacqueline Jones Royster, *Traces of a Stream: Literacy and Social Change among African American Women* (Pittsburgh, PA: University of Pittsburgh Press, 2000); and Janet Driftsman Cornelius, *When I Can Read My Title Clear: Literacy, Slavery, and Religion in the Antebellum South* (Columbia: University of South Carolina Press, 1991).

12. Sidney Kaplan and Emma Nogrady Kaplan, *The Black Presence in the Era of the American Revolution*, rev. ed. (Amherst: University of Massachusetts Press, 1989), 241.

13. Sheldon, *History of Deerfield* (Somersworth: New Hampshire Publishing Company in collaboration with the Pocumtuck Valley Memorial Association, Deerfield, 1972), 901.

14. Kaplan and Kaplan, *Black Presence*, 11.

15. Ibid., 91.

16. See, for example, the very excellent work of Julian D. Mason Jr., *The Poems of Phillis Wheatley: Revised and Enlarged Edition with an Additional Poem* (Chapel Hill: University of North Carolina Press, 2001); William H. Robinson, *Phillis Wheatley and Her Writings* (New York: Garland Press, 1986); and John Shields, *The Complete Poems of Phillis Wheatley* (New York: Oxford University Press, 1988).

17. For a fuller discussion of Wheatley as racial advocate and activist see Frances Smith Foster, *Written by Herself: Literary Production by African American Women, 1746–1892* (Indianapolis: Indiana University Press, 1993), 30–43.

18. See Mason, *Poems*, 104–5. According to Julian D. Mason Jr., a notation in the American Antiquarian Society's copy of Wheatley's book "identifies S. M. as 'Scipio Moorhead—Negro Servant to the Revd. Mr. Moorhead of Boston, whose Genius inclined him that way.'"

19. Mason, *Poems*, 104–5.

20. Ibid., 105.

21. Rosemary Fithian Guruswamy, "'Thou Hast the Holy Word': Jupiter Hammon's 'Regards' to Phillis Wheatley," in *Genius in Bondage: Literature of the Early Black Atlantic*, ed. Vincent Carretta and Philip Gould (Lexington: University Press of Kentucky, 2001), 191. Guruswamy offers a fascinating theory of Jupiter Hammon's work as pioneering "the discourse of 'African Americanism.'" Such a reading would offer additional support for the idea of continuities between eighteenth-century African American writers, artists, and thinkers and those of the twentieth. Like the speculations of Diouf and Judy mentioned earlier, her idea suggests great rewards to scholars who would give greater time and attention to pre-Emancipation theory and practice.

22. Henry Louis Gates Jr. and Nellie Y. McKay, eds., *The Norton Anthology of African American Literature*, 2nd ed. (New York: Norton, 2004), 165–68.

23. Other suggestions regarding Wheatley's African American sphere of influence come from her several letters to Obour Tanner in Newport, Rhode Island.

24. The quotation comes from Dorothy Porter, "The Organized Educational Activities of Negro Literary Societies, 1828–1846," *Journal of Negro Education* 5 (October 1936): 555–76. See also Elizabeth McHenry "Forgotten Readers: African-American Literary Societies and the American Scene," in *Print Culture in a Diverse America*, ed. James P. Danky and Wayne A. Wiegand (Urbana: University of Illinois Press, 1997), 149–72.

25. Kenneth D. Nordin, "In Search of Black Unity: An Interpretation of the Content and Function of *Freedom's Journal*," *Journalism History* 4.4 (1977–1978): 123.

26. Pride and Wilson, *History*, 10, 17.

27. *Freedom's Journal* 16 (March 1827): 1.

28. Susan Paul, *Memoir of James Jackson, the Attentive and Obedient Scholar, Who Died in Boston, October 31, 1833, Aged Six Years and Eleven Months, by His Teacher Miss Susan Paul*, ed. with an introduction by Lois Brown (1835, repr. Cambridge, MA: Harvard University Press, 2000), 1.

29. Jane Rhodes, *Mary Ann Shadd Cary: The Black Press and Protest in the Nineteenth Century* (Bloomington: Indiana University Press, 1998), 203.

KEITH D. LEONARD

"Bid the Gifted Negro Soar": The Origins of the African American Bardic Tradition

Listen all who never felt
For fettered genius heretofore—
Let hearts of petrifaction melt
And bid the gifted Negro soar.
                    —George Moses Horton, "A Poet's Feeble Petition"

In "A Poet's Feeble Petition," a poem he sent to the abolitionist Horace Greeley in a letter dated September 11, 1852, nineteenth-century slave poet George Moses Horton exemplifies in one quatrain the central claim to imaginative genius through poetic mastery and the accompanying claim to sympathy by which slave poets such as himself and African American abolitionist poets in general appealed to their white readers for an end to slavery. As such, the poem anticipates the way in which African American poets well into the twentieth century would construct poetic genius as the substance of an affirming racial self. It also provides the most persuasive terms for understanding eighteenth-century poet and slave Phillis Wheatley as the original African American poetic bard through her aesthetic, not just through her historical primacy. In the poem, Horton asks Greeley to recognize the slave poet's genius as an exemplar of Greeley's own imagination, an identification that would ideally melt Greeley's heart and motivate Greeley

From *Fettered Genius: The African American Bardic Poet from Slavery to Civil Rights*, pp. 19–49. © 2006 by the Rector and Visitors of the University of Virginia.

103

to bid Horton "soar" out of the fetters of slavery. And yet Horton's claim
to be a "gifted Negro" implies that he has already transcended those fetters
through the capacity to imagine that the poem exemplifies. This capacity distinguishes Horton from other slaves, frees Horton's mind, and thus
should justify the freedom of his body, if not the destruction of the entire
system of slavery. This self-contradictory idea—that his imaginative freedom is in jeopardy from the slavery that it has already transcended—enacts
a paradox in order to illuminate the fatal flaw of the ideology of absolute
difference by which slavery operates. The poem implies that this fundamental and shared human capacity, even in Horton's generous portion of it, can
be destroyed by lack of recognition or sympathy, even though Horton has
cultivated that genius without recognition. Also, Horton's distinction from
his fellow slaves paradoxically makes him representative of that community
in the fundamental humanity they share with Greeley, since the implication
is that if one African has imagination, all Africans might. Individuality and
imagination defined personal value, racial difference, and human community. And as the poetic encapsulation of all three, genius became the chief
political implication of Horton's art.

Thus, what matters about Horton's claim to genius is not exclusively
the very conventional appeal it makes to sentiment or sympathy or its relationship to the explicit protest Horton offers in other poems; rather, what
matters is the fact that such a claim implicitly depends upon the poem's construction of the poetic self as an ideal racial self. The significance of Horton's
claim—characteristic of most abolitionist poetry and central to Wheatley's
defining example—thus depends upon the fact that it constitutes a version
of what Stephen Greenblatt called *self-fashioning*. "Self-fashioning is in effect
the Renaissance version of . . . the cultural systems of meanings that creates
specific individuals by governing the passage from abstract potential to concrete historical embodiment. Literature functions within this system in three
interlocking ways: as a manifestation of the concrete behavior of its particular
author, as itself the expression of the codes by which behavior is shaped, and
as a reflection upon those codes" (4). A concrete historical embodiment of
the slave's denied abstract status as person, Horton's concrete act of imagination initiates a reflection on the codes of behavior that render Africans into
slaves and that should motivate Greeley's rejection of those codes based upon
other, related codes in the same social system. Horton has an agency here, in
other words, no matter the material effect of the poem, a capacity to participate somewhat in the construction of his identity in his culture. All African
American abolitionist poets used a version of this early-modern construction
of the individual to make claims upon society through their mastery of its
social codes of imaginative and moral personhood, claims enhanced even as

they were challenged by the poet's enslaved black body. For Wheatley, Horton, and Frances Ellen Watkins Harper, recognized poetic achievement was social participation, linking the abstract ideals of personhood and citizenship to the historically excluded black body, initiating through such conventionality the rewriting of conventional ideals of race, person, and nation. Scholars such as Henry Louis Gates have noted this association before but have not explored fully enough the aesthetic principles of the self-fashioning by which this association operates. Thus, the cultural agency of this mastery has been underestimated, since it has been linked primarily with literacy and self-defeating assimilation. By adapting ideals of sympathy and genius to their enslaved person, then, these poets made the poetic self a node of contention in the meaning of race, identity, and even nation. And Wheatley exemplifies this self-fashioning of genius, because the more fully these poets embraced communally shared literary standards of their time, the more fully their conventional poetics constructed an African self that was a convincing refutation of the ideologies of slavery.

In essence, I am suggesting that, paradoxically enough, the cultural assimilation of poetic mastery was the abolitionist poet's greatest act of resistance, an act exemplified by his or her self-constitution as genius as that self-concept was validated by the slaveholding and abolitionist reading public. Wheatley therefore became the originator of the central poetic practice of the African American formalist tradition because her work most fully engaged in the complicated antiracist meaning of literary genius. Unlike Horton's, Wheatley's claim to genius most fully associated her achievement with the cultural capacities of the entire race. By Wheatley's time, the term *genius* had come to mean a "personal quality ... which was assumed to reside in the blood," a conception that incorporated an aristocratic notion of race as inherited gentility into an ideal of individual talent (Hannaford 188). At the same time, the meaning of "race" had also shifted from the idea of a pre-Enlightenment aristocratic hierarchy to Montesquieu's related but broader idea of race as species of humanity, so that elitist hierarchy and shared biology overlapped in notions of racial identity and literary genius. As a result, formalist poetics allowed African American poetic "geniuses" to enact the idea that, as Arthur Schopenhauer put it, genius is both "energy, creativity, originality, inspiration and the capacity to bring meaning to matter" for the individual artist and a common imaginative capacity that "must exist in all men in smaller and different degree; for if not, they would be just as incapable of enjoying works of art as of producing them" (3). And as Barbara Will asserted in her discussion of Gertrude Stein's genius, attributing genius to a marginalized person, whether avant garde white woman or slave, challenges the notion that the marginalized are absolutely different and inferior (8).

By simultaneously exemplifying both individuality and community, distinction and commonality, these poets could place African imaginative selfhood at the center of a culture that had rendered it an absence, illuminating the cultural conjunction between notions of shared natural rights and artistic achievement that made the imagination the chief challenge to racism. It also meant that these poets garnered the public voice that refuted the "social death" characteristic of all of the practices of slavery in the world. Reading this verse as an ongoing practice of self-fashioning, then, I can suggest ways in which the intersection of discourses in the construction of that self by poet and audience constituted a construction of shared national ideals that included the poet in literary culture and, given the centrality of that culture to certain notions of nation, that thereby included them in a model of social and cultural citizenship. And that antiracist participation depended not upon protest but upon recognized talent, which in turn depended upon assimilating social and cultural discourses associated with that mastery. Though perhaps in some ways a less persuasive notion today, a "gifted Negro" in the time of slavery was more politically provocative than an angry slave would have been.

This bardic genius—as I will call it—transformed poetic achievement into a racial voice of freedom through poetic conventionality, an ideal that made social inclusion a genuine possibility and a genuine antiracist act. Thus, this conception of Wheatley as the originator of a model of imaginative genius that was the basis of social liberty and democratic citizenship provides an alternative to the tendency in the study of African American literary culture to treat literary conventionality, ideals of social integration, and practices of cultural assimilation as only capitulations to superior cultural power, as if some original, authentic, and essential black self were always already limited by the ideology of slavery, even in slaves who knew no other culture. Only in the broadest terms is this true. But when scholars attempt to assign that fixed black self to individuals or to lament its absence, they tend to come to dubious conclusions. For example, such simple oppositions of race politics led M. A. Richmond to assert that Wheatley's poetic mastery was evidence of her personal and political "lobotomy," the erasure of her personality and self-awareness by oppression (81). Using the same binary logic, Terence Collins concluded that her poetry was an exemplary "gauge of the depths to which . . . self-hate by blacks [was] based on interjection of the dominant culture's estimate of . . . worth" (147). To suggest that Wheatley's self was lobotomized is to make the false biological argument explicit. Not only does such essentialism reduce the complexity of African identity, it also leads such scholars to neglect that fact that, as Greenblatt suggests, any reading of the intersection of individual and cultural selfhood in literary self-fashioning "must address itself . . . to the interpretive constructions the members of the society apply to their experiences" (4–5). In other words, in embracing the culture of its time, African American poetic formalism *interprets* it, making such work evidence of something more than a lobotomy. This implicit interpretation is also more substantive than the idea that American culture is always an oppressive mask, a point through which scholars such as Rafia Zafar seek to rescue conventional writers such as Wheatley. Worse, scholars such as Richmond conclude that in the closing lines to his poem "On Liberty and Slavery," Horton "first struck the chord that has ever since dominated Afro-American poetry," a practice that, according to Richmond, made Horton a "pioneer" in black protest and black pride (81).

Instead of wearing early American culture as a mask or having her selfhood forcefully excised from her mind by some oppressive surgery, Wheatley constructed that self by wearing that culture as an ambivalent but ultimately empowering aspect of an ideal racial self worthy of poetic mastery and social inclusion. Therefore, a more persuasive conception of these dynamics of self-fashioning in general, and of Wheatley's remarkably successful case in particular, emerges when considered in terms of what Paul Gilroy aptly called the politics of fulfillment, the marginalized person's ideal that "a future society will be able to realise the social and political promise that present society has left unaccomplished," and that accomplished art can envision and motivate such fulfillment (37). Acting on the ideal that "bourgeois civil society [will] live up to the promise of its own rhetoric," Wheatley, Horton, and Harper fulfilled mainstream social codes in ways that provided an alternative—however minuscule—to the practice of those codes. After all, to be frank, the democratic ideals of the United States are well worth fulfilling, no matter how much racist social practices compromise those ideals, and that is exactly what these poets aspired to do by transforming poetic achievement into social participation. Certainly, it is more affirming to imagine that African American poets who were slaves would have created an ethnic tradition based on African culture, left to their own devices, but they were not left alone. To criticize them for not building an ethnic poetic culture seems to me to be worth doing only as a step toward understanding what they *did* build. Their politics of fulfillment was more self-assertion than abdication, a point conceivable only with a historically more persuasive attention to the meaning of poetic formalism in its time rather than in our own. It made good sense that slaves would want the nation to live up to its principles, and the African American poetic tradition is founded in this slightly self-deprecating but meaningfully self-assertive attempt to do just that. This pursuit is clearly a measure as much of their fettered situation as of their imaginative liberation.

I take the title of this chapter from Horton's poem, then, because, following the logic of Gilroy's assertion, the cultural assimilation that was a necessary precondition for inclusion into the imagined and historical body politic provided a rigid Eurocentric framework for African American identity and only the narrowest of spaces within which an affirming sense of self could be communally fashioned. But that space was broad enough to allow the "gifted Negro" to "soar" into public discourse through a mode of social participation derived from poetic self-fashioning and analogous to citizenship. It is the nature of this soaring that both unites and distinguishes these three poets as the progenitors of the African American formalist poetic tradition. In her 1773 volume *Poems on Various Subjects, Religious and Moral*, the first collection of poetry by a person of African descent published in the United States, Wheatley exemplified this soaring in her mastery of neoclassical poetics, Puritan religiosity, and discourses of natural rights. Her practice transformed the definition of African identity into the abstracted selfhood at the heart of what Andrew Burstein persuasively called "sentimental democracy"—"the connectedness of these people, their shared loyalty to national principles and the persistence of a common cultural idiom" as "zealous expressions of sympathy and affectionate ties joined with clear assertions of the reasoning intellect to promote national union" (xvii). For Horton, this self-fashioning was actually compromised by his claim to be an entirely distinctive poetic genius, a sense of individuality that resisted rather than confirmed this sentimental democracy and therefore compromised the politics of fulfillment. And Harper's advocacy for freedom through traditional moral integrity and explicit protest locates this sentimental democracy in the claim to conventional notions of womanhood. This self-fashioning of poetic genius was the central artistic and political achievement of these poets, and it is exemplified not by the more explicitly political Horton and Harper but by the still much-maligned Wheatley.

Thus I seek to reclaim Wheatley as an artist rather than an artifact by understanding more fully how her black body and slave status informed readings of her conventional artistic achievement as an expression of racial selfhood, allowing her claim to poetic gifts to function as the genius of citizenship. In these terms, the origin of the African American formalist poetic tradition starts with Wheatley's very existence. Brought to Boston from West Africa, a seven-year-old Phillis was bought by John and Susanna Wheatley in 1761 and soon proved herself to have intellectual gifts that refuted presumptions that Africans were incapable of higher thought, a contradiction to the racism of her society enhanced by her capacity to write poetry. The challenge was such that, as is quite well known by now, Wheatley had to prove to a panel of eighteen influential figures of the Massachusetts Colony that she was knowledgeable enough to have written her verse in order to get her volume published. As those worthies put it,

> We whose names are under-written, do assure the World, that
> the POEMS specified in the following Page, were (as we verily
> believe) written by Phillis, a young Negro Girl, who was but a few
> Years since, brought an uncultivated Barbarian from *Africa*, and has
> ever since been, and now is, under the Disadvantage of serving as
> a Slave in this Town. She has been examined by some of the best
> judges, and is thought qualified to write them.

This oral exam, as Henry Louis Gates called it, was the beginning of her self-fashioning. Though the volume would not have been published without it, this authorization would not have mattered without Wheatley's mastered artistry and her personal capacity to justify it with her knowledge. As one nineteenth-century reviewer put it, "The classical allusions [in Wheatley's verse] are numerous, and imply a wide compass of reading, a correct judgment, good taste, and a tenacious memory" such that Wheatley's volume was "perhaps the most favorable evidence on record, of the capacity of the African for intellect." Wheatley becomes, in this construction of her identity, the "unassisted Genius" that her publisher Archibald Bell described her to be (Robinson 16). And Wheatley's self is constructed here as a passage from "barbarian" to slave to qualified poet, even genius, a progression that she accepts and manipulates to her advantage. Not only does this racist narrative of evolution make her "soaring" possible, it also creates a notion of her genius that makes that racist narrative the paradoxical basis for her claims to citizenship.

More than even Gates has recognized, then, Wheatley participated in this racist public fashioning of her genius not as much through Africanist word-play as through identifying and defining as a component of her African heritage the imaginative gift that authorized her poetry and that was central to national unity. In her oft-anthologized poem "To the University of Cambridge, in New-England," for example, Wheatley revises the standard racist justification of slavery as the cultivation of barbarians by claiming that her imaginative life began before she was "cultivated."

> While an intrinsic ardor prompts to write,
> The muses promise to assist my pen;
> 'Twas not long since I left my native shore
> The land of errors, and *Egyptian* gloom:
> Father of mercy, 'twas thy gracious hand
> Brought me in safety from those dark abodes. (lines 1–6)

In addition to calling quite conventionally to the muses to motivate and authorize her artistry and requesting similar sanction from the Puritan God, proving her "wide compass of reading," Wheatley declares that she can write because she has an innate capacity that was ordained both by the muses and by the Christian God and that arose from her African self. Moreover, as in the spirituals in which slaves claimed biblical sanction for both spiritual and literal freedom by identifying with the Israelites and biblical Ethiopians, Wheatley's description of Africa as "Egyptian" and herself as an "Ethiop" later in the poem root her poetic authority in biblical prophecy, as in Psalm 68:31, which asserts, "Princes shall come out of Egypt; Ethiopia shall soon stretch forth her hands unto God." Just as her African identity preceded her conversion, then, and just as biblical ideals and prophecy preceded her enslavement, Wheatley's imaginative "ardor" for writing preceded her acculturation. Her desire to write—her imagination—is "intrinsic" to her personality and is thus a more fundamental authority for her verse than is her more readily apparent mastery of the classical allusions and heroic couplets of poetic neoclassicism. No matter its "errors" and "gloom," then; her "Egyptian" past was still the source of her ardor. This intrinsic ardor actually functions, in ways that Wheatley probably did not know entirely, as the substance of her claim to citizenship.

This claim to "intrinsic ardor" is one of Wheatley's most important antiracist gestures, because it ties her imaginative gifts to ideals of personhood central to the terms of her reception and fundamental to the definitions of citizenship emerging in colonial America. In her 1774 letter to Samson Occum, for example, Wheatley suggested as much. She declared herself to be "greatly satisfied with [Occum's] Reasons respecting the Negroes, and think highly reasonable what you offer in Vindication of their natural Rights." She goes on to explain that the work of missionaries in Africa

> reveals more and more clearly, the glorious Dispensation of civil and religious Liberty, which are so inseparably united, that there is little or no enjoyment of one without the other: Otherwise, perhaps the Israelites had been less solicitous for their Freedom from Egyptian slavery; I do not say they would have been contented without it, by no means, for in every human Breast, God has implanted a Principle, which we call Love of Freedom; it is impatient of Oppression, and pants for Deliverance; and by the Leave of our modern Egyptians I will assert, that the same Principle lives in us. (*Poems* 203)

Whether or not we here can equate sin directly with slavery, as Katherine Clay Bassard suggests, Wheatley clearly declares that the love of freedom, like her imaginative "ardor," is "intrinsic" to human personality, as it is "implanted" by God in "every human Breast" (42–44, 48). And Wheatley's conclusion to the letter emphasizes the relationship between her individual mind and these larger principles of human personality: "How well the Cry for Liberty, and the reverse Disposition for the exercise of oppressive power over others agree,—I humbly think it does not require the Penetration of a Philosopher to determine." Her ironic tone grants Wheatley the "Penetration" that she implies some of her alleged "superiors" lack, tying her intrinsic imaginative ardor to philosophical "penetration" and to a divine principle of freedom.

Likewise, seeing these antiracist effects of her assimilation of her culture, Betsy Erkilla and Houston Baker have discussed Wheatley's place in the rhetoric of the emerging democracy, but neither deals well enough with Wheatley as a poetic artist who used imagination and not the rhetoric of democracy as her ultimate authority. Erkilla has shown how Wheatley's poetry is invested in the rhetoric of democracy, offering admirable insights into the discursive context of Wheatley's art without examining aesthetic very fully. Baker, too, considers discursive effects, as in his persuasive reading of the frontispiece to Wheatley's volume, but has little to say about the poetry itself. In the context of her being an "Ethiop," Wheatley's capacity to speak becomes an assertion of individual personhood and of an intrinsic emotional capacity linked to the ideals of natural rights, two associations that render historically concrete in a slave's black body the abstract components of personhood that were denied her by her culture. And these terms of selfhood were so conventional that, in performing them, Wheatley makes the African self recognizable as a "human" self.

Even her otherwise conventional and apolitical verse participates in this self-fashioning as citizen, then, since this association between intrinsic imagination and the abstract personhood of sentimental democracy mirrored the transformation of social abstraction into social reality in Renaissance self-fashioning. In "On Imagination," for example, Wheatley might simply be read as defining the faculty of the imagination in the most boring of conventional gestures. But in the context of these ideological clashes created by her associations of African identity with universal human selfhood, her definition functions as a slave's link to her fellow Americans irrespective of race, class, or caste. So even though "*Winter* frowns to *Fancy's* raptur'd eyes / The fields may flourish and gay scenes arise":

> Such is thy pow'r, nor are thine orders vain,
> O thou leader of the mental train:
> In full perfection all thy works are wrought,
> And thine the scepter o'er the realms of thought.

> Before thy throne the subject passions bow,
> Of subject-passions sov'reign ruler Thou,
> At thy command joy rushes on the heart,
> And through the glowing veins the spirits dart.
>   (lines 23–24, 33–40)

These lines declare the sovereignty of the imagination over "subject passions" in order to imply its central role in the creation of human identity and connection, upon which Wheatley depends to authorize her public address in "To the University of Cambridge, in New-England." As Horton suggests in "A Poet's Feeble Petition," the imagination can defy material conditions—including slavery—to transport the poet into the realm of the ideal and her poetry into the minds and hearts of her readers. This ideal itself could be called genius since, in ways she could not have known, her verse enacted the notion of artistic genius that Schopenhauer would articulate forty years later on another continent. It is both a distinctive creativity and a common human capacity. More important, this definition of the imagination transforms the neoclassical ideals of sentiment into ideals of democratic human connection best exemplified, as Ralph Waldo Emerson and Walt Whitman would later so famously attest, by the poet herself.

In other words, her poem effectively characterizes the sentimentalist's faith in what Bruce Burgett called "a universal and pre-political point of affective identification for individuals otherwise divided through the imposition of an ideological 'code'" (23). If, as Burgett argues, social codes and hierarchical socially constructed identities separate one person from another and potentially prevent the fulfillment of the abstract ideals of individual value and communal connection necessary for democracy, then what unifies people, especially in democratic ideals of citizenship based on natural rights and sentiment, is this "affective identification" (see Morris). Wheatley's conventional definition of the imagination may have come across as analogous to this compassionate, human spirit, this "pre-political point" of identification, a component of democratic self-fashioning easily overlooked because it was not likely a conscious political commentary.

> We on thy pinions can surpass the wind,
> And leave the rolling universe behind:
> From star to star the mental optics rove,
> Measure the skies, and range the realms above.
> There in one view we grasp the mighty whole,
> Or with new worlds amaze th'unbounded soul.
>   ("On Imagination," lines 17–22)

This rhetorical "we," when warped and broadened by the lens of racial ideology and the conventions of sensibility, comes to include all poets and all people who share a common sympathetic reaction to common ideals of a sublime imagination, the capacity to "grasp the mighty whole." The poem is thus about a community held together by its members' equal access to the capacities of the imagination, a point that was the foundation of the poetic ideals of later republican thinkers like Percy Shelley, Emerson, and Whitman. Imagining new worlds in this context really means creating literary vision. But the experience of these literary creations can genuinely unite people, liberating them from the ideological codes that determine social identities. Perhaps a genuinely new world is therefore possible. Perceiving such sentiment in the slave's "unbounded soul" defied thinkers such as Kant, who claimed that "fundamental is the difference between [the black and the white] races of man, and it appears to be as great in regard to mental capacities as in color," or Hegel, who, when confronted with Africans, gave up on the universality of human experience and capacity so crucial to Enlightenment thinking. In other words, to paraphrase Greenblatt, Wheatley's literary self-fashioning revealed the construction of her social self as an extension of her "intrinsic ardor," which became embodied historically in her racialized and enslaved body. Its role as the source of community made this racialized ardor "democratic."

In these terms, Wheatley's very public cultivation of that ardor garners the force of subversive self-assertion because it constructs her poetic genius as a locus of cultural conflict and connection that both fettered and liberated her imagination. For example, "To Maecenas," the first poem in Wheatley's volume, transforms a conventional dedication to a patron into a construction of a sense of belonging based upon the "pre-political" identification that formed the foundation of literary expression as social participation and the cultural crossover that made that identification possible in art.

> Maecenas, you, beneath the myrtle shade,
> Read o'er what poets sung, and shepherds play'd.
> What felt those poets but you feel the same?
> Does not your soul possess the sacred flame?
> Their noble strains your equal genius shares
> In softer language and diviner airs.

> While *Homer* paints lo! circumfus'd in air,
> Celestial Gods in mortal forms appear;
> Swift as they move, hear each recess rebound,
> Heav'n quakes, earth trembles, and the shores resound.

Great Sire of verse, before my mortal eyes,
The lightnings blaze across the vaulted skies,
And, as the thunder shakes the heav'nly plains,
A deep-felt horror thrills through all my veins.
When gentler strains demand thy grateful song
The length'ning line moves languishing along.
When great *Patroclus* courts *Achilles'* aid,
The grateful tribute of my tears is paid;
Prone on the shore he feels the pangs of love,
And stern *Pelides* tend'rest passions move. (lines 1–20)

Cynthia Smith rightly asserts that in these two opening stanzas of the
poem, Wheatley makes the patron Maecenas into a writer ("What felt those
poets but you feel the same?") in order to affirm the nature of his sympathy
for other writers. But even more important, this gesture reveals Wheatley's
enactment of the literary-critical principles of sensibility and the sublime,
which I am suggesting are central to a definition of citizenship implicit in
her work. Her practice first implies that both she and Maecenas are great
readers. Wheatley identifies appropriately what makes Homer great for a
certain portion of neoclassical taste, gives credit to Maecenas for being able
to discern this quality also, and, crucially, affirms her own authority as
critic, since she too experiences the appropriate awe from the sublimity of
Homer's poetry. When she actually sees Homer's portraits as if they objectively existed, she is "thrilled" as she should be, and the "grateful tribute"
of her tears is "paid" where aesthetically and morally appropriate. Not only
a celebration of her actual patron—whether her owner or the Countess of
Huntingdon, who helped get the volume published—nor just a celebration
of Maecenas's generosity and of Homer's poetry, this poem is also a celebration of Wheatley's own sensibility. It is one of her most explicit claims to the
role of public leadership through poetic mastery, which I am calling "bardic
genius," and it is also her clearest representation of the liminal space of cultural mutation that refutes the racial absolutism by which white Americans
excluded her from the body politic.

In one of the many paradoxes of Wheatley's public self-fashioning,
then, her evocation of this abstracted sense of commonality became the
substance of her affirmation of her African identity, an affirmation that
makes her version of poetic genius simultaneously conventional poetic
mastery and unconventional ethnic self-definition. Even when she quite
conventionally declares in deference to Virgil, "But here I sit, and mourn
a groveling mind, / That fain would mount, and ride upon the wind" (lines
29–30), her poem belies that self-doubt with the affirmation of an African

poetic tradition as a version of the national community she would like to join. She expresses her envy of

> The happier *Terence*, all the choir inspir'd,
> His soul replenish'd, and his bosom fir'd;
> But say ye *Muses*, why this partial grace,
> To one alone of *Afric's* sable race. (lines 37–40)

Smith suggests that the Roman poet Terence, who was of African descent, is happier than Wheatley because, to Wheatley's eyes, he had a more appreciative audience, and this is certainly part of her point. But, more important, Wheatley is complaining directly to the muses that she has not been granted Africa's fair share of imagination and attention, effectively accusing her audience (as muses) of racism in their partiality. Without good reason, they fail to give Wheatley full credit. In this way, Wheatley implies a tradition of slave or African neoclassical artistry based in religious faith and the sublime, starting with Terence and including Scipio Moorhead, who was "Negro servant to the Revd Mr. Moorhead of Boston, whose genius inclined him that way." In "To S. M. a Young African Painter, on Seeing His Works," Wheatley implores the African painter

> On deathless glories fix thine ardent view:
> Still may the painter's and poet's fire
> To aid thy pencil, and thy verse conspire!
> And may the charms of each seraphic theme
> Conduct thy footsteps to immortal fame!
> . . . .
> But when the shades of time are chas'd away,
> And darkness ends in everlasting day,
> On what seraphic pinions shall we move,
> And view the landscapes in the realms above?
> There shall thy tongue in heav'nly murmurs flow
> And there my muse with heavenly transport glow.
>   (lines 8–12, 23–28)

The function of such praise is to align Wheatley's own religious accomplishment with what she sees in Moorhead's work. First, she validates the ideal that his religious vision of "deathless glories" will aid the artist's "fire," making their shared religion and, potentially, their shared race the sources of their "immortal fame." But, second, she recognizes that this "fame" may genuinely be immortal, because it may not be fully acknowledged (due to racism) until they both are dead and are offered the greater recognition of heaven. Wheatley is waiting for the day when heaven will remove her physical and poetic shackles and grant her and Moorhead the voices and recognition they deserve. The criticism is clear: race and slavery prevent the African poet from being recognized despite faith, talent, and tradition. Wheatley's conventionality functions as a celebration of her Africanness and a scolding for those of partial grace who grant attention to only one of "Afric's sable race" at a time. Her American genius is once again shown to be African in its intrinsic ardor *and* in its cultural cultivation.

Nonetheless, the most important implication of this paradoxical claim of an African tradition, like all of Wheatley's references to being African, is that it constructs out of this subtle emphasis on cultural difference the "pre-political" national self based upon inclusive social participation. And it does so in part and always by evoking the racist narrative of the cultivation of the barbarian. But since the barbarian's cultivation enhances an intrinsic ardor that also has a narrative of African cultivation, it enhances the politics of fulfillment more fully than it embraces the racist narrative. Instead of losing herself to cultural lobotomy, in other words, Wheatley was participating in what Phillip Richards describes as Wheatley's "gestures of self-deprecation," which were not just an African poet bowing to a superior white authority, though it was partly that. These gestures "were the rhetorical stock-in-trade of provincial American artists seeking to present themselves in [the] cosmopolitan tradition of English art" (170). Not only did such writers seek to bow down to that cosmopolitan tradition, as Richards emphasizes, they also implied their worthiness to join it. Wheatley's self-deprecation had a similar function, enhanced by its challenge to the logic of race politics: "While blooming wreaths around thy temples spread, / I'll snatch a laurel from thine honour'd head, / While you indulgent smile upon the deed" ("To Maecenas," lines 45–47). In these lines, Wheatley is actively snatching a laurel from what is by now clearly a figurative Maecenas who embodies Horace's actual classical patron, an ideal reader, and the halls of poetic fame in one figure. Instead of emphasizing the patron's "indulgence," as too many scholars do, I am emphasizing the act of "snatching" the laurel, which implies that Wheatley deserves the laurel. As a young writer and a slave, Wheatley was probably genuinely unsure of herself, but the two poetic conventions she had mastered—self-deprecation before a patron and celebration of the poet's gifts to justify the patron's attention—come into conflict to reveal a subtle and self-contradictory affirmation of the African poet's gifts and her "pre-political" identity. Like the authorizing note from the dignitaries of Boston, this patron's approval depends upon the inevitable recognition of Wheatley's verse that the poem implies. Not protest, this claim to fame still functions as a claim that she deserves social inclusion.

In effect, Wheatley's verse has constructed a hybrid African self that unites Homeric epic with an Ethiop's philosophical penetration, and the British tradition with an African poetic tradition, to suggest a "racial" self that is the substance of her claim to literary merit, cultural memory, and the social inclusion that both imply. Wheatley's elegies—her most numerous and most explicitly public poems—offer the most explicit and consistent definition of this ideal of social participation and abstract selfhood through literary merit that made Wheatley, in her verse, a citizen. In poems requested by whites or dedicated to them of her own accord, Wheatley offered doctrinal consolation for the deaths of loved ones. She almost always begins such poems with some invocation either to the "heav'nly muse" or to the classical ones and parallels those invocations to several implicit invocations to herself as African in order to authorize her most direct participation in public discourse. Moreover, Wheatley adopts the conventions of the elegy to her own imagination: "The choice of emphasis—celestial over terrestrial life, the Corporal Works of Mercy, the ancestral-like abode that Heaven is, and the conception of happiness in terms of the sense of sound over the sense of sight (Beatific Vision) as is traditionally the case—helps to give Miss Wheatley's elegies a stamp all her own" (Rigsby 252). For example, in the poem to a dead evangelist, "On the Death of the Rev. Mr. George Whitefield, 1770"—the poem that initiated her fame—Wheatley exhorts her reader to "Behold the prophet in his tow'ring flight! / He leaves the earth for heav'n's unmeasured height, / And worlds unknown receive him from our sight" (lines 11–13). Also, Wheatley adopts the voice and character of Whitefield in order to proclaim the joys of heaven and assert the exhortation to peace and faith to the grieving. Wheatley even vocalizes the adored Whitefield's heavenly advice to include Africans in the ancestral Christian community:

"Take him [Christ], ye wretched, for your only good,
Take him ye starving sinners, for your food:
. . . .
Take him, ye *Africans*, he longs for you,
Impartial Savior is his title due:
Wash'd in the fountain of redeeming blood,
You shall be sons, and kings, and priests to God."
          (lines 28–38)

The poem posits Wheatley as a bard not just for Africans who were slaves; she could also speak to and for whites and for God. In addition to associating her imagination with the democratic spirit and her accomplishment with social inclusion, in other words, Wheatley quite literally joins a mourning community as an equal or even as an advisor, as she had also done in speaking to the graduating students at Cambridge. God will make Africans equals; and, by speaking from the grave, Whitefield is implicitly attributing spiritual equality to Africans in his godlike way. This is not militant resistance by any stretch of the imagination, but it is a literal rewriting of a white divine's advice. The shared religious vision to which Wheatley claims to have greater access than her readers becomes the validation both of shared social ideals and values and of the African poet's unique perspective on those shared values.

Thus, in the few explicit protests or references to freedom in Wheatley's verse, the main mode of self-fashioning is through this pre-political identity of sentimental democracy whose validity was enhanced by the poet's experience of oppression or exclusion. The poem "To the Right Honourable William, Earl of Dartmouth, His Majesty's Principle Secretary of State for North-America, &c." is the best example of Wheatley's soft but serious version of political protest. The poem opens with Wheatley declaring that the ascendancy of Dartmouth as governor promises that "in thine hand with pleasure we behold / The silken reins, and *Freedom's* charms unfold" while "hated *faction* dies" (lines 7–8, 10). Wheatley then implies that such liberty as "silken reins" is a contradiction analogous to her own situation:

> Should you, my lord, while you peruse my song,
> Wonder from whence my love of *Freedom* sprung,
> Whence flow these wishes for the common good,
> By feeling hearts alone best understood,
> I, young in life, by seeming cruel fate
> Was snatch'd from *Afric's* fancied happy seat:
> What pangs excruciating must molest,
> What sorrows labour in my parent's breast?
> Steel'd was that soul and by misery mov'd
> That from a father seiz'd his babe belov'd:
> Such, such my case. And can I then but pray
> Others may never feel tyrannic sway? (lines 20–31)

Torn between loyalty to pagan Africa and to liberty-loving America, her own intrinsic love of freedom allows her "to suggest that the British values at work in the Revolutionary crisis have a wider applicability than the reader thought," especially since that love of freedom even here is tied implicitly to her status as "saved" and to her capacity for the sensibility necessary to imagine her parents' pain (Richards 185). Her sense of common good that justified "dissolving the Political Bands which have connected them with another" had less to do with direct protests of slavery and more to do with the appeal to "feeling hearts" for her bereft parents, an appeal that is potentially more effective than an appeal for sympathy for herself. Resistance both to slavery and to an unjust parent were metaphors that dominated the public justifications of the incipient revolution. Such gestures effectively participated in the "democratic" functioning of literary sentiment, allowing Wheatley to join the "empty space" of republican citizenship despite her enslaved body. Her poetry thus enacts Burstein's "sentimental democracy."

So while Wheatley was clearly no radical, her verse still offers a sophisticated poetic genius as the foundation of an African self that was in turn the foundation of a claim to be a member of the nation. Wheatley's acts of assimilation were her most substantive acts of self-definition and protest, then, and granted to her mastery of traditional poetics an extra register of meaning as a component of a racial self that the verse constructed in conjunction with its readers. This self-fashioning also made her verse more fully capable of changing her material circumstances. It is rarely worth measuring such material effects of poetry, but in Wheatley's case her material circumstances prove the efficacy of her assimilation. Wheatley's travels to Britain after the publication of her volume confirm how it managed to transform her from slave to citizen, even while she was still in bondage. Wheatley garnered audience with dignitaries in England while also receiving a letter of thanks from George Washington and his apologies for the lateness of his reply. She also got to meet him, though no record exists of what happened at the meeting. There are obvious flaws in such politics of fulfillment, namely an acceptance that the principles of the status quo are good in themselves and that the fulfillment of those principles is possible. But in the specific democratic principles that Wheatley's art implicitly evokes, this acceptance is not entirely problematic. What would be wrong with a slave claiming an inherent intellectual capacity that transcends social roles and categories? This approach obviates the need of present-day scholars to make dubious claims about anagrams that might link Wheatley to an African past or that might portray her as a trickster. If "loyalty to national principles" is at the heart of "sentimental democracy," then her emphasis on her relationship to those ideals constitutes a rhetorically legitimate construction of her resistance to "tyrannic sway." And, of course, she was manumitted, becoming a citizen indeed.

This conception of "bardic genius" as a pre-political abstraction not only illuminates the means by which Wheatley successfully claims citizenship, it also clarifies how Horton's sense of romantic genius was not as full a protest of the fetters of slavery as was Wheatley's neoclassicism. Horton was an even more fettered genius than Wheatley, in part because his assimilation of mainstream culture was not as entire nor was his engagement in it keyed enough to its emphasis on the communal to refute fully the racist cultural constructions in which he was bound. So while it is easy to see that his poetry is "better" than Wheatley's, in that it conforms more fully to contemporary tastes shaped more by British and American romanticism than by neoclassicism, readers must not allow that closeness to contemporary taste and the easily recognizable protest to obscure the nature of Horton's most important aesthetic achievement and political claim and the limited social implications of that claim. "A Poet's Feeble Petition," his most persuasive poem in these self-fashioning terms, reveals how Horton's claim to individual genius paradoxically undermined his claim to belonging in the national community.

> Bewailing mid the ruthless wave,
>   I lift my feeble hand to thee.
> Let me no longer live a slave
>   But drop these fetters and be free.
>
> Why will regardless fortune sleep
>   Deaf to my penitential prayer,
> Or leave the struggling Bard to weep,
>   Alas, and languish in despair?
>
> He is an eagle void of wings
>   Aspiring to the mountain's height;
> Yet in the vale aloud he sings
>   For Pity's aid to give him flight.
>
> Then listen all who never felt
>   For fettered genius heretofore—
> Let hearts of petrifaction melt
>   And bid the gifted Negro soar. (lines 1–16)

Claiming to be a "Bard," Horton begins his plea to Greeley—and to anyone who will listen—with the assertion that despair is the lot not primarily of the slave burdened by endless toil but of the *gifted* slave tied down by both physical and intellectual fetters. Unlike the transcendence of Wheatley's neoclassical genius and religious sublime, which links the gifted individual mind to an abstracted point of identification necessary for communal natural rights, Horton's images of thwarted transcendence are tied to the individual imagination alone. In this case, the "mountain's height" is an emblem of both artistic vision and physical freedom for the individual poet. The vale is therefore the poet's present condition as a slave, meaning that his characterization of limitation was less a matter of contradictions between social ideals and social practice than it was a matter of contradictions between the poet's individual ideal state and his reality. Horton is not engaged in pointing out a broad cultural hypocrisy through his social participation, in other words, and while Wheatley was not always aiming to do so either, her verse almost always did so because of the nature of her mastery. Horton's does not. In fact, he even calls on "Pity" to give him wings, as if the racist society could grant him poetic gifts as well as freedom.

In other words, the very effects of individual genius and self-assertive protest that make Horton's poetry "better" than Wheatley's essentially fetter its direct protest. As such, the images of flight and soaring, which John L. Cobbs rightly defines as the centerpiece of Horton's aesthetic, have their most significant appearances in his poems about poetry and the imagination, not in poems about freedom from slavery (446). Thus, Cobbs overstates their role in his direct protest. For example, Horton's poem "On the Poetic Muse," originally published in *Freedom's Journal* in the hopes of gaining subscribers before appearing in his volume *Hope of Liberty*, opens with what might be called this slave's "egotistical sublime":

> Far, far above this world I soar,
> And almost nature lose,
> Aerial regions to explore,
> With this ambitious Muse.
>
> My towering thoughts with pinions rise,
> Upon the gales of song,
> Which waft me through the mental skies,
> With music on my tongue. (lines 1–8)

The next three stanzas blend metaphors of fire, visual prospects of "wonders to survey," and the almost clichéd "quiet bliss of the soul / when in some calm retreat, / where pensive thoughts like streamlets roll" (lines 16, 17–19) to characterize the effects of imagination on mind, body, and soul. As such, Horton invests himself with the ideals of contemplation from which slaves would have been excluded. *His* ambitious muse provides music for *his* tongue as his wings gather the "gales" of that music in his individual "mental skies." Horton took his cue implicitly from the ideal that, as David Perkins put it, the romantic poem "ultimately . . . mirrors the struggle of genius against all limitation, and it leads to a glorification of yearning, striving, and becoming and of the personality of the artist" (8). What matters is the struggle of his genius against limitation, an ideal that other romantic poets successfully linked to democratic principles but that Horton does not, in part because of the nature of his conception and in part because of the ways in which he was constructed in the racial ideology of his time.

In fact, his conception of the pursuit of individual distinction even subtly compromises his explicit poetic protest. "On Liberty and Slavery" is not the communal voice Richmond and Collins make it out to be but is rather an assertion of individuality as a model for racial identity and political resistance. Any communal voice emerges as a secondary but compelling implication of the poet's individual and representative yearning:

> Alas! and am I born for this,
>   To wear this slavish chain?
> Deprived of all created bliss,
>   Through hardship, toil and pain!
>
> How long have I in bondage lain,
>   And languished to be free!
> Alas! and must I still complain—
>   Deprived of liberty.
>
> Oh, Heaven! And is there not relief
>   This side the silent grave—
> To soothe the pain—to quell the grief
>   And anguish of a slave?
>
> Come Liberty, thou cheerful sound,
>   Roll through my ravished ears!
> Come, let my brief in joys be drowned,
>   And drive away my fears.
>
> Say unto foul oppression, Cease:
>   Ye tyrants rage no more,
> And let the joyful trump of peace,
>   Now bid the vassal soar. (lines 1–20)

Clearly this protest is more likely to be stirring to the contemporary reader in its directness of resistance and the implications of pride in the poetic voice than Wheatley's more measured and even wimpish complaints. Moreover, given the insights Gates and others have offered about the inevitably public role of even the most private African American poetry, Horton's "I" here can easily be understood as a representative one rather than a personal one, and I suspect Richmond would concur with this reading (*Figures in Black* 4). After all, this poem clearly means to be representative as much as personal, claiming as Wheatley does that the individual genius of the slave poet is but a species of racial genius. The claim to genius justifies the "soaring" of the representative vassal in order to claim that soaring for the entire race. Nonetheless, there is a tension in this poem between that individual freedom and the eradication of slavery altogether, a tension that characterizes the space of discursive conflict into which Horton's poems enter. The speaker asks "Liberty to drive away *my* fears," personalizing the otherwise generalized vassal being bid to soar, with the relief being only for the grief of "*a* slave" and not "*the* slave." Horton's outrage is more effective when coupled with the admiration we are expected to have for the imaginative poet. In these terms, Horton's pleas both appealed to and resisted the "pre-political" point of affective identification that would make it both an ethnic and a human self and that would write it fully into the principles of democracy.

In other words, Horton's verse actually conforms to the usually misguided critique of romanticism as entirely individualistic, undermining in part Norton's ability to push the nation to live up to its promise through his claim to genius. The individualism of his self-fashioning reinforced rather than challenged the construction of race in Horton's time. Rather than being seen as proof of African capacities against racist expectations of its absence, and rather than being offered as a genius the reader can assume along with the poet, as Whitman proposed, Horton's individualist "genius" sometimes rendered him as something of a comic novelty or buffoon, an exception whose perceived pomposity proved the rule that Africans were a pale imitation of white Americans. As Joan Sherman explains, partly in Horton's own words:

> Chapel Hill students, the sons of wealthy planters, seemed more interested in sports, gambling, and pleasures of the table than in their studies.... The collegians, Horton wrote, "for their diversion were fond of pranking with the country servants," and they "pranked" with him by insisting that he "spout"; they made him "stand forth and address" the collegians extemporaneously, "as an orator of inspired promptitude." ... Since "oration was the highest type of literary effort developed in the ante-bellum South," it was fitting that the students transformed Horton into an orator. At first, the slave felt proud of his performance, he wrote, "but soon I found it an object of aversion, and considered myself nothing but a public ignoramus." Consequently, Horton abandoned these "foolish harangues and began to speak of poetry." On one or two known later occasions, however, he again "spouted" to order for the

collegians, and in his "Address" he called himself "your sable orator" and "your poor orator." (6–7)

This problem leads critics to take Horton lightly, and even some of Horton's white contemporaries believed that his "hope of liberty" was a matter of minstrel performance (Cobbs 443–44). But the problem with Horton's approach was less in his political consciousness, which J. Saunders Redding too simply characterizes as being that of a lackey for white pleasure, than in the difficulty he had challenging the roles into which he was placed by slavery and by the precursors to blackface minstrelsy, a role oddly reinforced by claims of individual rather than racial genius (17). If his individual capacity for expression sometimes distinguished him from the race, it did so by serving the sense among many slaveholders that talented slaves provided a mode of entertainment in their amusing and presumably inadequate imitation of white oratory or poetics. And because he was in the midst not of liberal-minded intellectuals, as Wheatley was, but of "pranking" college students, Horton's fame did not have the same broad cultural significance. These forces undermined the antiracist effects of Horton's self-fashioning as genius.

Horton did not strike the originating chord of the African American poetic tradition, then, because he did not fully engage in the construction of poetic genius invested in the mainstream culture of the time. By so successfully fulfilling the ideals of romantic genius, Horton did not embrace fully the range of social and cultural ideals available to link literary culture to the nation's political life. Horton's construction of bardic genius was thus an elaboration upon the artistic freedom of the individual genius without a thoroughgoing examination of the connections between that freedom and the racial discourses of the society. His protest, while stirring, was too narrow, as were his uses of formal innovation and individual distinction.

Frances Ellen Watkins Harper likewise did not originate the tradition. In fact, her artistry was fully a descendant of Wheatley's in terms of how its political effects—even its protests—depended upon its conventionality. Despite all apparent indications to the contrary, Harper's verse becomes perhaps the strongest proof of the primacy of Wheatley's model of poetic meaning as the origin of the aesthetic practice and political meaning of the African American formalist poetic tradition. On one hand, since she was freeborn and an abolitionist activist and lecturer; since she read her poetry as part of her lectures; since she was one of the most popular poets of the day; since she used proceeds from the sales of her books and her lecturing engagements to contribute to the Underground Railroad; and since she self-consciously devised her poetry explicitly for this purpose, her approach to poetry and politics comes closest to the twentieth- and twenty-first-century ideal implied by Richmond. In these terms, Patricia Liggins Hill is right: like 1960s poetic radicals Amiri Baraka, Haki Madhubuti, Nikki Giovanni, and Sonia Sanchez, who "base their oral protest poetry primarily on direct imagery, simple diction and the rhythmic language of the street to reach the masses of black people, Harper relies on vivid, striking imagery, simplistic language, and the musical quality and form of the ballad to appeal to large masses of people, black and white, for her social protest."

For Hill, this choice represents "an 'art for people's sake' aesthetic, rather than a Western Caucasian aesthetic assumption, 'an art for art's sake' principle." Melba Joyce Boyd concurs, declaring that Harper's consistent use of the ballad was central to her political purposes. The ballad, says Boyd, coincides with nineteenth-century mass culture and Harper's elocutionary format (67). Hill concludes that, even given her concern with all humanity—as in her temperance poems, for example—Harper "is primarily concerned with uplifting the masses of black people" (160).

Thus, her much-anthologized poem "Bury Me in a Free Land" bases its call to action on a claim to popular sentiments. It ends,

> I ask no monument, proud and high,
> To arrest the gaze of the passers by;
> "All that my yearning spirit craves
> Is—*bury me not in a land of slaves!*"

Clearly this poem presumes an audience of like-minded people and suggests that, unlike Wheatley and Horton, the poet identifies more with the slaves than with the slaveholders. This poem also asserts a principle of direct resistance to the entire institution, not just to the individual condition of the slave. Such a stanza suggests a meaningful difference between Harper's poetry and that of Wheatley and Horton.

But on the other hand, Harper's self-fashioning was based upon more than her claim of community with slaves. It was in fact a paradoxically radical pursuit of the politics of fulfillment, a self-fashioning predicated on being accepted in the mainstream as an embodiment of its moral and cultural principles pertaining to gender identity. Her poetry had its greatest effects, in other words, by articulating how the political principles and cultural mores of the nation should be transformed subtly in order to apply to slaves, especially slave women, creating community between Africans and white abolitionists through the contradictions in the morality that justified aspects of slavery. As such, the "genius" of the poet was as much her conventional moral sensibility as it was her political outrage, her formal mastery as much as her political protest. And these components of her poetic self came to be inextricable in the authorization of that self enacted by both the poet and the reading community. For example, the third stanza of "Bury Me in a Free Land" contains Harper's most characteristic gesture of protest:

> I could not sleep, if I heard the tread
> Of a coffle-gang to the shambles led,
> And the mother's shriek of wild despair
> Rise, like a curse, on the trembling air. (lines 13–16)

Though the individual genius is foregrounded as it is in Wheatley's and Norton's verse, the authority of that genius depends upon slavery's effects on mothers, an appeal that participates very deeply in nineteenth-century conceptions of feminine sensibility. The greatest sin of slavery that a female abolitionist could identify is the way it deprived mothers of their capacity to act as mothers. And the most powerful expression of outrage was to provoke the reader to an awareness of his or her moral investment in the condition of slave mothers. Rather than simply detailing the wrongs of slavery, then, the poem challenges the reader to understand his or her own moral compromises. In effect, Harper's claims upon the social community of white women destabilizes the very terms of its claim to unity, using that destabilized notion of "woman" to rewrite the "feminine" morality into a feminist racial community.

As with Wheatley's claim to ideals of liberty, Harper's destabilization of the category of "woman" derived from her almost complete fulfillment of its conventional, even conservative, premises. As Hazel Carby points out, Harper revised the nineteenth-century discourses of true womanhood and its four cardinal virtues (piety, purity, submissiveness, and domesticity) for her own political purposes. These principles included a delicacy of constitution and modesty readable in the size and color of the female body, the manipulation of charm—titillating sexuality—rather than overt sexuality, the pursuit of wifehood and motherhood, and the dominion over private life. Black women—especially those who were slaves—were excluded from these categories, serving as the physical and moral antithesis against which true womanhood was defined, since black female sexuality was linked to capital accumulation and illicit sexual behavior rather than heirs, and since the work black women did meant that their less-than-delicate bodies did not bear the conventional marks of virtue. By making slave women into "women," Harper's poetry simultaneously undermines the terms of exclusion of the feminine and fulfills the claims of unity upon which her poetry is based. As Carby points out, "Women [such as Harper] who spoke in public to mixed audiences [in the nineteenth century] were considered by most people to lack good sense and high moral character"; and since political life had an investment in morality, most spokeswomen had to define their public advocacy as God's work with a high moral purpose and display knowledge of the Bible to do so (Foster 11). Hence Harper's numerous temperance poems and the following assertion in the lecture "Woman's Political Future," given at the World's Congress of Representative Women at the 1893 World's Fair: "If the fifteenth century discovered America to the Old World, the nineteenth is discovering woman to herself" (Foster 436). This newly self-aware woman now anticipates the coming of political power, says Harper, and with that power comes great responsibility, "for power without righteousness is one of the most dangerous forces in the world." While her habit of exercising moral authority in the domestic sphere does not guarantee moral political leadership, the nineteenth-century woman should prepare herself to maintain that moral authority in the public sphere. In these terms, Harper used conventions of womanhood to do what women were not supposed to do—speak in public—and to associate those same conventions with black women, who had been excluded from them. Her poetic genius thus genders genius, making the mastery of womanhood and poetic conventions associated with it—like sentimentality—a means by which she could revise racist and sexist exclusion.

The effect of this revision is a complex, hybrid notion of a "feminine" abolitionist community as the foundation of a just national community. Harper's practice also enacts a model of political poetic meaning through poetic conventionality that reiterates Wheatley's bardic genius. "The Slave Mother," one of Harper's most-anthologized poems, exemplifies Harper's broadening of conventional femininity to create this "national" community. The poem opens with a direct address to the reader that, formally, is perfectly appropriate to the kind of appeal Harper makes:

> Heard you that shriek? It rose
>   So wildly on the air,
> It seemed as if a burden'd heart
>   Was breaking in despair.
>
> Saw you those hands so sadly clasped—
>   The bowed and feeble head—
> The shuddering of that fragile form—
>   That look of grief and dread? (lines 1–8)

In keeping with the sentimental appeal associated with the literature of sensibility and with the fact that Harper probably read this poem at abolitionist meetings, the poem's opening question brings the reader directly into the anguish of the victim whose cry rose "so wildly on the air." It is also a way to place a woman's public address in a "proper" moral context. Posed as a series of questions, the poem's first three stanzas challenge the reader's ability to identify with this pain. If the implied reader does not hear the shrieks, the poem implies, the coldness of that reader's heart—its "petrifaction," if you will—will be revealed. In addition to this appeal, the poem asserts three times that the child whom the mother seeks to protect "is not hers," despite "the mother's pains"—presumably of labor—and despite the fact that "her blood / Is coursing through his veins!" (lines 19–20). Even among slaves, the poem argues, the bonds of family are real, the sympathy of mother and child is real, and the slave mother is a true woman, even if the society's laws and social practices do not recognize it. And the fact that the female speaker of the poem—Harper herself, of course—knows this moral truth authorizes the poem as much as its masterful ballad stanzas and crisp imagery do. This poem thus resembles Wheatley's poem to the Earl of Dartmouth, in which she refers to the suffering of her parents.

Community in this context is predicated on unifying sensibilities that are posited as universal, but instead of linking them directly to national community or to literary readership as Wheatley does, Harper associates those sensibilities with family. For example, the speaker points out that the defining horror of slavery derives from the fact that, in sending family members away from the mother, "cruel hands" have the capacity to "tear apart" the "wreath of household love / That binds her breaking heart" (lines 21–24). The poem concludes by associating the wreath with the natural beauty of sentimental human communion that becomes aligned in the poems with national belonging.

> His lightest word has been a tone
>   Of music round her heart,
> Their lives a streamlet blent in one—
>   Oh, Father! must they part?
>
> They tear him from her circling arms,
>   Her last and fond embrace.
> Oh! never more may her sad eyes
>   Gaze on his mournful face.
>
> No marvel, then, these bitter shrieks
>   Disturb the listening air:
> She is a mother, and her heart
>   Is breaking in despair. (lines 29–40)

Slave women bear children and feel the emotional connections of mother-hood, but they are not defined as such due to their race. But the speaker of the poem and the freeborn Harper are tied by bonds of race to these women, a contradiction that is revealed as one of the most fundamental horrors of slavery. Slave mothers are mothers, and once this fact is clear, the reader must acknowledge the astounding travesty that the family is destroyed by this peculiar institution. The great tragedy, then, is that the family "circle," hinted at in circle imagery throughout this passage, is torn asunder, meaning that the familial foundation of moral sensibility and national union is torn asunder. Most of Harper's poetic speakers, presumably Harper herself, thus occupy a space of "righteous" quasi-feminist moral self-assertion mirrored by Harper's conventional artistry and validated by this paradoxical appropria-tion of traditional domesticity for public unity. J. Saunders Redding is partly right when he notes that, though she was "immensely popular as a reader ('elocutionist'), the demands of [Harper's] audience for the sentimental treat-ment of old subjects sometimes overwhelmed her" (40). But he misses the fact that this sentimentality was a trenchant political use of poetic achieve-ment. Sentimentality was for Harper the substance of the moral heroism of black female selfhood, of the moral character women were bringing to the public sphere and national life, and thus the terms by which abolitionists should move to end slavery and all people should embrace female sensibility as the foundation of nation.

In these terms, the individualism central to national identity became the foundation of a mode of "feminine" heroism in which Harper yokes "true womanhood" to masculine heroic ideals of adventure and self-assertion to validate this simultaneously conventional and alternative model of woman-hood. For example, in "Eliza Harris," Harper transforms the sentimental moral martyrdom that is the substance of the meaning of "The Slave Mother" into a brave and active heroism that otherwise would be considered mascu-line. As Eliza escapes from slavery by crossing the Ohio River with her child, Harper writes:

> She was nearing the river—in reaching the brink,
> She heeded no danger, she paused not to think!
> For she is a mother—her child is a slave—
> And she'll give him his freedom, or find him a grave!
> ("Eliza Harris," lines 5–8)

It is telling that the only reason Harper gives for Eliza's motivation is simply that she is a mother. In the similarly titled "The Slave Mother (A Tale of Ohio)," Harper elaborates upon the apparently "heroic" story of a different

slave mother—a historical one rather than one from *Uncle Tom's Cabin*—
who did in fact find her children a grave, an act depicted as heroism twisted
by the horror of slavery, but heroism nonetheless. In these passages, Harper
has articulated the moral source of heroic action in the implications of "true
womanhood" for a slave woman presumed to be capable neither of morality nor of heroism. No longer damsels in distress awaiting knights, these
mothers act, and they do so in the best interests of their children within the
circumscribed circumstances in which they find themselves. And in finding
themselves, these characters become like the poet in their capacity to destabilize the boundaries and conventions of womanhood by daring to serve as
a public example of the moral principles—"the zealous expression of sentiment" and the "reasoning intellect"—necessary for national union.

What mattered for Harper's use of poetry to protest slavery, then, was
not primarily outrage but mastery. She assimilated conventions of womanhood in order to define a black female consciousness exemplified by the poet
that asserted the slave's individuality and collective human commonality in the
terms of rationality and sensibility, imagination and genius, that were current
at the time. As with Wheatley's sublime, Harper's moral outrage, channeled
through bardic mastery, presupposes and pursues the "pre-political" point of
identification on which to build the political ideal of citizenship for the slave.
So when Maryemma Graham pointed to Harper's use of the vernacular in
her Aunt Chloe series, she was partly right to emphasize the heroism of folk
wisdom in Harper's verse. But since this emphasis on folk culture functions as
an ethnic authenticity that excludes a consideration of femininity, it does not
tell the whole story. Also, since Graham implies that Aunt Chloe's wisdom
is alternative simply because it is asserted in an early version of vernacular speech, her claim underestimates how fully conventional Aunt Chloe's
wisdom was and how fully that wisdom was a component of the alternative
"true womanhood" that Harper offered as a Reconstruction extension of her
abolitionism. All of these elements of her verse are predicated in some substantial part on the "bardic genius"—the antiracist implications of the "gifted
Negro"—that is the centerpiece of African American abolitionist verse.

In essence, for the African American abolitionist poet, especially the poet
who was a slave, artistic self-assertion became an effectual challenge to the
racist exclusion of the poet from ideals of national belonging, including the
notions of absolute difference that allegedly justified slavery. Where Wheatley
constructed citizenship from religiously authorized poetic genius, and where
Horton constructed an artistic subjectivity that almost entirely authorizes
itself (and almost fails) in its resistance to limitation, Harper authorized her
protest through her role as a conventional woman. These three poets together
exemplify the broad continuum of antiracist meaning available to the African

American formalist poet from the public self-fashioning enacted through his or her mastery of traditional poetics. This range of "protest" is best illuminated by the terms of the literary conventions these poets mastered as those terms related to the racial ideology current at the time. Given this continuum, it becomes clear that, whatever we think of the actual quality of Wheatley's verse or of her conservative politics, her verse and public role exemplify the potentially subversive character of formalist poetic mastery and its associated cultural assimilation, anticipating the central forms and function of African American formalist poetics well into the twentieth century. In this verse, cultural assimilation is the locus of conflicting ideas about race, culture, and cultural achievement that transforms the self-assertion of artistic creation into the agency of racial protest. This practice also transforms the mainstream culture, becoming instrumental in the freedom of the slaves. This complex relationship between formal poetic structure and political effect is the defining antiracist effect of the African American poetic tradition. And it is built upon Wheatley's construction of herself as bardic genius.

PAULA BERNAT BENNETT

Rewriting Dunbar:
Realism, Black Women Poets, and the Genteel

The complete assimilation of American culture will equip the Negro with the "refinement" and "taste" requisite to writing in a tradition utterly alien to his temperament.[1]

In 1924, Allen Tate, Southern Fugitive and New Critic-to-be, reviewed *An Anthology of Negro Poetry*, edited by Newman Ivey White and Walter Clinton Jackson. Although Tate called the volume "useful," he did not, in fact, have much use for it. On the contrary, if the anthology is representative of the bulk of African American poetry "from its beginning in Phyllis [*sic*] Wheatley down to Countee P. Cullen," Tate wrote, "[I]t is just as well that the entirety of poetry in this field . . . isn't generally available, for . . . it is on the whole . . . worthless, and the good would . . . be submerged in the . . . bad."[2] The only black writer whom Tate fully exempts from this condemnation is Jean Toomer, author of the widely hailed, experimental *Cane* (1923) and to Tate "the finest Negro literary artist that has yet appeared in the American scene."[3] Of Clinton and Jackson's many sins, Tate views Toomer's omission as among the most egregious.

Tate's admiration for Toomer may be token; but his praise has a credible ring. Anticipating by a year one of Alain Locke's key arguments in *The New Negro* (1925), Tate is disturbed by the anthologists' privileging of an aesthetic

From *Post-Bellum, Pre-Harlem: African American Literature and Culture, 1877–1919*, pp. 146–161. © 2006 by New York University.

that he views as a whitening of the black man's soul. Tate asserts that Toomer "is interested in the interior of Negro life, not in the pressure of American [*sic*] culture on the Negro." In favoring poets like William Braithwaite, the editors chose authors "only Negro by an accident of blood, [having] as little of the Negro temperament as Longfellow."[4] Black writers who failed to embrace what Tate calls "the interior of Negro life" but that he defines only in terms of what Toomer was not (i.e., not Longfellow) were, quite simply, not black.

Because of the implosion of identity politics in the early 1980s, the essentialist approach in Tate's review to race, not to mention literature, no longer seems as self-evident as it was in 1924. Flawed or not, however, his argument cuts to issues that were roiling in the black literary community in his day. By 1924, modernism was well underway, and, like their white counterparts, African American writers were increasingly engaged, as Henry Louis Gates Jr. puts it, with "matters of language and voice." Behind their focus lay the question of "the absence or presence of the black voice in the text" that had plagued African American poetry from Wheatley on, and that the publication of Paul Laurence Dunbar's internally divided work only made more urgent.[5] Increasingly sensitized to the gulf between their strivings toward gentility and post-Emancipation realities, black writers between Dunbar and Hurston sought, Gates argues, to fashion a language more directly expressive of the varieties of African American experience as they knew them.[6]

Gates's observations represent a fundamental insight into the way black poetry evolved in the post-bellum–pre-Harlem years. This essay will expand upon his comments in relation to the writing of four black women poets, all of whom chose to challenge the genteel aesthetic governing Clinton and Jackson's anthology as a standard for measuring black social and cultural progress. Through most of the nineteenth century, the genteel was the dominant style, used by all authors, whatever their class, ethnic, or racial backgrounds, with relatively few exceptions. To suggest, as Tate and Locke do, that black writers' adoption of this style was imitation or mimicry, where white writers' use of it was not, is consequently misleading.[7] Unless employing dialect or writing satire, a nineteenth-century poet was expected to write this way. At the same time, performatively and culturally, the genteel was a highly problematic discourse for African Americans to employ.

Tate to the contrary, the real difficulty with the genteel was not its "whiteness," however, but its self-conscious poetical-ness. Almost another language, it announced itself not only by romantic vagueness and idealism but also by anachronistic turns of phrase (such as "doth" and "thee"), exclamations and apostrophes, and frequently inverted syntax. Given how embedded these devices were in the middle-class American literary imaginary—an imaginary shaped by Shakespeare, Milton, and other writers of the elite British tradition—even the most black-identified poet could not use them without sounding white, and middle-class to boot. In reaching towards a more specifically black voice and content, the poetry written by the four women I discuss here—Lizelia Augusta Jenkins Moorer, Maggie Pogue Johnson, and the sisters Priscilla Jane and Clara Ann Thompson—reflects their efforts to find ways of writing more compatible with their experience than was the genteel—a shift in priorities for which Dunbar's intervention was crucial. In this way, they helped move black poetry toward a language of its own—one that, in the standard or in the vernacular, was Other and American at once, sometimes in surprisingly powerful ways.

Paul Laurence Dunbar

Viewed by many as the most talented black poet between Wheatley and Hughes, Dunbar is a puzzle without a solution. Nor will this essay offer one, not only because I am skeptical that one exists but also, far more importantly, because it was precisely his contradictions that made him such a generative figure for other poets. An extraordinarily prolific and versatile writer, Dunbar published eleven volumes of poetry, four short story collections, and four novels in thirteen years. Blessed with a lyric gift that could spin gold from straw, he earned his reputation during the post-bellum–pre-Harlem years largely by writing dialect poetry wherein, some claim, he exploited the racist conventions of minstrelsy and of white Plantation School authors—Thomas Nelson Page, Joel Chandler Harris, James Whitcomb Riley—for commercial gain.[8]

Although elsewhere in his writing Dunbar denounced slavery passionately, he undeniably wrote many dialect poems that romanticize it, such as "The News," "The Deserted Plantation," "Chrismus on the Plantation," and "A Banjo Song," in which black speakers lament their masters' deaths, fondly recall their lives in slavery, and tout their fidelity and banjo playing.[9] Of such poems, William Dean Howells, the highly influential critic and father of realism, said, "Paul Dunbar was the only man of pure African blood and of American civilization to feel the Negro life aesthetically and express it lyrically. . . . [H]is . . . achievement was to have studied the American negro objectively, and to have represented him . . . with . . . entire truthfulness."[10] In a mean-spirited mood one could translate this as, "Dunbar's unique achievement was to take slavery's victims, and by aestheticizing them, turn them into *objets d'art* for white, middle-class readers like myself to learn from and enjoy."

As is well established, Dunbar was far more ambivalent about his vernacular poetry than were Howells and other white magazine editors. Viewing it as a narrowing of his talent, he resented the pressure they put on him to write it. His opinion was certainly true, but when Dunbar blames editors for his writing dialect poetry, his complaint begs some important questions, including what led him to write it in the first place, and, no less striking, why he wrote it so well. If Dunbar really devalued dialect poetry so much, how could he bring such sympathy, wit, and wisdom to his writing of it? And coming right down to it, why do so many of his dialect poems—such as "Accountability," "An Ante-Bellum Sermon," "When Malindy Sings," "Little Brown Baby," "In the Morning," and "A Negro Love Song"[11]—seem alive in ways that his standard verse, which he valued more, does not? If, as I believe, the strengths of Dunbar's dialect poetry and the weaknesses of his standard verse share a single root—his unswerving loyalty to a genteel aesthetic—then Howells was right: Dunbar's most important literary contribution lay in his vernacular verse.

When Dunbar began writing, the problem that Howells and other white editors confronted was that which Tate and Locke both identify: the genteel's inability to incorporate the real. By the 1880s, the push toward realism, spearheaded by Howells, had already started to undermine the genteel's dominance as a literary practice—no surprise, since it had been in use for rather too long anyway. Tired of repeating their precursors and themselves, fiction writers and poets began to reinvigorate their writing by turning to more realist modes such as local color and regionalism. In these works, dialect served as the real's linguistic signature, no matter how faked it actually was. Taking dialect from whatever cultures they could find it in—Chinese, southern, black, Jewish, rural, urban, or Native American—poets and storytellers alike used it to bring verbal novelty and seeming touches of reality to their work.

To judge by the contradictions embedded in Howells's praise for Dunbar's dialect poetry (Can something that is aestheticized also be "objective" and "true"?), it would seem that what realism's father really saw in the young black poet was not the truth of black lives, of which he had little or no direct knowledge, but the answer to his own aesthetic dilemma. Dunbar's vernacular verse, which was neither strictly realist nor strictly genteel but partook of both styles at once, allowed Howells, who only gave up writing genteel poetry himself in the 1890s, to have his cake and eat it too.[12] By taking poetry down from the heights where the genteel had imprisoned it and giving it over to black speakers, Dunbar had succeeded where Howells himself had failed. He had revitalized the aesthetically oriented lyric and filled it with the wonder and beauty of everyday life—moves he effectively allegorizes in "When Malindy Sings," when he gives his unschooled black singer the advantage over her genteel white competitor, Miss Lucy. This was no mean achievement; and its influence on Dunbar's contemporaries and on his successors was, as Gates suggests, immense.[13]

At the same time, because Dunbar never abandoned genteel aesthetics wholly in his lyric verse, he did not carry the realism of his vernacular poetry to its logical conclusion, either in the dialect poems themselves or in his standard verse. His dialect poems have black speakers and settings, but, faithful to genteel aesthetic principles, they avoid anything close to a realistic representation of the painful, ugly sides of pre- and post-Emancipation life. On those occasions when his standard poems do confront the latter, as in "To the South on Its New Slavery," "The Haunted Oak," and "Douglass," their claim to authenticity—that is, to being the expressions of an African American voice—is subverted by their use of the genteel's signature rhetorical gambits: in particular, verbal and syntactic archaisms such as "pinions foul," "I trow," and "with amaze."[14] Poems such as "We Wear the Mask," "Sympathy," and "The Poet,"[15] where Dunbar brings together a black speaker, black reality, and contemporary standard speech patterns, are simply too rare to challenge the general impression of out-of-dateness and derivativeness that his continued reliance on genteel rhetorical strategies creates.

As I see it, these are the contradictions that Dunbar left unresolved at his premature death in 1906. As such contradictions often are, they were a boon to later writers, who struggled to cohere what Dunbar could not: a distinctively black voice speaking of distinctively black experience in the vernacular and the standard alike. If Gates is right that this desire was not fully satisfied until Hurston's *Their Eyes Were Watching God* (1937),[16] then the four post-bellum–pre-Harlem women poets I discuss here, none of whom possessed one-tenth of Dunbar's or Hurston's talent, nevertheless represent significant steps along the way to this conclusion.

Lizelia Augusta Jenkins Moorer, Maggie Pogue Johnson, and the Thompson Sisters

Neither of the first two women, Lizelia Augusta Jenkins Moorer and Maggie Pogue Johnson, remotely qualifies as a professional poet. By her own account, Moorer, a teacher at Claflin University, South Carolina's first black college, decided to publish because she was frustrated with the way both northern and southern writers misrepresented southern blacks; and she wanted to tell "the unvarnished truth." "Seeing that the one cannot get at the facts, while the other will not, I reach the conclusion that the story must be told by a Negro—one who is a victim to the inconveniences of prejudice."[17] Most of *Prejudice Unveiled: and Other Poems* (1907) is dedicated to this mission. Much less is known of Maggie Pogue Johnson. However, based on the subtitle to her sole volume, *Virginia Dreams* (1910)—"Lyrics for the Idle Hour, Tales of the Time Told in Rhyme"—and her brief statement that she published at the request of friends,[18] it seems she was a coterie poet, producing entertaining verse, half of which consisted of dialect poems, for her own crowd.

To realize just how seriously Moorer took her mission to tell "the unvarnished truth," one only need look at the titles of her poems: for example, "Prejudice," "Jim Crow Cars," "The Peonage System," "Injustice in the Courts," "Lynching," "The Truth Suppressed."[19] Item by item, each offers a searing indictment of a society whose glut of post-bellum–pre-Harlem evils, as Dunbar asserted, made the Old South seem relatively benign by comparison. But this is also where the cutting difference between Dunbar and Moorer lies. Ever the genteel poet, Dunbar frames his appeal to the South in the high-minded rhetoric of an earlier time, even as he tactfully implies, but does not detail, its new cruelties, and he further weakens his poem's edge by loading his comparison to chattel slavery with "homely joys" and "chubby children."[20] On the other hand, Moorer utterly strips away any hint of "the mask that grins and lies,"[21] as in the following lines from "The Peonage System":

> Oft we find an overseer with a gun and club and whip,
> Who at night within the stockade locks the Negroes, lest they skip,
> If they offer a resistance for their treatment in this cage,
> They are clubbed into submission in the overseer's rage.[22]

To be sure, there are moments of light among Moorer's jeremiads, and she praises Lincoln, Theodore Roosevelt, and two southern-born educators—who, by supporting blacks, jeopardized their careers. Overall, however, she paints a grim picture, sacrificing beauty repeatedly to truth, and the ideal to the real. Of the Jim Crow car, she writes, "Legalized humiliation is the Negro Jim Crow car" (8);[23] of what goes on in lynching, "Then the flesh is cut in pieces and the souvenirs begin; / Each must have the piece allotted for the friends at home to see."[24] Of jury trials, she says, "When a mob has forced a jury to a stand against the right, / All the waters of the ocean cannot make the conscience white."[25] One would have to return to the antebellum period to find poetry this saturated with anger, this ruthless in expression. Confronting everything from separate and (un)equal schooling to corrupt politicians and courts, Moorer, whose nonpolitical poetry more or less conforms to genteel standards, avoids it here by using unadorned language to tell the truth, and letting the chips (including the very prosey quality of her verse) fall where they may.

Speaking from her subject position as a black woman educator, Moorer uses truth to undo the genteel, by this means recapturing something of the fierce energy and uncompromising anger of abolitionist poetry. Johnson, on the other hand, modeled herself on Dunbar, to whom she dedicated a worshipful poem, and her poetry might, therefore, seem a step backward from the real. Yet, by drawing her vernacular vignettes from the lives of post-bellum–pre-Harlem African Americans whose attitudes and speech patterns were close to their slave roots, she managed to avoid the nostalgic romanticization of slavery that mars so many of Dunbar's vernacular poems. Instead, she creates space for a more faithful social real.

What gives Johnson's poetry special interest is her speakers. These blacks are neither objects of sympathy nor exotics, as the genteel tradition would have them, nor are they the Plantation School's carefree "darkies" of bygone days. Rather, they are hard-working, somewhat frazzled men and women, who revel in nothing more than a table groaning with food (in the poem "What's Mo' Temptin' to de Palate?" the speaker recites her favorite edibles dish by dish),[26] good company, and swapping stories—and, of course, active participation in church services. Alongside the local minister, their hero is "Booker T.," but they are equally voluble on the virtues of "Brudder Wright's mule."[27] They are curious about new fashions for women and men, but slyly mocking of them as well; they look back on slavery with equanimity, not nostalgia; they look forward with hope and pride. They love their children even when scolding them, and each other, as long as each pulls his or her own weight.

Johnson's poems are too long to quote in full, but the following lines from "Krismas Dinner"—partially based on Dunbar's "The Party"—will illustrate these points, and the way in which the speakers' reality emerges through the thicket of mauled speech. This reality is that of free men and women who briefly gather to enjoy the fruits of their labor in the way they love best—by eating. Where Dunbar's "Party," even if meant as parody,[28] is improbable in the extreme, Johnson's poem, while teasing, is sufficiently similar to family gatherings this writer has attended to possess the ring of truth:

Parson Reuben Jones was called,
To say de blessed wuds,
En as he 'gin to cle'r his throat,
His inmos' soul was stirred:—

"Heabenly Fodder look down on us,
En dis earfly blessin',
We thanks De fer dis possum roast
All brown wid ash-cake dressin,

"We thanks De fer dis sausage,
En squirrel cooked wid beans,
En all dis nice fried chicken,
Dese onions en dese greens;—

"En as we goes to eat it,
Wilt Dou be our frien',
To keep us all from dyin,
We ax dis, en amen." . . .

Den we 'menced to eatin'.
Dat was a stuffin' time,
Case no one said a wud
To pass away de time.

Jis''cept to ax fer eatin's,
Den in a quiet way,
Dey w'ud cle'r der throats
En hab a wud to say.

You talk about folks eatin'!
But neber in my rouns'
Has I eber eat up so much grub
As I did at brudder Browns.

De wimmen dey was near de stove,
En I tho't dat dey wud melt,
But dey jis kept on a' eatin'
'Till dey had to loose dey belts.

En when dem folks did git up,
Dat table was cleaned up right,
Possum carcass, chicken bones,
Was all dat's lef in sight.[29]

As gentle in tone and ambiance as Moorer's poems are tense with outrage and frustration, Johnson's dialect vignettes register the other side of post-bellum–pre-Harlem black life, the side that, one suspects, made survival possible through all the horrors that Moorer describes.

* * *

What distinguishes the Thompson sisters is that, unlike Dunbar, Moorer, and Johnson, who are primarily interested in describing events, they are more concerned to expose the causes behind them. Whether Priscilla Jane and Clara Ann Thompson decided to rewrite Dunbar's material out of disgust with the way in which Howells misread him, or with the way in which Dunbar lent himself to misreading, their poems on slavery and the post-bellum–pre-Harlem African American experience offer the most explicit critiques of his work that I have found by the period's women poets. Like Dunbar, the Thompsons largely avoid the kinds of physical brutalities that made enslavement hell for its victims. However, in a small number of poems they explore with raw truthfulness the skewed personal interactions between blacks and whites, and the various ways in which slaveholders made not just their slaves' but also their own lives miserable—subjects that Dunbar deals with elsewhere but not in his poetry.

Like Johnson, the Thompsons self-published, and therefore were not burdened with white patronage or its constraints. Acute students of slaveholder psychology, they portray the "masters" of men and women as destroyed by the very power they cherish. Indeed, like early abolitionists, the Thompsons appear to view slaveholding as an addiction, making victims not just of slaves but of slaveholders as well, who became uncontrollably dependent on those they feared, hated, and abused. As the Thompsons depict this dynamic, slaveholders needed slaves not only to pick cotton, serve dinner, or swat flies but also emotionally, in ways that give a bitterly ironic twist to the trope of the faithful slave.

In "Freedom at McNealy's," Priscilla Thompson, writing in the standard, turns this overexploited trope—used by Dunbar, among others—ugly side out. The war lost and his plantation in ruins, McNealy assembles his two hundred slaves to tell them they are free. As Thompson describes McNealy's slaves, they are "[m]en of middle age all palsied," "blighted youths and orphaned infants," and women to whose skirts cling children "through whose veins his own blood runs." "Void of learning, inexperienced," they are "launched upon the crafty world" by their erstwhile owner, but not before McNealy tries to obtain their pity. "With quivering voice and husky, / [He] Tells them of his heavy losses, / Meanly seeking sympathy." Having "soft hearts," Thompson tells us, the newly emancipated slaves oblige, pushing lifelong cruelties aside to shake "his tyrant hand." Then, except for two, they leave. Aunt Jude and Uncle Simon, old, helpless, and frightened, beg McNealy to let them stay: "Told him, all their days remaining, / They would gladly give to him,"

> And McNealy, pleased and flattered,
>   With no feeling of remorse,
> Takes them back into his service,
>   As you would a faithful horse.[30]

To appreciate the full power of this last stanza, one must consider conventional treatments of the faithful slave trope such as Dunbar's "The Deserted

Plantation" (in which the speaker revisits the abandoned site of his bondage and, awash in nostalgia, vows to "stay an' watch de deah ole place an' tend it / Ez I used to in de happy days gone by")[31]—or his even more egregious "Chrismus on the Plantation," whose similar "farewell" scene ends not with one slave remaining but all, voluntarily, after their erstwhile master tearfully tells them that he cannot pay them wages:

> All de women was a-cryin', an' de men, too, on de sly,
> An' I noticed somep'n shinin' even in ol' Mastah's eye.
> But we all stood still to listen ez ol' Ben come f'om de crowd
> An' spoke up, a-try'n' to steady down his voice and mek it loud.[32]

Perhaps both "ol' Ben," who initiates the slaves' self-sacrificial gesture in this poem, and the speaker of "The Deserted Plantation" are also Uncle Simons, so broken they could not survive elsewhere. However, Dunbar presents it as slaveholders saw it. In their version, they could perpetrate obscene crimes, including selling their own children, and still be forgiven; they could rape and still be loved; they could burn, mutilate, and torture, and still be served willingly. Finally, when their own arrogance lost them everything, they could still expect those whom they abused to pity them. In "Freedom at McNealy's," Thompson exposes the narcissistic foundation of a thought process that allowed men like McNealy to do unforgivable evil and never know it. In Dunbar's poems, on the other hand, the (former) slaves who freely volunteer their services enable slaveholders and their apologists, past, present, and future, to retain their ignorance.

In such instances, the genteel's inability to confront evil made it evil's unwitting accomplice. The coarse final stanza of "Freedom at McNealy's" contains all the brutal clout the situation deserves. Does this degrade the former slaves, taking away a dignity and decency that, as some argue,[33] Dunbar restored to them? Possibly, but to this writer, at least, that seems preferable to letting slaveholders off the hook, especially given that apologists for slaveholding, if not the slaveholders themselves, are still with us.

In "The Favorite Slave's Story," Priscilla Thompson again pinpoints the narcissistic foundation of slaveholder neediness. In this poem we learn of its impact on a single slave family: the mother, Maria, and her three children, Peter, Susan, and Simon, "the favorite slave" who narrates the poem. Speaking in the vernacular, Simon, now a family man himself, tells his daughter's fiancé about his life under slavery. As in the narratives of Olaudah Equiano and Harriet Jacobs, what emerges is not a tale of consistent brutality but of irrational inconsistencies, where periods of "spoiling" and abuse alternate at the slaveholders' whim. One minute, Miss Nancy, having caught her husband abusing Maria, threatens to leave him; the next, she joins him in the abuse. No "Angel in the House," Miss Nancy eventually allows her husband, both a profligate and an alcoholic, to sell all her slaves with the exception of Simon, her "pet." Whites, Simon learns, even in the best of times were not to be trusted, and he relays this message:

> I tell you son de good white-folks,
>   Wus good in times uv ease;
> But soon as hawd times cummed tha' way,
>   Dey'd change, quick as you please.[34]

And Simon transmits other, equally depressing insights. Before selling the faithful Maria down the river, for example, Miss Nancy manipulates circumstances so as to justify her criminal intent: "One mawnin, jest to pick a fuss, / She said she missed a pie; / . . . / An' ef [Maria] didn't bring it back, / She'd have her whooped an' sold."[35]

The consequence of this sort of behavior is constant emotional mayhem. Those with power scream, weep, and lie; those without it live in terror, one that finally overwhelms the white family as much as it does the slaves—if not more so. The husband dies, a raving madman, of alcohol poisoning; and, as the war begins, Miss Nancy is left to wring her hands, "cryin' day an' night, / An' beggin' [Simon] to stay" as other slaves begin "a-walkin' off, / To suit their own free mind."[36] Contrary to her expectations and to the myth of the faithful slave, Miss Nancy's "favorite" leaves too, taking wife and children. At poem's end, we see Simon not nostalgically mourning for "de happy days gone by," but contentedly ensconced in his own home, patriarch of his household.

Like spoiled children who know nothing of limits, Priscilla Thompson's slaveholders cannot appreciate why those on the giving end might hate them. Rather, they remain fixed in their immaturity, possessing the power of gods and the temperaments of two-year-olds. The irony—one ubiquitously present in the literature on slavery—is that, as with children, this spoiling makes the slaveholders miserable. Never possessing enough, they cannot achieve the closure that freedom from desire would bring. In this sense, they are even more trapped by slavery than their slaves. Though their slaves never satisfy them, they make slavery their god.

In a canny move, Clara Thompson extends her sister's insights on the relationship under slavery among excessive power, narcissism, and immaturity to the relationships during the post-bellum–pre-Harlem era between whites and blacks. In "Uncle Rube and the Race Problem," whites ask the poem's narrator, the garrulous Rube, to tell them how he would "solve de Negro Problum," and

Rube gives them answers they do not much care for, beginning with the suggestion that whites change the way they talk to blacks:

'How'd I solve de Negro Problem?'
    Gentlemen, don't like dat wo'd!
'Mind me too much uv ol' slave times,
    When de white man wus de lo'd.
Spoutin' roun' about 'My niggahs',
    Knockin' us fum lef' to right,
Sellin' us, like we wus cattle,
    Drivin' us fum mawn till night—[37]

Whites, Rube says, only know how to give orders, and they blame African Americans for everything and praise them for nothing: indeed, they tear down any black who does manage to "mak[e] a mawk."[38] Furthermore, where whites are quick to see blacks' faults, they never see their own; they worry about non-concerns like amalgamation, and they refuse to "play faiah."[39] Twice, Rube points to the success of European immigrants in fitting into American mainstream society. Adopting genteel attributes worked for them, he argues, but not for blacks, because whites do not permit it:

'Don't know whaur to place de black man?'
    He will fin' his place;—You'll see!
Like de foreign whites is doin'
    When you learn to let him be.[40]

Rube's "solution"—to leave a black man like him alone instead of "git[ing] into his way"[41]—is sound, but the whites who seek his advice do not hear a word he says. What they want from him (or, better, need) is not the truth but his absolution. As with McNealy and Miss Nancy, the hand-wringing whites in this poem expect blacks to redeem them from the situation they themselves created. If these whites would accept responsibility for what they have done, Rube says, then they would now know what to do without his telling them; but this is not what they want, insuring that the "Negro Problum" will persist indefinitely into the future, which, of course, it has.

In "Uncle Rube and the Race Problem," Clara Thompson deliberately uses an ungenteel speaker (a "rube") to stress both the gulf between blacks and whites and the need for plain talk over that divide. The main point that emerges from this unsuccessful interchange is that becoming genteel (or "uplift," as it was known) failed as an answer to the "Race Problem," not because gentility was incompatible with African Americans (Tate's view) but because, in focusing only on elevating the black community, it tacitly ceded to white racism the power to dictate the grounds. This is precisely what Rube is challenging when he insists that the problem will not be resolved until whites change. There was just so much even the most genteel of blacks could do. The rest was in the hands and hearts of those who had set the conditions and who alone had the power to change them.

In this poetry, one can, I think, hear the door shutting on black optimism, especially the belief that the acquisition of gentility in itself could bridge the gap racism made. To this day, African Americans remain the single minority for whom cultural assimilation, not to mention an enormous contribution to American culture in all its branches, has not been enough. At the same time, however, one can also hear another door opening—that which made space for African American women poets to write their lives as they knew them, free of genteel restraints, in voices recognizably their own, whether in the standard or in the vernacular—the very great gift that Dunbar, more than any other single figure, gave them.

Notes

1. Allen Tate, "Negro Poetry," in *The Poetry Reviews of Allen Tate, 1924–1944*, ed. Ashley Brown and Frances Neel Cheney (Baton Rouge: Louisiana State University Press), 21–22.

2. Ibid., 21.

3. Ibid., 22.

4. Ibid., 22.

5. Henry Louis Gates Jr., *The Signifying Monkey: A Theory of African-American Literary Criticism* (Oxford: Oxford University Press, 1988), 174.

6. Ibid., 178–79. Although I have "translated" Gates's language into my own terminology, I have tried to be true to his basic intention in this seminal passage, and throughout his discussion of the role Dunbar played in the birthing of a black literary voice. In this sense, Gates's comment that Dunbar "drew upon dialect as the medium through which to posit this mode of realism" (176)—by which he means a realism designed to refute Plantation School stereotypes of African Americans—is the starting point of my essay.

7. See Tate, "Negro Poetry," 21–22; and Alain Locke, "The New Negro" in *The Norton Anthology of African American Literature*, ed. Henry Louis Gates Jr. and Nellie Y. McKay (1925; repr. New York: Norton, 1997), 961.

8. See Joan R. Sherman's introduction to *African–American Poetry of the Nineteenth Century: An Anthology* (Urbana: University of Illinois Press, 1992), 12–14; and William M. Ramsey, "Dunbar's Dixie," *Southern Literary Journal* 32 (1999): 30–34.

9. Joanne M. Braxton, ed., *The Collected Poetry of Laurence Dunbar* (Charlottesville: University of Virginia Press, 1993), 136–37, 67–68, 137–38, 20–21.

10. William Dean Howells, introduction to *Lyrics of Lowly Life*, in *The Complete Poems of Paul Laurence Dunbar*, ed. Howells (New York: Dodd, Mead, 1944), viii–x.

11. Braxton, *Collected Poetry*, 5–6, 13–15, 82–83, 134–35, 190–91, 49.

12. Julie Bates Dock, "William Dean Howells," in *Encyclopedia of American Poetry: The Nineteenth Century*, ed. Eric L. Haralson (Chicago: Fitzroy Dearborn Publishers, 1998), 224–29.

13. Gates and McKay, eds., *Norton Anthology*, 961.

14. Braxton, *Collected Poetry*, 216, 219, 208. The Dunbar poems in this essay are quoted with permission of the University of Virginia Press. For an illuminating and sympathetic discussion of "black-white-ness" in Dunbar's poetry, see Shirley Eversley's entry "Paul Laurence Dunbar" in Haralson, ed., *Encyclopedia of American Poetry* 138–40.

15. Ibid., 71, 314, 191.

16. Gates, *Signifying Monkey*, 173–74.

17. Lizelia Augusta Jenkins Moorer, *Prejudice Unveiled: and Other Poems* (1907; repr. Boston: Roxburgh, 2004), 5. American Verse Project, University of Michigan, http://wwcv.Hti.Umich.Edu/cgi/t/text/text-idx?.

18. Maggie Pogue Johnson, *Virginia Dreams: Lyrics for the Idle Hour, Tales of the Time Told in Rhyme* (n.p.: John M. Leonard, 1910), 5. New York Public Library. Digital Schomburg: African American Women Writers of the Nineteenth Century. http://digdib.nypl.org/dynaweb/digs/wwm9712/@'Generic_BookView.

19. Moorer, *Prejudice Unveiled*, 7, 14, 17, 42, 31, 62.

20. Dunbar, "To the South," in Braxton, *Collected Poetry*, 218.

21. Dunbar, "We Wear the Mask," in Braxton, *Collected Poetry*, 71.

22. Moorer, *Prejudice Unveiled*, 18.

23. Ibid., 14.

24. Ibid, 32.

25. Ibid., 43.

26. Johnson, *Virginia Dreams*, 31.

27. Johnson, "Dat Mule ob Brudder Wright's," in *Virginia Dreams*, 32–33. All of Johnson's poems in this essay are quoted with permission of the New York Public Library.

28. Braxton, *Collected Poetry*, xxv.

29. Johnson, *Virginia Dreams*, 12, 13, 14.

30. Priscilla Jane Thompson, *Gleanings of Quiet Hours*, in *Collected Black Women's Poetry*, ed. Joan R. Sherman, vol. 2 (1907; repr. New York: Oxford University Press, 1988), 66–69. All of Thompson's poems in this essay are quoted with permission of the New York Public Library.

31. Braxton, *Collected Poetry*, 68.

32. Ibid., 137.

33. Ibid., xxvi–xxviii.

34. Thompson, *Gleanings*, 55.

35. Ibid., 56.

36. Ibid., 61.

37. Clara Ann Thompson, *Songs from the Wayside*, in *Collected Black Women's Poetry*; ed. Joan R. Sherman, vol. 2 (1908; repr. New York: Oxford University Press, 1958), 33. Thompson's poems in this essay are quoted with permission of the New York Public Library.

38. Ibid., 35.

39. Ibid., 37.

40. Ibid., 38 (see also 36).

41. Ibid., 36.

LENA AHLIN

The Harlem Renaissance:
Depicting the "New Negro"

If previous research on Johnson, Fauset, and Larsen long lacked critical focus on the fictional European episodes and the interdependence of black and white artistic life, the question remains to be asked: why? One way of interpreting this lack is to see it as an effect of the establishment of what Paul Gilroy calls "the great ethnocentric canon of African American literature" (186). The focus has been on experiences of African cultural retention or on the struggle for recognition in American society. Arguably, this "ethnocentricity" has historically been a response to being denied literacy and "history," or a cultural heritage. The aesthetics of writing was from the outset coupled with social and political aims. In the introduction to the *Norton Anthology of African American Literature*, Henry Louis Gates and Nellie McKay claim that:

> African American slaves, remarkably, sought to write themselves out of slavery by mastering the Anglo-American bellettristic tradition [...] In a very real sense, the Anglo-African literary tradition was created two centuries ago in order to demonstrate that persons of African descent possessed the requisite degrees of reason and wit to create literature, that they were, indeed, full and equal members of the community of rational, sentient beings, that they could, indeed, write. (xxvii–xxviii)

From *The "New Negro" in the Old World: Culture and Performance in James Weldon Johnson, Jessie Fauset, and Nella Larsen*, pp. 38–56. © Lena Ahlin 2006.

Through their writing, the ex-slaves sought to prove their humanity, and at the beginning of the twentieth century the Harlem Renaissance writers sought to prove through their art that they were worthy of full citizenship as Americans. African-American artistic production was thus from the start seen as a means of gaining social rights. To claim "a literature of one's own" formed part of an attempt to gain acceptance as artists and citizens. Behind this work is a belief in literary language as a performative speech act, that is, through their literary works early African-American authors established themselves as intellectual and creative subjects with a story to tell. In addition, this has implications for the writer's responsibility as a representative of the race. McKay and Gates go on to describe the author and her/his works as a "synecdoche, a part standing for the ethnic whole" (xxxiv). This indicates the relationship between race and historical representation and documentation, that is, the responsibilities, limits, and possibilities of representing a history of oppression.

In this chapter, the cultural event usually referred to as the Harlem Renaissance is probed. Some of the vital questions that concerned artists and intellectuals of this time are addressed in order to situate Johnson, Fauset, and Larsen in the historical context in which they were writing and to discuss what was at stake for the artists in representing the "New Negro" on the stage or in literature. These questions primarily concern the subject matter and form of African-American literature, debates in which the notion of cultural authenticity and the representation of primitivism and particularly female sexuality figure importantly. The notion of place is also of moment here, as the trans-Atlantic interchanges between Harlem and Paris are explored. A discussion of how the symbolism of Europe is related to the idea of cultural authenticity is initiated here.

It should perhaps be added as a preliminary that, having two publication dates (1912 and 1927), Johnson's *The Autobiography of an Ex-Colored Man* in its original, anonymous version preceded the literary (re)naissance of the inter-war years. The second publication took place during the heyday of this creative historical period, and Johnson was indeed, in his novel as well as his critical and poetic work, very much a writer and personage of the moment.

The "Old Negro"

African-American writers of the early twentieth century took issue with the images of African Americans that were circulated in popular culture and that formed the way black Americans came to be perceived by white Americans. They were the first to claim that common ideas of "black folk" had come into being out of a specific historical context and were not to be seen as objective reflections of actual circumstances. What is more, as they could be identified and analyzed, these largely negative images could be changed. These images can be read as semiotic signs, similar to the linguistic signs of the language. Like words, images are signs with certain meanings that can be understood by relating them to their context. For example, Roland Barthes's reading of images in advertisements has shown how messages are encoded in the signs (114–16). These messages can be understood through cultural codes. Pictures belong to a signifying system analogous to that of language and, like the signs in the linguistic system, images can be read as "text." Like the literary text, images like that of the *tom* and the other stereotypes studied by Bogle—described below—are not merely descriptive but "world-making." Music and dressing are additional examples of signs that convey meaning and that are relevant to the particular context of this study.

In his history of early American film, Donald Bogle identifies five recurrent images through which a black cultural presence was registered. These five basic types were the tom, the black buck, the coon, the tragic mulatta and the mammy (Bogle 4–18). Early versions of these characters were stock characters of the nineteenth-century minstrel shows, such as the plantation rustic Jim Crow and the urban dandy Zip Coon (Lott 23).

The tom is of course named after the protagonist of Harriet Beecher Stowe's *Uncle Tom's Cabin* and refers to a subservient, docile character who, throughout any hardship, remains true to his white master and his Christian faith. The coon is a slow-witted, backward country type. Versions of this type could sometimes appear in the guise of a child, a "pickaninny," or an elderly, quaint "Uncle Remus." The buck is brutal, savage, over-sexed and especially desirous of white women. The tragic mulatta is a mixed-race character, always very beautiful and sexually attractive. Her balancing act between the two separated racial worlds of black and white leads to her inevitable downfall. Finally, the mammy is typically a very black, obese domestic who is more loyal to the white family she works for than to her own biological family. About these types Bogle writes:

> Fun was poked at the American Negro by presenting him as either a nitwit or a childlike lackey. None of the types was meant to do great harm, although at various times individual ones did. All were merely filmic reproductions of black stereotypes that had existed since the days of slavery and were already popularised in American life and arts. The movies, which catered to public tastes, borrowed profusely from all the other popular art forms. Whenever dealing with black characters, they simply adapted the old familiar stereotypes, often further distorting them. (Bogle 4)

In addition to the mammy figure, two more female stereotypes were often used in literature by white southern writers of the slavery and Reconstruction era: the concubine and the conjure woman (Christian 3–19). These representations were conceived in contrast to idealized representations of white womanhood. For example, the mammy is black, fat, nurturing, religious, kind, strong, and enduring, as opposed to the southern mistress who is white, beautiful, frail, and incapable of doing hard work. Most importantly, "all the functions of the mammy are magnificently physical. They involve the body as sensuous, as funky, the part of woman that white southern America was profoundly afraid of. Mammy, then, harmless in her position as a slave, unable because of her all-giving nature to do harm is needed as an image, a surrogate to contain all those fears of the physical female" (Christian 2). These images, then, were widely circulated in American popular culture, in literature as well as in early film and advertisement, and were part of the "Old Negro" images that the Harlem Renaissance authors sought to replace with new, more positive concepts of African-American identity. One response was to revise these figures, such as the tragic mulatta, in their own fiction (these revisions are probed in the following section).

These "Old Negro" stereotypes were also part of the inspiration for the anthology *The New Negro*, which was published in 1925 and marks the formal launching of the Harlem or New Negro Renaissance, as it was then often called. The editor, Alain Locke, identifies the most important points of the work in his introductory essay, also entitled *The New Negro*. Here, he analyzes the psychological effects of discrimination and stresses the importance of taking issue with the denigrating images of black people that were widely circulated and often caused an inferiority complex. The "Old Negro," says Locke, is "more of a myth than a man [. . .] more of a formula than a human being" (3). He calls for the replacement of this myth, which was often internalized by blacks themselves, with a positive, forward-looking attitude and the refusal to see oneself as "a social burden." Thus exhorting his fellow African-Americans not to accept these negative images Locke aims to instill in them "race pride." "The New Negro" that he visualizes is characterized by self-respect and self-dependence.

There were a number of factors that coincided to make the historical moment of the 1920s auspicious for the introduction of the "New Negro." To begin with, there had been a great migration from the segregated south to the north before and during World War I. In this process of transplantation, says Locke, the African-Americans have also been transformed (6). While they previously shared only "a condition" (of segregation and subjugation) the move north and the consequent gathering together in urban centers led to "a common consciousness." There was increased inter-racial contact:

where previously only workers had met, on the farms or in factories, now other segments of the black community came together. This stronger, more unified community wanted their full share in the country's institutions and thus underscoring their previous marginalization they drew attention to the discrepancy between American social creed and social practice. Now, the "New Negro" aimed to be an active collaborator and participant in American civilization. In fact, Locke declared that this new man would be guided by a "sense of a mission of rehabilitating the race in world esteem from that loss of prestige for which the fate and conditions of slavery have so largely been responsible" (14). Art and other forms of cultural production were at the center of this work of restoration. By proving their artistic and intellectual capabilities Locke and his contemporaries hoped that they would qualify for full and equal social status.

In the eyes of white Americans this "New Negro" (so recently freed from slavery) seemed to have found a capacity for enjoyment of life that was largely lost to their own post-war generation. It is striking that the "New Negro" appears at a time when European Americans used images like a "waste land" and a "lost generation" to account for their situation and outlook on life. By contrast, *The New Negro* "exudes a quality suspiciously like joy" as Arnold Rampersad put it in his 1992 introduction to the anthology (xxiii). To the white American, then, the "New Negro" was both a threat—since he claimed increased social space—and a promise.[10]

The Tragic Mulatta and the Literature of Passing

James Weldon Johnson, Jessie Fauset, and Nella Larsen all make specific use of mulatto characters, and passing, in their works. Of the novels included here, Johnson's *The Autobiography* is the only one to deal with passing in the traditional sense, while Larsen's *Quicksand* offers a reversal of the passing novel. Significantly, all three novels employ metaphors of masking.

Literature featuring mulattoes light-skinned enough to pass as white questions the idea of the body as a truthful signifier of difference and destabilizes the polarized identities of "black" and "white." In addition, the mulatto calls into question the power of vision, by which bodies are ordered in racial categories. As a literary figure, the mulatto appears most frequently in the post-Reconstruction era, at a time when the segregation of blacks and whites was institutionalized. It was the least offensive of the black stereotypes and the one with the greatest potential for social critique. Today, the literature of race passing has gained significance as a part of post-modern investigations into the "grand narratives" of Enlightenment and emancipation. Through the concept of passing, categories and classifications such as "race" are deconstructed and the fictions behind them revealed. In the introduction to the anthology *Passing and the Fictions of Identity*, Elaine K. Ginsberg writes that "[i]n its interrogation of the essentialism that is the foundation of identity politics, passing has the potential to create a space for creative self-determination and agency: the opportunity to construct new identities, to experiment with multiple subject positions, and to cross social and economic boundaries that exclude or oppress" (16). Despite its origin in a deprivation of rights, passing can thus be interpreted positively, as a subversive strategy for eschewing a legally assigned social identity, involving a destabilization of the "colorline."

The result of a union between black and white, the mulatto character functions as a device for exploring the relationship between the races (Carby 89). His or her intermediary position between two separate worlds suggests the close but separate co-existence of black and white. The fictions of Nella Larsen and Jessie Fauset are modern revisions of the literature of the tragic mulatta, which was most often employed in works with a female protagonist. The genre was initiated in the nineteenth century by works such as William Wells Brown's *Clotel, or, the President's Daughter* (1853) and Frances E. W. Harper's *Iola LeRoy, Shadows Uplifted* (1892), the first published novel by a black woman. There were also white authors who made use of this literary figure, such as George Washington Cable and William Dean Howells.[11] In *The Politics of Color in the Fiction of Jessie Fauset and Nella Larsen* (1995), Jacquelyn Y. McLendon shows how Fauset and Larsen developed the nineteenth-century stereotype of the tragic mulatta as used by these, and other, white authors. In their fiction, the figure of the mulatta becomes a vehicle for exploring "the concept of doubleness as it inheres in the experience of African Americans generally, and to satirize the bourgeois class" (11). As they do this, McLendon observes, they are particularly concerned with how issues of identity and difference relate specifically to being female.

The works in which early African-American novelists made use of the figure of the tragic mulatta were written mainly for a white audience and sought to refute prevalent stereotypes of the black woman. Owing to the prevalent myth of the super-sexuality of the black woman and its severe historical consequences, the issue of sexuality was often submerged in early African-American women's literature. For example, in the works of Frances Harper and others, sexuality is submerged or denied. In *Quicksand*, Nella Larsen confronted the denial of sexuality, making Helga Crane "the first truly sexual black female protagonist in Afro-American fiction" (Carby 1987: 174).

The novels featuring the tragic mulatta raise fundamental questions about the institution of slavery. By their very existence, the mulatto figures are an indictment of the ideology that proclaimed them to be less than human beings since they are the product of a union between white and black. The tragedy of the literary mulatta is that she is caught between the black and white worlds. If she exhibited characteristics thought to derive from her white heritage, such as sensitivity or capacity for intellectual work, they could not be expressed in her daily existence within the black world. In fact, her situation was often perceived as so untenable that the novel's resolution demanded her death. In relation to plot, the mulatta as a literary figure allows for the movement between the black and the white world. Thus, she underscores the theme of traveling and identity of the novels dealt with here, drawing attention to the trope of border crossing.

Passing relates fundamentally both to the performance perspective on identity and to place as it connotes the (physical) passing from one side of the color line to the other. Passing was the topic of Fauset's second novel, *Plum Bun*, as well as of Nella Larsen's second novel, *Passing* (both published in 1929). In an analysis of *Plum Bun*, Sonja Kroell uses a spatial metaphor when she likens passing from one's own black world into the white world to being an expatriate (40). There were people who passed only on occasion, but the passer often had to leave her or his family and give up all ties with the black community. In *Plum Bun*, for example, Fauset depicts how the protagonist Angela denies her own sister before the white man she hopes to marry one day. The connection between space and race, which is a fundamental part of passing, is retained and queried throughout this study. The passage to Europe means entering into a white world, leaving all ties with the black community.

"The Negro in Art": Race (Wo)man or Exotic Primitive?

The issue of literary representation was a topic of lively debate among African-American intellectuals in the 1920s. The main points of the debate are worth recapitulating as they indicate that, regardless of their individual persuasions on these matters, the authors of the Harlem Renaissance shared a belief in the performative potential of language. They saw in literature a possible means of transcending or transforming their present untenable social situation.

In sum, the debate was centered on three questions. First, should the black author be emphatically a black author? That is, should the art s/he produced be "racial" or "universal"? Second, should the black author cater to the demands of the largely white-dominated reading public? What this audience expected (and therefore what sold best) were often descriptions of low-life, night-life scenes in Harlem spiced up with the characters' display of uninhibited sexuality. While depictions of this kind may have reflected one part of black life, they ran the obvious risk of reinforcing common stereotypes of African Americans. This led to the third issue of debate, which concerned what responsibility the black authors should take for portraying only the positive aspects of the African-American characters. Should the authors indeed defend, and even sometimes glorify, the race in order to counter all the negative images of African Americans that already circulated within American culture, or should they opt for a more honest art of portraying their people as they happened to find them, good or bad? These questions arise as the audience for black literature changes from being primarily white for earlier authors, such as Paul Laurence Dunbar or Charles Chesnutt, to being mixed, black and white. They are contested issues that have continued to be of concern for African-American authors during the twentieth century. Alternatively, this can be formulated as a debate about the relationship between art and propaganda. The leading black intellectual of the time, W.E.B. Du Bois, wrote in the October, 1926, issue of *The Crisis* that "all art is propaganda and ever must be, despite the wailing of the purists" (296). However, the primitivist expectations were figured differently for men and women. The issue of gender and how it affects Fauset and Larsen on the one hand and Johnson on the other is addressed in connection with the analyses in chapter 3.

The two polarities of the contemporary debate are represented by Langston Hughes and George Schuyler. In 1926, the two authors both published articles discussing the question of whether the black artist was just another American, or if there really was a specific African-American art. In "The Negro Art-Hokum," Schuyler stressed the similarity between black and white Americans and argued that there was no genuinely black art. Hughes, on the other hand, in "The Negro Artist and the Racial Mountain" relates with sadness the story of a friend who expressed the wish to be "a poet—not a Negro poet." Hughes believed that this desire really stemmed from a wish to be white, as he denounces the "urge within the race toward whiteness" (Huggins, *Voices* 305). Having said this, Hughes goes on to expresses his regard for jazz and black folk art in order to claim that the black artist must above all be free to be himself. However, this notion of freedom seems somewhat paradoxical given the opening of the article, where any inclination towards what could be connected to whiteness or universalism was dismissed as deplorable. Most important perhaps, the often-quoted finishing lines of Hughes's article assert that, whatever the writer may choose to write about, s/he should not be governed by public opinion:

> We younger Negro artists who create now intend to express our individual dark-skinned selves without fear or shame. If white people are pleased we are glad. If they are not, it doesn't matter. We know we are beautiful. And ugly too. The tom-tom cries and the tom-tom laughs. If colored people are pleased we are glad. If they are not, their displeasure doesn't matter either. We build our

temples for tomorrow, strong as we know how, and we stand on top
of the mountain, free within ourselves. (Huggins, *Voices* 309)

The portrayal of African Americans was also debated in a series of articles
published between March and November, 1926, in *The Crisis*, under the
heading "The Negro in Art: How Shall He Be Portrayed?" Jessie Fauset
was one of several authors who were asked to answer a number of questions
on the topic. Others were Sinclair Lewis, Sherwood Anderson, and Countee Cullen. Here, Fauset expresses clear ideas on the roles of both audience
and publishers. Publishers have a fixed idea of what topics and characters
are appropriate to African-American literature. Therefore, it is right to
criticize authors for refusing works that portray educated and accomplished
African Americans in favor of those works that include "the sordid, foolish
and criminal among Negroes convincing the world that this and this alone
is really and essentially Negroid." The reading public also has an important
role to play. Best sellers are made—not born, Fauset says, as she urges black
readers to actually go out and buy the books they clamor for, that is "good
novel[s] about colored people by a colored author" (71). In her own work,
Fauset refused to comply with the demand for "primitivist" literature.

James Weldon Johnson and Nella Larsen also had to negotiate the
demands of the white and the black audience. In the essay "Double Audience
Makes Road Hard for Negro Authors," originally published in the *Philadelphia Tribune* on November 29, 1928, Johnson describes the predicament of
the black author who had to face a double audience of black and white readers: "[M]ore than a double audience it is a divided audience, an audience made
up of two elements with differing and often opposite and antagonistic points
of view" (Wilson 409). While the African American audience expected him
to deal only with "their best points," the Euro-American audience expected
entertaining diversion in accordance with plantation stereotypes. The challenge, then, was to try to write "so as to fuse white and black America into one
interested and approving audience" (412). In chapter 3, I discuss how Johnson's *The Autobiography* negotiates the balance between the mixed demands
of his audience in greater detail. There are a few matters I want to bring up
at this point, however. In *The Autobiography*, Johnson lets his characters state
opinions that he was later to voice himself in other contexts. For example, a
friend of the narrator (the doctor he meets on his passage back to America
from Europe) declares a belief that sounds very much like the credo of the
Harlem Renaissance: "Every race and every nation should be judged by the
best it has been able to produce, not by the worst" (114). Johnson's own work
certainly deals with a highly accomplished man, moving between jobs, coun-
tries and languages without any problem. While the book refers to Club life

in NYC, and includes scenes of gambling, violence, and theft on the part of its black characters, the superior intellect and accomplishments of the narrator balance the negative aspects of these scenes. In addition, the artistic achievements of African Americans are continually referred to as a source of pride. In the novel, the narrator vents his theory on the matter of artistic achievement and its social consequences:

> It is my opinion that the coloured people of this country have done four things which refute the oft-advanced theory that they are an absolutely inferior race, which demonstrate that they have originality and artistic conception, and, what is more, the power of creating that which can influence and appeal universally. The first two of these are the Uncle Remus stories, collected by Joel Chandler Harris, and the jubilee songs, to which the Fisk singers made the public and the skilled musicians of both America and Europe listen. The other two are ragtime music and the cake-walk. (63)

The same four examples are referred to by Johnson in the preface to *The Book of American Negro Poetry* (10). Johnson was an important promoter (as well as creator) of African-American arts. Like Fauset, he worked as both author and editor of works of contemporary poets. In his critical as well as his fictional work, Johnson chooses to celebrate African-American achievement. However, the main point for Johnson is not that they are African-American achievements, but that they are American. As Sondra Kathryn Wilson notes in the introduction to *Lift Every Voice and Sing* (vii), Johnson was always a universalist. Recognizing the distinctiveness of African Americans, he still emphasized their similarity with other Americans. To him, the cultural production of black and white Americans was differently figured as a result of social and material differences, rather than intellectual or moral differences. These differences could be overcome if the social and material conditions were altered. Johnson's own writings were acts designed to buttress this theory.

Nella Larsen's novel about Helga Crane reflects "the quicksands of representation," as Hazel Carby put it (163). At a time when the primitivist trend encouraged depictions of African-Americans as sexually uninhibited, it was a precarious task to try to give a complex presentation of a young black woman's sexuality. This was a charged topic, given the very recent history of slavery and the widespread stereotypes of the promiscuity of the African American woman that were used to legitimize sexual slavery. Carby writes: "Racist ideologies proclaimed the black woman to be a rampant sexual being, and in response black women writers either focused on defending their morality or displaced sexuality onto another terrain. Larsen confronted this denial directly in her fiction" (174). As we see in the novel, Helga Crane is positioned between the extremes of virtuous mother-woman and promiscuous black concubine. Ultimately, her alternatives come to depend on men through the ideology that dictates that female sexuality is only to be given outlet within marriage. The result of Helga's limited choices is tragic. The terrain of sexual independence turns out to be a quicksand for Helga, who at the end of the novel is nearly dying from too-frequent childbirths in her precipitate marriage with a Southern preacher.

The content of the art was not the only point of contention, however. . . .

Josephine Baker—A Primitivist Icon

The most successful of all African American artists in Europe at this time was dancer and singer Josephine Baker. In 1925, she became an overnight success in Paris with her *danse sauvage* (the savage dance), in which she made the most of the contemporary primitivist fad. She would enter the stage half naked, dressed only in feathers, and start dancing with rolling eyes and angular body movements. While her stage persona owed more to French exotic fantasies than to African culture, Baker's performance was steeped in the traditions of African-American jazz and vaudeville. Contemporary African-American press was divided in its comments on Baker's overseas success. Some expressed pride in the fact that a black woman had made it in the white world and was able to mix with European aristocracy. Baker even married a French Count, Pepito de Abatino. Others considered her a sell-out to white values and felt disappointed that she had abandoned her home country (Lemke 103–104). The example of the world-famous dancer and revue artist Josephine Baker offers a vivid illustration of the stakes involved in primitivist representation, and of the role of Europe in this representation, for the African-American artist. Indeed, Baker emblematizes the significance of performance, in relation to both stage and social appearances, and of the role of Europe in African-American culture at this time. Baker's persona, both on and off-stage, was a conscious production, and thus, Sieglinde Lemke suggests, "prototypically modernist" (106). To Ann duCille, Baker is an icon of the eroticized black woman in Western civilization (73).

Baker's European experiences were to be partly fictionalized by African-American author Nella Larsen. In fact, Helga Crane adapts a kind of stage persona for Danish social circles much like Josephine Baker's in her Parisian revues. In fact she is made, both literally and figuratively, into an object of art, to be gazed and often gaped at. In *Quicksand*, Helga's Danish uncle Poul "detest[s] tears," and when he sees Helga weeping he finds her "insufficiently civilized." Such a comment might lead us to suspect that uncle Dahl himself is overly civilized, as it were. This was actually a real anxiety during the first decades of the 20th century. Freud's exposition of civilized man's repression of basic instincts had helped increase the interest for what was thought of as more "primitive" lifestyles. Furthermore, the Great War had dealt the ultimate blow to the belief in constant rational progress and led to a loss of faith in Western civilization. Now, the African, and the African American, who had long been dismissively ascribed an irrational, naive, and spontaneous approach to life, were suddenly valued for these same qualities. Painters like Picasso and Braque were already looking to African art to find inspiration for a new aesthetic idiom. White Americans turned to Harlem clubs for black music and entertainment, hoping to gain some lost quality for enjoyment of life. The African American thus came to represent the hope for a reinvigoration of Western culture. For example, jazz music was one of the first cultural products that were exported from the USA to Europe. In Larsen's *Quicksand*, there is an ambivalence regarding primitivism and civilization, which can also be found in Josephine Baker's European experiences. On the one hand, primitivism was associated with anti-modernism, a longing for a return to a pre-rational life. On the other hand, the primitivism of the 1920s was a kind of ultra-modernism: it was in fact the primitivism of African cultures that would provide regeneration for a Western civilization threatened with degeneration.

DuCille notes a resurgence of interest in Josephine Baker in the 1990s, evidenced by the British documentary *Chasing a Rainbow* (1987) and the movie *The Josephine Baker Story* (1991). Furthermore, two films featuring Baker from the 1930s were re-released and shown in movie theaters as well as made into video cassettes (duCille 168). Many of her recordings were collected and produced as CDs in the 1990s as well. This leads duCille to draw parallels between the cultural moment of the late twentieth century and that of Baker in the 1920s and 30s, and prompts her to ask: "Are we, in our attempts at cultural criticism, modern-day primitivists? Are our Afrocentric interests and our vernacular theories and our feminist concerns for female agency colluding with primitivist proclivities like those that helped to bring the black 'other' into vogue in the 1920s? Are we, like the moment in which they lived and worked, inventing these artists as icons?" (duCille 85). This she asks apropos of her observation that the blues artists of the 1920s, like Ma Rainey and Bessie Smith, have been constructed by many feminist critics (for example Angela Y. Davis, Cheryl Wall and Hazel V. Carby) as sexual icons as well, but in more affirmative terms. The blues artists are conceived of as more grounded in the experiences of the majority of African Americans, and as being able to voice a more independent black female sexuality. Not only was the blues an art that had grown out of the folk and reached the folk. In addition, the blues singers were freer to express themselves in affirmative, sexual terms, claiming independence and status as sexual subjects in their own right. DuCille concludes that this privileging of the blues artists as superior representatives of black culture needs to be questioned, since it postulates that certain versions of blackness and the black experience are considered more authentic than others when dealing with the 1920s. This has led to the privileging of a "blues aesthetic" over literary works of arts, such as the novel, and a writer like Zora Neale Hurston. With this perspective, the art of Larsen and Fauset, although eschewing Baker's kind of primitivism and dealing with middle-class characters, using the novel as medium, is conceived of as less authentic. . . .

Harlem and Paris: Centers of African-American Culture on Two Sides of the Atlantic

Place and geographical movement were of central importance to the historical period in which Johnson, Fauset, and Larsen worked. In the 1920s, the ongoing African-American cultural flowering was usually referred to as "the New Negro Renaissance," suggesting that this was a formative moment in the history of a collective African-American identity. The period has subsequently become known as the Harlem Renaissance[12] in recognition of the fact that Harlem was a major cultural center attracting many of the best known artists of the time. The name change not only emphasizes the significance of place to this moment of cultural production, but points to a significant relationship between place and subjectivity. The name also refers back to the European Renaissance, which suggests a desire to be linked with the European tradition. An important part of that earlier Renaissance, as of the Harlem Renaissance, was the idea of a new man, a man of education and a strong sense of self-consciousness in the place of a concept of self that was associated with a less enlightened past.

Demographic shifts and the war experiences form the background for the cultural flourishing of the Harlem Renaissance. In the Great Migration of the first decades of the twentieth century, large numbers of African Americans who were disillusioned with the continued racial segregation in the post-Reconstruction South traveled north. Often, they gathered in urban centers, such as New York's Harlem, where a new racial consciousness and self-assertiveness were expressed. By the sheer force of numbers, African Americans now felt they could be a political force. The experiences of black Americans in France also played a part in this development. Black soldiers who were returning home from the war were faced with continued racial segregation, and the inconsistency between the values of freedom and democracy that the soldiers had been fighting for on foreign ground and the treatment they received on their return to their native country was glaring. During the "Red Summer" of 1919, race riots erupted all over the country and led to the lynching of eighty-three blacks. Another important event in 1919 was the publication of Claude McKay's sonnet "If We Must Die" in the New York socialist magazine *Liberator*. McKay's poem voiced a bold defiance of oppression and, perhaps even more significantly, showed what an important part literature could play in the communication of a new racial consciousness. The sonnet was featured in African-American newspapers and magazines throughout the country and led Jessie Fauset, who was made literary editor of the NAACP magazine *The Crisis* in November 1919, to announce that "[t]he portrayal of black people calls increasingly for black writers" (Davis 132).

The New Negro or Harlem Renaissance emerged out of this post-war tumult, with the aim of creating an image of the New Negro: "one who would not allow himself, his family, or his race to be victimized without fighting back" (Davis 131–32). The authors of the period thus sought to refute previous literary stereotypes and create a new, positive self-concept for African Americans. To talk of a "New Negro" was to claim a specific identity, a particular set of shared characteristics for African Americans—characteristics related to a shared history and a culture that could function as a source of pride and yield increased self-respect. It was felt that legitimacy and recognition as a people and a culture required a heritage. The search for self-definition that was part of the Harlem Renaissance thus often occasioned an interest in history and the folk tradition. The aim was twofold: formulating a positive image of a modern, urban, educated African American marked by her/his distance from the "Old Negro" of plantation slavery would not only inspire African Americans but also help motivate demands for equal rights in the eyes of white Americans. Art had a central position in this struggle, and in the introduction to *The New Negro* Alain Locke stresses the role of the artists and intellectuals as leaders and interpreters of their people. The engineers of the "New Negro" movement, such as Locke and Charles S. Johnson, conceived of a new, positive black identity that could be "taught" by an educated elite, the Talented Tenth. Although the purpose was positive, as they were trying to change derogatory images of black people, any new "prescription" of what an African-American identity could or should be also had to rely on very particular, exclusive ideas of what this identity was supposed to mean. Johnson, Fauset, and Larsen tackled this issue in various ways in their novels, as we will see in the following, and Europe figures as an important space affecting their renditions of "blackness."

The works of the Harlem Renaissance authors usually have a national, American perspective, dealing with American settings and specifically American experiences, such as life in Harlem. Alternatively, in their attempt to articulate an African-American cultural tradition, some Harlem Renaissance writers, such as Jean Toomer and Zora Neale Hurston, turned to the American South to trace the folk traditions established there since slavery. The project of "digging up one's past" also involved relating to African cultural forms in order to define what was distinctly African American in American culture. Whereas many of their contemporaries are concerned singularly with the American experience in the American setting, Johnson, Fauset, and Larsen are among the handful of authors who have attempted to relate African-American culture to European culture through fictionalized accounts of the meeting between "the New Negro" and Europe. They turn outward, to Europe, in order to comment on America. In doing so, they draw our attention to the international tendencies of the Harlem Renaissance, built on a long tradition of African-American writing about Europe.

As indicated above, France played a part in the self-consciousness of the "New Negro" as the black soldiers felt they received better treatment there than in their home country. Many chose to stay on, especially in Paris. Tyler Stovall, in *Paris Noir: African Americans in the City of Light* (1996), observes that the black GIs laid the foundations for the formation of a black community in Paris after the war. He writes: "The classical music of black America, jazz has always played a key role in the life of Paris's black community during the twentieth century, and it was the African American GIs of World War I who first introduced it to the French people" (Stovall 20). The community was a loose formation, centered mainly on jazz clubs, which also provided meeting places between black and white Americans. Paris was of course an artistic center that attracted many Americans at this time, be it aspiring writers or tourists come to have a good time. Some of the best-known writers that resided in Paris during the 1920s are Ernest Hemingway, F. Scott Fitzgerald, and Gertrude Stein, but many African-American artists went there as well. Paris has in fact been called the "second home" of the Harlem Renaissance, as most of the artists connected with the movement lived there at some point (Griffin & Fish 168). Jessie Fauset, Gwendolyn Bennett, Claude McKay, and Langston Hughes are a few of them. During this time the African-American expatriate literary community in Paris was neither as large nor as close as the one created by the white American authors of the Lost Generation. There does not seem to have been much artistic collaboration or interaction between the African-American authors and their Anglo-American counterparts in Paris. For example, Jessie Fauset sought contact with Sylvia Beach (the owner of the famous English book store Shakespeare and Company) but was rebuffed (Lewis 124). When *Quicksand* had just been published, Nella Larsen sent a copy to Gertrude Stein, together with a letter in which she praises Stein's portrayal of the African-American characters in "Melanctha" (Davis 251). Respectfully, Larsen asks for a meeting with Stein, but this was never to come about.

Travel is in itself a part of the modernity of the "New Negroes." There was a larger number of educated middle-class black Americans with the financial means to travel abroad than ever before. In the inter-war years, approximately as many black as white Americans came to Europe. According to Michel Fabre,

> [m]others of soldiers killed in France came on pilgrimages to the battlefields from Flanders to Alsace; tourists sought culture and freedom, trying to forget the "red summer" of 1919 and the increasing number of lynchings. Black and white alike were fleeing from prohibition and Puritanism. They took advantage of the strong dollar to have a good time at little expense. The Europe they encountered was imbued with jazz and Negro art. (3)

Here, Fabre indicates that Europe played a part in the valorization of music and art of African origins. In the early twentieth century, traveling to Europe was, in fact, not only a way of getting in touch with a European heritage but also a means for African Americans to gain a better sense of themselves in relation to other blacks in the diaspora. Again, place and subjectivity are significantly connected. Paris, which has been called "the gateway to Africa," often served as a meeting place between blacks from America, the Caribbean, and Africa (Griffin & Fish xvi). Traveling to Europe could thus be a step on the way to gaining the self-consciousness that the "New Negroes" sought but that was so hard to attain on American soil. In this sense, Paris is—along with Harlem—at the center of modern black experience. During the inter-war years, movements like Pan-Africanism and negritude brought blacks from America, Africa, and the Caribbean together in Paris. For example, in 1919 the Pan-African Congress, which W.E.B. Du Bois and 15 other African Americans attended, was held there. So, while the New Negro Renaissance artists aimed to claim space for themselves in American society, much of their work sprung out of international connections, and their search for space was often rerouted via Europe, where new enactments of self could be staged.

"Home . . . What Is Home?"

Many of the central questions that these authors addressed, and that I examine in the present study, are dealt with by Jessie Fauset in an article titled "Nostalgia," which was published in *The Crisis* in August, 1921. Here, Fauset points to a crucial difference between the African Americans and the other immigrants that populate America, concerning the meaning of "home." The article describes Fauset's meeting with a young black soldier who has just returned from the war in France. On his return to America, he finds himself feeling not relieved but confused: "Home [. . .] is it where mentally and spiritually he is recognized and taken for what he is? What is home?" Feeling that he has been "taken for what he is" in France, he is starting to doubt whether France is not more of a home than his native country, America. Fauset expands on his predicament:

> It is from the spiritual nostalgia that the American Negro suffers most. He has been away so long from that mysterious fatherland of his that like all the other descendants of voluntary and involuntary immigrants of the seventeenth century,—Puritan, pioneer, adventurer, indentured servant,—he feels himself American. The past is too far past for him to have memories. Very, very rarely does he have a backward reaching bond, be it never so tenuous. (157)

What Fauset is saying here is that Africa does not mean anything in terms of home to the African American of the 1920s.[13] He is American, and as such, linked to the descendants of Europe and a part of the culture of the "West." However, as long as America fails to live up to its constitutional ideals, the country will not be a home to its black population. "Nostalgia" ends with a wistful query: "the black American is something entirely new under the sun. Shall he ever realize the land where he would be?" (158). The artists of the Harlem Renaissance were seeking to attain their constitutional rights and, by extension, a home by means of their art. As they were not quite accepted in their new homeland America, and so many generations removed from Africa, Europe appeared as an alternative place to search for acceptance and a home. Fauset's essay hence offers part of a motivation for African-Americans to leave for Europe at this time.

As Gertrude Stein put it with regard to the stream of Americans who came to Paris in the 1920s: "It was not what France gave you but what it did not take away from you that was important" (Marks and Edkins 201). The statement seems to suggest that freedom—and restrictions of freedom—is spatially enacted. Concordantly, the reason why the protagonists of *There Is Confusion*, *The Autobiography of an Ex-Colored Man*, and *Quicksand* decide to leave the US for Europe is that they feel their possibilities are, in some way, limited at home. The connection Stein makes between space and freedom leads to the question of how place affects what kind of social and cultural roles the African Americans—as represented in the fiction of Johnson, Fauset, and Larsen—were allowed to play.

Notes

10. Locke was, however, very cautious in political terms saying that separatism must not be a goal, only full inclusion in American democracy, and calling the New Negro a "'forced radical,' a social protestant rather than a genuine radical" (11).

11. See, for example, Cable's *Madame Delphine* (1881) and Howells' *Imperative Duty* (1891).

12. There has been a lively debate concerning the period, for example, whether Harlem was in fact the only Northern urban center to function as an important creative center or if Washington DC could not be considered of equal importance. Other issues debated concern the duration of this "Renaissance" since different authors see different years as its starting-point and ending respectively; the "success" or "failure" to achieve the political aims of the art; the elitism inherent in the work of the Talented Tenth; and the alleged failure to represent the majority of African Americans.

13. There were, of course, those who were of another opinion, notably Marcus Garvey, founder of the Universal Negro Improvement Association. Within this organization, Garvey worked for the repatriation of black Americans to Africa (Lewis 34–44).

EMILY BERNARD

A Familiar Strangeness:
The Spectre of Whiteness in the Harlem Renaissance
and the Black Arts Movement

> We younger Negro artists who create now intend to express our individual
> dark-skinned selves without fear or shame. If white people are pleased we
> are glad. If they are not, it doesn't matter. We know we are beautiful. And
> ugly too. The tom-tom cries and the tom-tom laughs. If colored people are
> pleased we are glad. If they are not, their displeasure doesn't matter either.
> We build our temples for tomorrow, strong as we know how, and we stand
> on top of the mountain, free within ourselves.
> —Langston Hughes, "The Negro Artist and the Racial Mountain," 1926

"I would like to be white." This phrase ends the first sentence of Langston Hughes' formidable 1926 essay, "The Negro Artist and the Racial Mountain." This statement is not autobiographical. Rather the sentiment is Hughes' translation of a declaration made by an unnamed poet—Countee Cullen—about his preferred professional identity.[1] Cullen told Hughes that he wanted to be known as "a poet—not a Negro poet" and Hughes heard behind Cullen's words a lamentable self-loathing, a pitiable hankering for whiteness. The path from Cullen's sentiment to Hughes' interpretation is circuitous at best, however, and there are, finally, multiple ways in which Cullen's desire could be understood. Surely, Hughes, in his long acquaintanceship with Cullen, perceived myriad subtleties inherent in Cullen's

From *New Thoughts on the Black Arts Movement*, pp. 255–272. © 2006 by Rutgers, the State University of New Jersey and by individual contributors.

resistance to the label "Negro poet," and experienced his own ambivalence about such labels. But Hughes' interest in Cullen's words here is not philosophical but polemical. Only in this reduced and distorted version does Cullen's language serve a significant role in Hughes' essay. It provides an occasion for the exposure and condemnation of the black middle class, reviled here as the most eminently insidious agent of white supremacy. But while Hughes' essay pretends to curse Cullen and his kind—black imitators of pernicious whiteness—his explicit objective is belied by the essay itself, which depends on Cullen's putative self-loathing for its own declaration of self-love.

Whiteness and black agents of white supremacy are similarly "condemned" all over the rhetorical landscape of the Black Arts Movement. In *Are We Not Men? Masculine Anxiety and the Problem of African American Identity* (1996), literary critic Phillip Brian Harper identified interracial conflict as having a central function in the rhetoric of Black Arts nationalism, and the same mechanism works in the idiom of the Harlem Renaissance. In addition, Harper's analysis applies to interracial conflict in both the Black Arts and New Negro Movements. In other words, just as social divisions within the black community as perceived by Black Arts intellectuals were never meant to be resolved but instead actually served, in Harper's words, to "solidify the meaning of the Black Aesthetic," black struggles with white power were similarly meaningful to both Black Arts and Harlem Renaissance ideology.[2] Both movements built their foundations upon a common belief that authentic black art could only be produced when black artists liberated themselves from white influence. Anxieties about white control were often figured in sexual terms, and the racial discourses historically linked to both the Harlem Renaissance and the Black Arts Movement brim with heteronormative directives. Finally, black creativity in both movements depended upon white influence in various guises—both material and non-material—to enable *and* to handicap it. Ultimately, an examination of the Harlem Renaissance and the Black Arts Movement reveals that intimate relationships—whether generative or repressive—with whiteness are not extraneous or even peripheral to authentic black experience, they are defining aspects *of* that experience.[3]

* * *

The resounding lines that serve as this chapter's epigraph have often been quoted to represent not only the spirit of "The Negro Artist and the Racial Mountain," but the essence of Harlem Renaissance ideology, as well. Langston Hughes composed "The Negro Artist" as a response to "The Negro Art-Hokum" (1926), an essay by George Schuyler that lampoons the idea that a distinct black art could ever exist in a context in which "the Aframerican is subject to the same economic and social forces that mold the actions and thoughts of the white American."[4] Among its other accomplishments, Schuyler's essay effectively provided a platform for Hughes to codify his own aesthetic politics in what biographer Arnold Rampersad describes as "the finest essay on Hughes' life."[5] "The Negro Artist" reverberates with Hughes' triumphant convictions that authentic black art not only existed but thrived and would be essential to the cultural salvation of the race.

The rhetoric of liberation that runs through "The Negro Artist," however, as well as through much of the language of the New Negro movement, depends upon a constant invocation of all that inhibits and compromises fearless and shameless artistic expression from actually being realized, namely the black middle class. Countee Cullen serves "The Negro Artist" as a perfect—and perfectly despicable—representative of the black bourgeoisie, who are, in Hughes' definition, "people who are by no means rich yet never uncomfortable or hungry—smug, contented, respectable folk, members of the Baptist church."[6] In Hughes' formulation, the black middle class not only fails to fulfill the promise of black progress, it is also the most sinister impediment to "younger Negro artists" and to positive African American group identity, in general. With their "Nordic manners, Nordic faces, Nordic hair, Nordic art (if any)" they present "a very high mountain indeed for the would-be racial artist to climb in order to discover himself and his people."[7]

Cullen and his bourgeois milieu are not the only enemies to black progress that Hughes castigates. Another foil is his "Negro clubwoman in Philadelphia" who disdains spirituals in favor of the "drab melodies in white folks' hymnbooks."[8] Together, Cullen and the Negro clubwoman function in "The Negro Artist" as personifications of the ideological hurdles that stand between the black artist and the "serious radical art" that he would produce. Formidable enemies though they may be, all is not lost, Hughes informs us. Real, unmitigated, unspoiled blackness flourishes: "But then there are the low-down folks, the so-called common element, and they are the majority—may the Lord be praised!"[9] Once the dead layer of faux whiteness is rhetorically vanquished, authentic blackness is revealed and celebrated, only to be buried again under more references to its black oppressors. Obviously, the real adversary to black progress here and everywhere is white supremacy, but I'd like to explore the particular threats that its black ambassadors are understood to offer to the integrity of black identity.

A potent current of disgust for the black middle-class runs energetically through the discourse of the Harlem Renaissance, the Black Arts Movement, and beyond.[10] In their aping of "white" ways and values, the black middle class is figured as more pernicious, more insidious than whiteness itself. Why?

As Zora Neale Hurston described the ambivalent response of Eatonville's modest citizens to Mayor Jody Starks' middle-class ways in *Their Eyes Were Watching God* (1937): "It was bad enough for white people, but when one of your own color could be so different it put you on a wonder. It was like seeing your sister turn into a 'gator. A familiar strangeness. You keep seeing your sister in the 'gator and the 'gator in your sister, and you'd rather not."[11] What this suggests is chilling and obvious: if your sister could so easily turn into a 'gator, then maybe your sister and the 'gator weren't so different in the first place. The "familiar strangeness" that alienates Eatonville from Starks created a hysteria during both the Harlem Renaissance and the Black Arts Movement that fed on itself and informed both movements with meaning; it revealed the true proximity to whiteness that blackness could never actually escape, even though attempts to do so have always been central to black experience. Distinguishing the "'gator" from your sister was a fixation in both movements, and it demanded a constant vigilance.

What is finally most important here is not the actual disunion of sister from "'gator," but the ritual inherent in the attempt. In other words, these black foils were effectively not *obstacles to* but *essential to* the ideological constructions of black identity in both the Harlem Renaissance and the Black Arts Movement. The threats they posed were necessary and productive. The "The Negro Artist and the Racial Mountain" is theoretically a paean to Hughes' "low-down folks," but word-for-word, Hughes spends much more time in his essay focused on the self-hating elitists he claims to pity and despise. After his first reference to his celebrated authentic black folk, he returns again to his Philadelphia clubwoman, ostensibly to bemoan her shame for jazz. "Years of study under white teachers, a lifetime of white books, pictures, and papers, and white manners, morals, and Puritan standards made her dislike the spirituals. And now she turns up her nose at jazz and all its manifestations—likewise almost everything else distinctly racial." Hughes sees it as a duty of the "younger Negro artist, if he accepts any duties at all from outsiders, to change through the force of his art that old whispering, 'I want to be white,' hidden in the aspirations of his people, to 'Why should I want to write? I am a Negro—and beautiful!'"[12] But the energy of his essay is provided by the conflict itself, not by the promise of its resolution.

In *Are We Not Men?*, Phillip Brian Harper reveals that similar contradictions were inherent features of the black nationalist project, and argues that "the response of Black Arts nationalism to social division within the black populace is not to strive to overcome it, but rather to articulate it in the name of black consciousness."[13] Putatively nationalist, the Black Arts Movement based its very existence upon the idea that there were those who could never be incorporated into the fold. As Amiri Baraka announced in

Raise Race Rays Raze (1969): "There are people who might cry BlackPower, who are representatives, extensions of white culture. So-called BlackPower advocates who are mozartfreaks or Rolling Stones, or hypnotized by Joyce or Hemingway or Frank Sinatra, are representatives, extensions of white culture, and can never therefore signify black power."[14] Addison Gayle, Jr., editor of *The Black Aesthetic* (1971), believed there was a cure: "The Black Aesthetic then, as conceived by this writer, is a corrective—a means of helping black people out of the polluted mainstream of Americanism, and offering logical, reasoned arguments as to why he should not desire to join the ranks of a Norman Mailer or a William Styron."[15] The continuous need to weed out the righteous from the fallen, the "blacks" from the "Negroes," was not really a necessary, recuperative step on the way to group solidarity, however; finally it served as the essence of the project of Black nationalism itself.

An ambiguity and ambivalence inherent in the objectives of the movement itself accounts for the intraracial tensions invoked so commonly by Black Arts artists. Harper's analysis of Amiri Baraka's poem "SOS" (1969) makes plain that "the threatening unpredictability of exactly what will issue from the essentially contradictory nationalist urge accounts for Baraka's decision not to project beyond the call manifested in 'SOS': 'Calling black people.'"[16] Group solidarity could not be achieved because the practical purpose of this solidarity was never clear. The urgent, relentless effort to ferret out those blacks who were potentially hurtful to black progress was finally a ruse that serves to distract even Black Arts leaders themselves from the contradictions that threatened the ostensible cohesion and focus of the black nationalist project.

A very similar strategy was at work in the New Negro Movement, whose complications began with the term "New Negro" itself. As Henry Louis Gates, Jr. reminds us in "The Trope of a New Negro and the Reconstruction of the Image of the Black" (1988), the term "New Negro" was not invented in the 1920s but had, in fact, been circulating in African American public discourse since the 1700s. This figure was composed, in part, by blacks attempting to correct the negative stereotypes about them that were already in play by the time they arrived in the New World. "Almost as soon as blacks could write, it seems," Gates explains, "they set out to redefine—against already received racial stereotypes—who and what a black person was, and how unlike the racist stereotype the black original indeed actually could be."[17] Black people attempted to convert popular stereotypes about blacks from those based upon absence (of morality, intelligence, and other basic features of humanity) to presence. Those who participated in the circulation of this figure, "the New Negro," believed that this semantic strategy would have serious political and cultural ramifications in the lives of black Americans. A preoccupation with this term, and the liberation it represented, became a near-obsession for Harlem Renaissance intellectuals. In fact, Gates suggests that the Negro Renaissance was finally nothing more than a vehicle created to contain the "culturally willed myth of the New Negro."[18]

But the term "New Negro" does not make sense without its counterpart—"Old Negro." In fact, the terms are hardly in opposition at all. Instead, they are in dialectical harmony and fundamentally necessary to each other; a definition of one term is only possible in light of the other. In other words, the New Negro is finally only what the Old Negro is not, and vice versa. Gates discusses the contradictions built into the terms "Old Negro" and "New Negro":

> The paradox of this claim is inherent in the trope itself, combining as it does a concern with time, antecedents, and heritage, on the one hand, with a concern for cleared space, the public face of the race, on the other. The figure, moreover, combines implicitly both an eighteenth-century vision of utopia with a nineteenth-century idea of progress to form a black end-of-the-century dream of an unbroken, unhabituated, neological self—signified by the upper case in "Negro" and the belated adjective "New." A paradox of this sort of self-willed beginning is that its "success" depends fundamentally upon self-negation, a turning away from the "Old Negro" and the labyrinthine memory of black enslavement and toward the register of a "New Negro," an irresistible, spontaneously generated black and sufficient self.[19]

The inextricability of the terms "Old Negro" and "New Negro" presented a problem for black intellectuals intent upon severing the relationship between the two types, embracing the latter while turning the collective racial back on the former, thereby obliterating forever the ugly history of shame and servility that the Old Negro represented. But the progress promised by the New Negro Movement could be evident only in relation to this agonizing history. Continuous comparisons were necessary, and that meant that the figure of the Old Negro had to be kept alive and in the center of discussions about racial progress. It was finally impossible for Harlem Renaissance intellectuals to leave the Old Negro behind; they needed to maintain a concentrated focus on this symbol in order to remind themselves exactly what they were shedding, and conversely, what precisely it was that they were becoming. The necessity of keeping close at hand the very image that they were so desperate to cast off created an acute anxiety among Harlem Renaissance intellectuals whose relief was attempted by a seemingly continuous celebration of the symbolic death of the Old Negro. The compulsion to create distinctions between an

Old Negro ideology—imbedded in white expectations—and a New Negro framework—free from preoccupations with white standards—was a compulsion that necessitated and effectively created its own antagonists.

Harlem Renaissance writers were eminently aware of their status as members of a cultural vanguard, yet they lacked clear, physical evidence of the progress that their art was supposed to have achieved. The acute self-reflexivity of this moment in African American literary history apparently left its black writers with few alternatives but to look inside the movement itself for the source of their problems.[20] Bt the middle of the 1920s, when the Harlem Renaissance was in full swing, those black writers casting about frantically to identify the outdated features of black cultural identity that were preventing them from self-actualization found useful targets in each other, as Hughes exemplifies in his treatment of Countee Cullen in "The Negro Artist and the Racial Mountain." The Harlem Renaissance, then, can be characterized by mechanics of exclusion that are similar to those that travel through the rhetoric of the Black Arts Movement.

"Negro life is not only establishing new contacts and founding new centers, it is finding a new soul," Alain Locke proclaimed in the opening pages of *The New Negro* (1925).[21] African American arts of the 1920s was intoxicated with the idea that it had invented itself, not only in terms of its creative ambitions, but as a locus of a new black identity. A version of the same fantasy characterizes the Black Arts Movement. "We advocate a cultural revolution in art and ideas," Larry Neal echoed in 1966.[22] In his introduction to *The Black Aesthetic,* Addison Gayle, Jr. summarized the objectives of the Black Arts Movement: "Speaking honestly is a fundamental principle of today's black artist. He has given up the futile practice of speaking to whites, and has begun to speak to his brothers."[23] Gayle posits the Black Arts strategy as historically unique, but his gesture itself is actually redundant, Alain Locke and Langston Hughes being among those Harlem Renaissance artists and intellectuals who precede him. Like the Harlem Renaissance, the Black Arts Movement articulated its objectives in powerful but pointedly abstract language that was finally more confusing than illuminating. How a black artist "could speak to his brothers" without any white mediation proved more confounding than Black Arts leaders were willing to concede. But if the Black Arts Movement wasn't clear on how it would get where it was going, it was very clear on where it was *not* going, and that was in the direction taken by the movement against which it continuously measured itself: the Harlem Renaissance.

A central project of the Black Arts Movement was to correct the mistakes made by the Harlem Renaissance: "The Black Arts Movement represents the flowering of a cultural nationalism that has been suppressed since the 1920s. I mean the 'Harlem Renaissance'—which was essentially a failure."

It failed, Neal explains, because it did not "address itself to the mythology and the life-styles of the black community."[24] In the first chapter of *The Crisis of the Negro Intellectual* (1967), Harold Cruse sees white patronage as having played a significant role in the failure of the New Negro Movement. In his view, "the Harlem Renaissance became partially smothered in the guilty, idealistic, or egotistical interventions of cultural paternalism."[25] Like Addison Gayle, Jr., Harold Cruse felt that the Black Arts Movement should serve as an "ideological tonic that cures misguided assimilationist tendencies."[26]

In opposition to the Harlem Renaissance, the Black Arts Movement strived to succeed without white influence. In *Blues People* (1963), LeRoi Jones sized up the role whiteness played in the New Negro Movement:

> The rising middle class-spawned intelligentsia invented the term New Negro and the idea of the Negro Renaissance to convey *to the white world* that there had been a change in tactics as to how to climb onto the bandwagon of mainstream American life. The point here is that this was to be conveyed to white America; it was another conscious reaction to that white America and another adaptation of the middle-class Negro's self-conscious performance to his ever appreciative white audience.[27]

Like other Black Arts Movement spokesmen, Jones often used the terms "Negro" to refer to, in his own words, "white-oriented schizophrenic freaks of a dying society,"[28] African Americans he considers less progressive, less revolutionary than his own cohort. Elsewhere in Jones' writing, "Negro" is simply a synonym for "black."[29] African Americans have been debating nomenclature as long as they have been struggling with the burden of representation, which is to say, since the inception of African presence in this country. But whether or not terminology has material or symbolic impact on the African American condition, the debate itself, in all of its variations, is consistently front and center in all of the major historical shifts in African American experience, and always represents an evolving interpretation *of* that experience. More than simply a semantic shift, the mythological distance between "Negro" and "black" was as necessary, meaningful, and mysterious to the Black Arts Movement as was the stretch between "Old Negro" and "New Negro" for the Harlem Renaissance.

The safest way to ensure one's status as "black" during the Black Arts Movement was to snitch on the Negroes. "The colored people, negroes, who are Americans, and there are plenty, are only colored on their skin. They are white murderers of colored people," proclaimed Baraka in *Raise Race Rays Raze*.[30] The essays in *Raise* are peppered with distinctions between "Negro artists" and "Black Artists" (98); references to deluded "hip negroes" (139) and the potential for "negro politics" to result only in "negro egos aggrandized at the expense of the ultimate development of the Black nation." Baraka warns: "We cannot lose our values and become negroized" (160). To become negroized would have been a fate worse than death—but reversible.

In *New Day in Babylon* (1992), cultural historian William Van Deburg describes the elaborate process by which Negroes could become black.[31] Whether or not you were worthy of the moniker "black" depended on how far at bay you held "whiteness." Conversely, an immediacy to "whiteness" compromised the authenticity of your "blackness." The same equations were in effect during the Harlem Renaissance, but just as Harold Cruse points out, so much of the Harlem Renaissance was connected to white support that it was—and is—impossible to determine where it ended and unalloyed black art actually began. Langston Hughes describes the significance of the title of the 1926 vanguard journal *Fire!!* in his 1940 autobiography, *The Big Sea:* "the idea being that it would burn up a lot of the old, dead conventional Negro-white ideas of the past, *épater le bourgeois* into a realization of the existence of the younger Negro writers and artists."[32] Countee Cullen worked as a personalization of these "dead conventional Negro-white ideas" in "The Negro Artist," and as such, had to be rhetorically cast from the Edenic racial landscape of Hughes' manifesto. But even *Fire!!*, as a realization of an authentic racial dream, could not have existed without white financial support. Wallace Thurman, the magazine's editor, lamented the fact that *Fire!!* could not burn "without Nordic fuel," even as he sought help from his current lover, who was white, and Carl Van Vechten.[33] This type of dependence played a crucial role in the eviscerating assessments made by Black Arts Movement intellectuals about the Harlem Renaissance.

Just as some Harlem Renaissance intellectuals needed to distinguish themselves from peers whom they considered to be too focused on the expectations of whites, Black Arts Movement spokesmen clarified the racial purity of their own objectives and beliefs by juxtaposing them against the "interracialism," as Harold Cruse characterized it, practiced by the Harlem Renaissance. "Learn to kill niggers/ Learn to be Black men," commands Nikki Giovanni's 1968 poem, "The True Import of the Present Dialogue: Black vs. Negro."[34] Hughes' "The Negro Artist and the Racial Mountain" never advocated murder, but the brutality inherent in the language he uses to dismiss Countee Cullen ensures that readers will not associate him with the "old, dead conventional Negro-white ideas" that Cullen is charged to represent.

This rhetoric of purification is central to the ritual of separation that preoccupies both Harlem Renaissance and Black Arts Movement spokesmen. Upon Malcolm X's assassination, LeRoi Jones famously left his white

wife and family to move uptown, to Harlem, the "black Mecca." In his autobiography, Jones describes how his birth into blackness, Black Power-style,
took a predictable course:

> The middle-class native intellectual, having outintegrated the
> most integrated, now plunges headlong into what he perceives as
> blackest, native-est. Having dug, finally, how white he has become,
> now, classically, comes back to his countrymen charged up with the
> desire to be black, uphold black, & c . . . a fanatical patriot![35]

But even in this moment of total immersion in blackness, a full rejection
of whiteness, though proclaimed, is ultimately impossible. As Phillip Brian
Harper argues, even though Black Arts poetry derives much of its power
through its presentation as a black-only product, "it achieves its maximum
impact in a context in which it is understood as being heard directly by whites,
and overheard by blacks."[36] The constant iterations of murderous fantasies
about whites that are staples of Black Arts poetry are finally most effective
if they are directed at white people, Harper explains. To speak these fantasies *to* a white listener effects a symbolic annihilation, which is immeasurably
important considering the great improbability that its physical counterpart
would ever actually take place. According to Harper's argument, Black Arts
poetry was meant to be only *overheard* by blacks, who were then meant to
experience envy and awe for the racial righteousness being espoused. So, even
within this decidedly black-only movement, white influence was inescapable.
Indeed, efforts to elaborate on the meaning of blackness depended on invocation of whiteness. Literary critic David Lionel Smith points out that Hoyt
Fuller, in the lead essay in *Black Aesthetic,* must quote at length from a white
writer, George Frazier, in order to effectively illustrate the enigmatic superiority of black style. Ironically, Fuller excuses Frazier for being "a white writer
who is not in the least sympathetic with the likes of LeRoi Jones."[37] These
sorts of contradictions, I believe, impelled Black Arts Movement thinkers to
use strategies that became more and more desperate in order to purge the
whiteness without and within.

In another instance of this ritual of separation, Black Arts Movement
prolocutor Eldridge Cleaver used James Baldwin as a handy target in his
own rhetoric of purification, utilizing him in the same manner that Hughes
employed the symbolic figure of Countee Cullen in "The Negro Artist." In
Soul on Ice (1968), Eldridge Cleaver warned his readers about the wolves in
sheep's clothing—"'gators" disguised as sisters—with a fanatic intensity. "Those
truly concerned with the resurrection of black Americans have had eternally
to deal with black intellectuals who have become their own opposites, taking

on all the behavior patterns of their enemy, vices and virtues, in an effort to aspire to alien standards in all aspects," Cleaver railed.[38] To Cleaver, Baldwin represented the quintessential "intellectual sycophant . . . a white man in a black body. A self-willed automated slave, he becomes the white man's most valuable tool in oppressing other blacks."[39] Cleaver was not alone in his judgments of Baldwin. According to Amiri Baraka, Baldwin was "Joan of Arc of the cocktail party" with a "spavined whine and plea" that was "sickening beyond belief."[40] Ishmael Reed described him as "a hustler who comes on like Job."[41] While it is important to note here that several of these Baldwin-haters have since revised their positions on the man, and now understand the stances they took then as a function of the times, it is meaningful to recognize how central these denunciations of James Baldwin were to the establishment of a kind of racial authenticity for those who perpetuated them. "A new generation, so it seemed, was determined to define itself by everything Baldwin was *not*," concluded Henry Louis Gates. "By the late sixties, Baldwin-bashing was almost a rite of initiation."[42]

Cleaver's disdain for Baldwin's counterfeit whiteness was inextricably bound up in his anxieties about Baldwin's sexual orientation. Cleaver's racial objections to Baldwin were always sexualized, and he believed homosexuality to be a white man's plague. He wrote in *Soul on Ice,* "Many Negro homosexuals, acquiescing in this racial death-wish, are outraged and frustrated because in their sickness they are unable to have a baby by a white man."[43] According to Cleaver, if the middle-class black was dangerous, then the black homosexual was deadly: "The white man has deprived him of his masculinity, castrated him in the center of his burning skull."[44] Thus zombie-fied, the black gay man, in Cleaver's fantasy, had the potential to undermine all of African American progress. The ugliness of Cleaver's distortions of Baldwin had more to do with anxieties around black masculinity than it did with any authentic hatred of James Baldwin as an individual. The stridency in Cleaver's language finally only represents the weaknesses in the movement's message about manhood. But as Phillip Brian Harper maintains, this is a "masculine anxiety that is rendered no less potentially oppressive by the sense of vulnerability it conveys."[45]

Virtually all crises in African American culture have been historically portrayed as crises of black heterosexual male authority. Heterosexism is by no means unique to African American culture, of course, but the historical intersection of heterosexual masculinity with the discourse of authenticity in African American identity is central to the discussion.[46] Figured as perennially at risk, African American ideologues have privileged the recuperation of black heterosexual masculinity as primarily important, and then exhibited its recuperation as a "best foot forward" gesture in the continuous struggle for race uplift. Historically, homosexuality has been implicitly understood to be simply incommensurate with the ideal of the black male hero. At worst it has been considered detrimental to racial progress. This latter assumption, of course, reached a volcanic intensity during the Black Arts Movement, and it found an individual target in James Baldwin. The sexualization of Black nationalism is inherently connected, of course, to its proponents' portraits of the Harlem Renaissance as an effeminate movement. Harold Cruse wrote, tellingly, that the failures of the New Negro Movement left it, not only whitened, but "emasculated."[47]

When it comes to the legacy of the Harlem Renaissance (and beyond), the intersection of anxieties about black male heroism and homosexuality finds an important expression in the controversy surrounding one black cultural icon: Langston Hughes. Commonly idealized by black communities with histories of competing interests, Hughes' status as a cultural hero, historically and presently, depends upon a public "whitewashing" of two features of his life that would otherwise tarnish his image as the ultimate race man: his presumed homosexuality, and the degree and quality of his involvement with whites.

There is an implicit imperative at work that demands that all discussions about Hughes' possible homosexuality be swiftly repressed in order for Hughes to maintain his central place in the annals of African American cultural history. The most remarkable instance of this repression occurred around the release of the 1989 film *Looking for Langston*. The film, directed by Isaac Julien, is a meditation on gay male culture during the Harlem Renaissance through the vehicle of the enigmatic sexual identity of Langston Hughes. When Julien and other members of the black British film collective, Sankofa, showed the film to the Hughes estate, officials there refused to grant permission unless every direct visual and textual reference to Hughes' sexuality was removed from the film. The panic generated by even this speculation about Hughes' homosexuality itself testifies to the centrality of heterosexuality to the discourse of black male heroism. Ada Griffin, then director of the New York City–based Third World Newsreel, the distributor for *Looking for Langston*, bolstered this argument when she suggested that many of those involved in the production and distribution of the film were simply unaware of the degree of resistance they would encounter from the members of the "black bourgeoisie" who consider Hughes "a racial icon."[48] Clearly, Hughes' status as an icon has consistently been implicitly contingent upon the assertion of his heterosexuality. And conversely, the repression of discussions about the possibility of his homosexuality has been necessary to the conservation of this status.

Equally threatening to Hughes' status as a "race man" are specific representations of his relationships with whites. I have discussed elsewhere how crucial the figure of white promoter Carl Van Vechten was to the younger generation of New Negro writers who manipulated Van Vechten's symbolic presence to differentiate themselves from their older, more conservative counterparts.[49] Van Vechten has always been considered to pose a particular threat to Langston Hughes, both as a mentor and as a friend.[50] That Carl Van Vechten, who was married for more than forty years to Russian actress Fania Marinoff, also enjoyed erotic relationships with men only increases the level of danger associated with him. The determination with which contemporary historians and scholars consistently attempt to sever or downplay relations between Van Vechten and Hughes results from the intersection of Van Vechten's public identity as a homosexual and a discourse about Hughes that prevents even the speculation that he might have had an intimate affiliation with gay male culture during his lifetime. But Langston Hughes enjoyed a textured, long-term relationship with Carl Van Vechten and many other white people, gay and straight, both formally and informally.[51] The possibility of a legitimate, mutual beneficial relationship between Hughes and Van Vechten jeopardizes Hughes' status as a racial icon, a status that demands black male heterosexuality and forbids close, positive associations with whites.

The demonization of homosexuality, as an agent of white power, was central to Black Arts Movement discourse. According to the philosophy of the Black Arts Movement, the central lesson of the Harlem Renaissance was that white power, in all its forms, was perilous, even lethal. "We hated white people so publicly, for one reason, because we had been so publicly tied up with them before," Baraka explains provocatively in *The Autobiography of LeRoi Jones/Amiri Baraka* (1984). Baraka's "before" refers directly to his own life, and it also speaks to the generational congruities of interracialism in African American cultural history. The final, incontrovertible purging of whiteness from black lives was, both collectively and individually, the central object of the Black Arts Movement, and its constituents pursued this mission with convert-like fervor. But all projects hatched toward this end were almost always necessarily distributed through white-controlled institutions.[52] "What's needed now for 'the arts' is to get them away from white people," Amiri Baraka announced in "What the Arts Need Now," and this tenet is echoed in other essays in his 1969 collection *Raise Race Rays Raze*. Does Baraka contradict himself by publishing these words with Random House?[53] The note to the first paperback edition of *Black Fire: An Anthology of Afro-American Writing* (1968), edited by LeRoi Jones and Larry Neal, apologized for the omission of work by several authors, and then explained:

We hoped it wd be in the paperback, but these devils claim it costs too much to reprint. Hopefully, the 2nd edition of the paperback will have all the people we cd think of. The frustration of working thru these bullshit white people shd be obvious.[54]

In its candid language and innovate syntax, the above note emblematizes the passion and purpose of the Black Arts Movement. But finally, the "bullshit white people" called out by the editors are the same "bullshit white people" that make such a calling out possible in the first place. In other words, it was only by the grace of the white "devils" at William Morrow that, in this case, the flames of black fire were able to blaze.[55] Did the editors of *Black Fire* see the ironic connection between their own inconsistencies and that of the conundrum in which the editors of the 1926 journal *Fire!!* found themselves? The implicitly revisionist intentions of *Black Fire* serve as a microcosm for the equally ambitious, equally contradictory imperatives that kindled the Black Arts Movement as a whole. In both movements, the spectre of whiteness that hovered ambiguously over black art generated multiple crises whose resolutions were never as important as the fertile heat they ignited.

The crisis mentality that characterizes African American cultural history is responsible for the anxieties occasioned by the personas of Hughes and Baldwin, among others. African American culture has been continuously represented as a culture of crisis; witness the obvious significance of the appellation of one of the most important African American periodicals to date, *The Crisis*. The hysteria created by this crisis mentality accounts for the insistence upon nomenclature revisions, as well as the paranoid, short-sighted fantasies about weeding out internal enemies. In an essay about contemporary feminist discourse, literary critic Carla Kaplan argues that a parallel phenomenon impacts the language of contemporary feminism. According to Kaplan, the ubiquitous "language of crisis does not so much *represent* the current state of affairs as *construct* it in particular—and particularly disadvantageous—ways."[56] Kaplan's argument provides a provocative lens through which we might understand something fundamental about African American culture. African American culture has been historically figured by ideologues as troubled, fragmented, and in need of re-unification. The imperative to re-name and root out internal enemies are common strategies employed to resolve these perpetual crises; resolutions are proclaimed in declarations of the birth of another "renaissance."[57] Obscured in these rituals are not only the substantial problems that continue to drain black communities, but also the fact that the language of crisis serves mainly to produce more crises, among them the perpetuation of heterosexism within the black community, which itself only serves to represent, yet again, how useful this divisiveness is within the black community in the continuing drama of the pursuit of racial authenticity. In other words, those who identify homosexuality as aberrant, a threat to black male heterosexuality, only further underscore how crucial homosexuality is to the articulation of heterosexual masculine identity—as essential as whiteness is to blackness.

* * *

I'm looking for a house
In the world
Where the white shadows
Will not fall.

There is no such house,
Dark brothers,
No such house
At all.

—Langston Hughes, "House in the World" (1931)[58]

I have conceived this essay, in part, as a response to Toni Morrison's *Playing in the Dark: Whiteness and the Literary Imagination* (1992), in which she discusses the "dark, abiding, signing Africanist presence" that hovers like a shadow over American literature.[59] My purpose here is not to propose that the shadow of whiteness performs an identical function in African American literature, mainly because the relationship between white and black power is not, and has never been, equitable. What I have attempted to explore here is the degree to which the spectre of whiteness—and black embodiments of that spectre—has informed two important episodes in African American cultural formation: the Harlem Renaissance and the Black Arts Movement. The examples upon which I base my argument are not meant to epitomize the totality of either movement, but are rather only intended to suggest something meaningful about the nature of this feature common to both episodes in African American cultural history. In its indirect, ambiguous, non-material forms, white influence has impacted black culture powerfully, and engendered equally powerful, even desperate, attempts by black people to finally extinguish it. Those attempts involve efforts to purge the whiteness from within—to wrest the noble sister from the pernicious "'gator." Such attempts are meaningful but futile: your sister and the "'gator" were always intertwined.

"House in the World" sighs resignedly at the impossibility of ever separating the righteous from the reptilian, therefore evoking a very different spirit than Hughes' 1926 essay, "The Negro Artist and the Racial Mountain." If his 1926 essay celebrated black freedom from white (and black) expectations, this

1931 poem wearily cedes the impossibility of ever extricating black identity from the constancy of the white normative gaze. The mood of the poem more closely resembles Hughes' tone in his 1940 autobiography, *The Big Sea*, when he writes about the Harlem Renaissance. "As for all those white folks in the speakeasies and night clubs of Harlem—well, maybe a colored man could find some place to have a drink that the tourists hadn't yet discovered."[60] Hughes' metaphor of the house represents the conviction devotedly espoused during the Black Arts Movement that institution-building would be the key to black political, cultural, and ideological liberation from white power. The poem also portends the futility of such an enterprise to do the work with which it is *really* charged, which is to protect blackness from white influence not only materially but symbolically, as well. The linguistic distinction—"white shadows" and "dark brothers"—is about as close as you can get. But if "House in the World" is a lament on the unrelenting power of whiteness—a whiteness so powerful it can permeate physical structures—then it is also an honest reckoning with it, a meditation on the inevitability of white presence as a constant—and significant—feature of black life.

Truly, the white normative gaze has always been at work in African American culture. It has played a fundamental role in structuring black cultural forms at every significant moment in African American cultural production. Because white support *and* corruption have been central to every episode in the evolution of African American creativity, we can safely name it as a crucial part of what makes African American art exactly what it is. In other words, there would be no black creativity without white influence.

Even more than artistic expression, the centrality of whiteness to black cultural *identity*, along with attendant anxieties about that centrality, are fundamental features of black American experience. Efforts to denounce and extinguish white presence from black life are important dynamics in the evolution of African American identity. The contradictions I assert here are deliberate; they resonate absolutely with the essentially contradictory nature of black American experience. The patron saint of Black nationalism during the Black Arts Movement, Amiri Baraka, himself explains: "The paradox of the Negro experience in America is that it is a separate experience, but inseparable from the complete fabric of American life."[61] Intimate struggles with whiteness are perhaps the only continuous—*essential*, if you will—aspects of black identity. White shadows make blackness, as we know it, visible.

Notes

1. "If I am going to be a poet at all," Countee Cullen told a *Brooklyn Daily Eagle* reporter in 1924, "I am going to be a POET and not a NEGRO POET." Quoted in Stephen Watson, *The Harlem Renaissance: Hub of African-American Culture, 1920–1930* (New York: Pantheon, 1995), 78.

2. Phillip Brian Harper, *Are We Not Men? Masculine Anxiety and the Problem of African-American Identity* (New York: Oxford University Press, 1996), 45.

3. My essay borrows from the groundbreaking work done by generations of scholars on the inherently and "incontestably mulatto"—to use the phrase made famous by Albert Murray—nature of American culture.

4. George S. Schuyler, "The Negro-Art Hokum," *The Nation* 121 (June 16, 1926): 3180, reprinted in *The Portable Harlem Renaissance Reader*, ed. David Levering Lewis (New York: Penguin, 1994) 97–98. In *Authentic Blackness: The Folk in the New Negro Renaissance*, J. Martin Favor's thoughtful interpretation of Schuyler's position expands upon and enlivens traditional scholarly discussions that have dismissed "The Negro-Art Hokum" as accommodationist and counterproductive to the race uplift ideology spearheaded during the Harlem Renaissance and beyond. See J. Martin Favor, *Authentic Blackness: The Folk in the New Negro Renaissance* (Durham: Duke University Press, 1999), 120–26.

5. Arnold Rampersad, *The Life of Langston Hughes*, Vol. I (New York: Oxford University Press, 1986), 130.

6. Ibid., 175.

7. Ibid., 176.

8. Ibid., 178.

9. Ibid., 176.

10. In *Authentic Blackness*, Favor identifies the equation of "folk" identity with authentic black experience as a fundamental feature in African American cultural discourse. Hazel Carby makes similar arguments in the essays that make up "Fiction of the Folk," a section of her essay collection, *Cultures in Babylon: Black Britain and African America* (London: Verso, 1999).

11. Zora Neale Hurston, *Their Eyes Were Watching God* (New York: Harper-Collins, 1998), 48.

12. Langston Hughes, "The Negro Artist and the Racial Mountain," *The Nation* 122 (23 June 1926): 3181, reprinted in *The Black Aesthetic*, ed. Addison Gayle, Jr. (Garden City, NY: Doubleday, 1971), 180.

13. Harper, *Are We Not Men?*, 44.

14. Amiri Baraka, *Raise Race Rays Raze: Essays Since 1965* (New York: Random House, 1969), 43.

15. Addison Gayle, Jr., *The Black Aesthetic*, xxiii.

16. Harper, *Are We Not Men?*, 52.

17. Henry Louis Gates, "The Trope of a New Negro and the Reconstruction of the Image of the Black," *Representations* 24 (Fall 1988): 131.

18. Ibid., 132.

19. Ibid.

20. In "What He Did for the Race: Carl Van Vechten and the Harlem Renaissance," I argue that, by 1926, one of the most successful strategies by which the "younger Negro artists" Hughes champions in "The Negro Artist and the Racial Mountain" distinguish themselves from their more conservative peers and mentors, was to claim public support for Carl Van Vechten and his 1926 novel, *Nigger Heaven*. I discuss the 1926 magazine *Fire!!* in its primary significance as a vehicle for the deployment of this strategy.

21. Alain Locke, ed., *The New Negro* (New York: Atheneum, 1968), xxvii.

22. Larry Neal, *Visions of a Liberated Future: Black Arts Movement Writings* (New York, Thunder's Mouth Press, 1989), 63.

23. Addison Gayle, Jr., "Introduction" to *The Black Aesthetic*, xxi.

24. Neal, *Visions of a Liberated Future*, 78.

25. Harold Cruse, *The Crisis of the Negro Intellectual* (New York: William Morrow & Company, 1967), 38.

26. David Lionel Smith, "The Black Arts Movement and Its Critics," *American Literary History* 3: 1 (Spring 1991): 95.

26. LeRoi Jones, *Blues People* (New York: William Morrow & Company, 1963), 134.

27. Imamu Amiri Baraka, "The Need for a Cultual Base to Civil Rites & Bpower Mooments," in *Raise Race Rays Raze*, 46.

28. In his 1963 study, *Blues People*, Jones' use of the term "Negro" does not contain the politically charged meaning that it takes on in his writing after 1965, the year Malcolm X was assassinated and Jones moved uptown to begin his journey into blackness.

29. Baraka, *Raise Race Rays Raze*, 39.

30. William L. Van Deburg, *New Day in Babylon: The Black Power Movement and American Culture, 1965–1975* (Chicago: University of Chicago Press, 1992). See pages 53–55.

31. Langston Hughes, *The Big Sea* (New York: Alfred A. Knopf, 1940), 235.

32. Quoted in Arnold Rampersad, *The Life of Langston Hughes*, Vol. I, 137.

33. Quoted in Harper, *Are We Not Men?*, 195.

34. Amiri Baraka, *The Autobiography of LeRoi Jones/Amiri Baraka* (New York: Freundlich Books, 1984), 202.

35. Harper, *Are We Not Men?*, 46.

36. Smith, "The Black Arts Movement," 95.

37. Eldridge Cleaver, *Soul on Ice* (New York: Dell, 1968), 100.

38. Ibid., 101.

39. LeRoi Jones, "brief reflection on two hot shots," in *Home: Social Essays* (New York: William Morrow & Company, 1966), 116.

40. Quoted in *Thirteen Ways of Looking at a Black Man* (New York: Random House, 1997), 12.

41. Ibid., 12.

42. Cleaver, *Soul on Ice*, 100.

43. Ibid., 101.

44. Harper, *Are We Not Men?*, 73.

45. Recent scholarship by Cathy J. Cohen, Phillip Brian Harper, J. Martin Favor, Dwight McBride, and Mason Stokes, among others, explores this topic in fascinating depth. See Cathy J. Cohen, *The Boundaries of Blackness: AIDS and the Breakdown of Black Politics* (Chicago: University of Chicago Press, 1999); Dwight McBride, "Can the Queen Speak? Racial Essentialism, Sexuality, and the Problem of Authority," in *The Greatest Taboo: Homosexuality in Black Communities* (Los Angeles: Alyson Books, 2001): 24–43; and Mason Stokes, *The Color of Sex: Whiteness, Heterosexuality & the Fictions of White Supremacy* (Durham: Duke University Press, 2001).

46. Cruse, *The Crisis*, 37. The equation of the progression of black identity with the recuperation with manhood stays with us even today. Phillip Brian Harper argues that inherent in the "cultural-political reclamation supposedly represented by the widespread adoption of the term African-American" is the equation of the term with "the achievement of manhood, a good twenty-five years after the similarly significant advent of *black*." (Harper, *Are We Not Men?*, 68).

47. Douglas Sadownick, "Protest from Poet's Estate Keeps Film Out of Gay Festival" *Los Angeles Times,* July 12, 1989, part 6, p. 2.

48. Emily Bernard, "What He Did for the Race: Carl Van Vechten and the Harlem Renaissance," *Soundings* 80: 4 (Winter 1997): 531–42.

49. Faith Berry provides an excellent example of this current of suspicion that circulates in discussions about the relationship between Van Vechten and Hughes in her 1976 essay, "Did Van Vechten Make or Take Hughes' Blues?" In this essay, Berry attempts to reaffirm Hughes' status as an authentic literary forefather by belittling Van Vechten's importance to his career. *Black World* (February 1976): 22–28.

50. See Arnold Rampersad, *The Life of Langston Hughes,* Vols. I and II (New York: Oxford University Press, 1986, 1988).

51. I do not mean to suggest here that black-run institutions, like Broadside Books, for instance, did not meet with success during the Black Arts Movement. For a thorough discussion of the accomplishments of Broadside Books, see Julius E. Thompson, *Dudley Randall, Broadside Press, and the Black Arts Movement in Detroit, 1960–1995* (Jefferson, NC: McFarland & Co, 1999).

52. To his credit, Baraka (Jones) owns up to the contradictions he veritably embodied in his autobiography, *The Autobiography of LeRoi Jones/Amiri Baraka.*

53. LeRoi Jones and Larry Neal, eds., *Black Fire: An Anthology of Afro-American Writing* (New York: William Morrow & Company, 1968), xvi.

54. For a description of the Ford Foundation's role as a source of support for the Black Arts Movement, as well as a larger discussion of the continuing tensions between black art and white money, see Henry Louis Gates, Jr., "The Chitlin Circuit," *The New Yorker* (February 3, 1997): 44–55.

55. Carla Kaplan, "The Language of Crisis in Feminist Theory," *Bucknell Review* 36: 2 (1992): 68–89.

56. For examples of this continuing phenomenon, see Trey Ellis, "The New Black Aesthetic," *Callaloo* 12 (Winter 1989): 233–50. The October 10, 1994 cover of *Time* magazine featured a photograph of Bill T. Jones with the caption: "Black Renaissance: African American artists are truly free at last."

57. Langston Hughes, "House in the World," in *The Collected Poems of Langston Hughes,* ed. Arnold Rampersad and David Roessel (New York: Alfred A. Knopf, 1998), 138.

58. Toni Morrison, *Playing in the Dark: Whiteness and the Literary Imagination* (Cambridge, MA: Harvard University Press, 1992), 5.

59. Hughes, *The Big Sea,* 128.

60. Amiri Baraka, *Home: Social Essays* (New York: William Morrow & Company, 1966), 111.

JAMES SMETHURST

Lyric Stars:
Countee Cullen and Langston Hughes

Many people have considered the work of Countee Cullen and Langston Hughes to represent two antagonistic strands of Harlem Renaissance thinking about the role of the black artist, the nature of African American literature, and indeed whether something called "Negro Literature" existed. It is unquestionably true that the two poets themselves to some extent felt such an antagonism, as seen most famously in Hughes' 1926 essay "The Negro Artist and the Racial Mountain," that began with a sort of racial syllogism attributed to an unnamed Negro poet in which the statement "I want to be a poet—not a Negro poet" becomes "I would like to be white." While Hughes does not name the poet, the opening premise of this syllogism closely resembles a statement Cullen made during a 1924 interview in which he declared, "if I am going to be a poet at all, I am going to be POET and not NEGRO POET."[1]

Hughes, too, is well known as the progenitor of a new black vernacular lyric poetry, particularly the genre of blues poetry, while the statement "White folks is white" in the first line of Cullen's "Uncle Jim" represents practically the entirety of his published verse directly utilizing some version of a distinctly African American idiom. Though Cullen agreed that one could talk about poetry by Negro authors, he vigorously disputed notions of a distinct "Negro poetry," put forward not only by Hughes but also by

From *The Cambridge Companion to the Harlem Renaissance*, pp. 112–125. © Cambridge University Press 2007.

such "midwives" of the Harlem Renaissance as Alain Locke and James Weldon Johnson:

> Negro poetry, it seems to me, in the sense that we speak of Russian, French, or Chinese poetry, must emanate from some country other than this in some language other than our own. Moreover, the attempt to corral the outbursts of the ebony muse into some definite mold to which all poetry by Negroes will conform seems altogether futile and aside from the facts. This country's Negro writers may here and there turn some singular facet toward the literary sun, but in the main, since theirs is also the heritage of the English language, their work will not present any serious aberration from the poetic tendencies of their times.[2]

Yet both Hughes and Cullen were the literary descendants of the turn of the century writers, particularly Paul Laurence Dunbar, who grappled with the political, cultural, and ideological impact of the rise of Jim Crow and the final collapse of most of the institutions and ideals of Reconstruction. Like many in the New Negro Renaissance, Langston Hughes (born 1902) and Countee Cullen (born 1903) were part of the first generation of black artists and intellectuals to grow up after the final triumph of Jim Crow in the South signaled by the infamous Supreme Court decisions that legitimated "separate, but equal" (Plessy v. Ferguson in 1896) and the various devices and strategies designed to restrict the access of African Americans to the ballot (Williams v. Mississippi in 1898) despite the continued presence of the Fourteenth and Fifteenth Amendments in the Constitution.

They also matured during the second wave of Jim Crow that saw the establishment of often extraordinarily rigid patterns of residential segregation in the cities of the North and South. This process began in earnest during the first decade of the twentieth century, greatly gaining in scope with the beginning of the "Great Migration" of African Americans from the country to the city, North and South, and from the South to the North. Cullen's foster father, Frederick Asbury Cullen, began the Salem Methodist Episcopal Church in a Harlem storefront with a handful of members in 1902 as part of an effort by the downtown St. Mark's Methodist Episcopal Church to reach the growing black community of Harlem still scattered in small pockets across the neighborhood.[3] By the time Cullen was adopted in 1918, Harlem's African American residents numbered in the several tens of thousands, replacing white Harlemites who fled what they frequently described as a black "invasion" (Osofsky, *Harlem* 109). When Hughes and his mother joined his stepfather in Cleveland in 1916, they lived in a basement apartment in the emerging ghetto on the East Side. This period saw not only the black population of Cleveland swell exponentially (308 percent between 1910 and 1920), but also a dramatic increase in segregation in the city. For example, despite the rapid growth of the African American community, the number of census tracts reporting no Negro inhabitants more than doubled from seventeen to thirty-eight. During this same period, the number of Cleveland's 112 elementary schools that were all-white went from seventeen to thirty. Where, in 1910, no census tract reported a Negro population greater than 25 percent, by 1920, ten were recorded as a quarter or more Negro with two over 50 percent.[4] As Hughes later noted, the World War I period also saw a concomitant local increase in Jim Crow practices in public accommodations despite Cleveland's history as a liberal city that frequently elected socialists to office.[5] Beyond the personal histories of Cullen and Hughes, Woodrow Wilson's increasing segregation of Federal jobs, the increasing number and intensity of violent racist incidents in the North and the South, and the growth of the Ku Klux Klan into a mass organization of millions that essentially ran governments of many southern and northern cities and states, attested to the growth of Jim Crow as a national phenomenon.

In short, by the time Hughes was in Central High School in Cleveland and Cullen in DeWitt Clinton High School in New York, Jim Crow was in many respects intensifying and reaching North in ways that went beyond the longstanding patterns of discrimination in employment, housing, education, and so on. Both, especially Hughes, credited the teachers and students at their predominately white high schools with doing much to introduce them to a larger artistic and intellectual life beyond the increasingly rigid boundaries of the ghetto. Yet even in Hughes' 1940 account of his days at Central High, there is a sense that it was a short moment of a school in transition. Within ten years of Hughes' graduation, he notes, only 3 percent of Central High's student body was white (*Big Sea* 29–30).

Given their coming of age during this second wave of Jim Crow, it is not surprising that both Hughes and Cullen looked back to Paul Laurence Dunbar as a crucial literary ancestor. Hughes in particular felt an early attachment to Dunbar's poetry, claiming that, other than Longfellow's *Hiawatha*, it was the only verse he liked as a young child (*Big Sea* 26). He also recalled that in his first serious efforts as a poet in high school, his two literary models were Carl Sandburg and Dunbar (*Big Sea* 28–9). As a mature poet, Hughes continued to acknowledge the impact of Dunbar on his work (and on the readers of his work, especially black readers), as in the collection *The Black Mother and Other Dramatic Recitations* (1931), a self-published chapbook aimed at the primarily African American audiences of his early reading tours in the South that declared the pieces to be in the tradition of Dunbar's vernacular work.

Far less is reliably known about Cullen's early life, which was apparently spent largely in Louisville, Kentucky. Still, it is clear that Cullen, too, saw Dunbar as a model. In part, the attachment of Cullen (and Hughes) to Dunbar stemmed from what Cullen called "his uniquity as the first Negro to attain to and maintain a distinguished place among American poets, a place fairly merited by the most acceptable standards of criticism" (Cullen, "Foreword" x–xi).

Dunbar's influence on Cullen and Hughes also derived from his "uniquity" as the best-known and perhaps the most powerful literary articulator of an African American dualism in the early Jim Crow era. African American dualism in its various expressions revolved around the notion that there were huge (and in many respects increasing) political, legal, social, cultural, and psychological contradictions between "Negro" and "American," so that the term "Negro American" might seem like an oxymoron. Like others in his age cohort, such as W. E. B. Du Bois and James Weldon Johnson, Dunbar was a product of a paradoxical time. He grew up during Reconstruction, came into young adulthood with the growth of Jim Crow, and achieved artistic success as the Supreme Court put its imprimatur on "separate, but equal." This bifurcated legal and political status was mirrored by a similarly double and ambivalent position in the simultaneous emergence of a relatively distinct African American transregional popular culture and of the linked and "mainstream" popular culture fueled significantly by the "coon song" and the related ragtime craze (in which Dunbar participated as a librettist).

The problem of dualism, whether in the Du Boisian semi-psychological sense of two more or less unintegrated consciousnesses existing simultaneously in one body or in a more strictly legalistic sense of post-Reconstruction Jim Crow segregation, is the problem of being a citizen and yet not a citizen (and, by extension, of being legally human and not quite human) in an increasingly urbanized, industrialized, and imperial United States. How does one respond? By proving oneself to be worthy or by withdrawing? Or through a sort of integration through self-determination in which African Americans force white people to recognize them as full citizens through political, educational, economic, and cultural self-development? And if one tries to represent the distinctly African (American) portion of this divided identity, what might that be? How does one represent and/or re-create black culture without being contaminated by the stereotypes of minstrelsy and plantation literature, by popular and so-called "high" culture appropriation or misappropriation? How does one deal with the doubleness of popular culture as seen in the cakewalk, ragtime, and the ambivalence of African American minstrelsy and "coon songs"?

Dunbar's engagement of these questions in "We Wear the Mask" is the most influential literary expression of African American dualism after *The*

Souls of Black Folk. With the possible exception of "Sympathy" (and its famous dualistic line "I know why the caged bird sings!"), "We Wear the Mask" is almost certainly Dunbar's best-known and most anthologized poem today. Formally, it is a fairly straightforward rondeau—an old French form that enjoyed a vogue in English poetry at the end of the nineteenth century. The most arresting and most remembered aspect of the poem is, of course, Dunbar's metaphor of the mask. It may seem obvious, but, appropriately enough, this metaphor (and its relation to the logic of the poem) is more complicated than it might first appear. After all, the speaker of the poem identifies with a "we" who are compelled to mask "our" true identities and true emotions from "the world." Yet there is a sort of game of doubling in this revelation of concealment. The speaker weirdly stands outside him- or herself, describing the existence and something of the nature of "the mask" that he or she as part of the "we" wears. On the other hand, the speaker contradictorily proclaims that "the world" never really sees "us," only the disguise "we" put on. This confession would seem to involve a lowering of the mask—unless the revelation about the mask is a mask.

In other words, there is an endless regress in which the possibility of a double-consciousness is asserted, but without the comfort of any stable features or boundaries. This contradiction between concealment and revelation resembles that of Du Bois' notion of "the veil" and a "double-consciousness" that prevents or inhibits genuine African American self-reflection and self-consciousness, while provoking endless introspection about the nature of the self and identity. The metaphor of masking makes obvious the act of concealment and its coerced motivation, underpinning militant and historically pointed social criticism, suggesting a new way of reading African American minstrelsy and other forms of African American popular culture as well as Dunbar's own work. The metaphor of the mask invites (or challenges) the reader to change the way she or he reads apparently conventional dialect poems.

Also, can Dunbar the "high" poet exist without Dunbar the "dialect" or "popular" poet? If the so-called "low" or popular work did not exist, wouldn't the "high" poetry be less powerful, less well-defined? And, of course, without the "high" poetry and the split proposed between "real" and "mask," between "art" and box office rooted in a representation and/or re-creation of the African American voice, wouldn't the dialect poetry seem far shallower and much more easily conflated with the plantation tradition and the minstrel tradition in some uncomplicated way? In other words, "high" and "low," "standard" literary and "dialect," are inextricably linked and opposed. This strategy allowed Dunbar both to affirm himself as a poet and to re-create the black speaking subject on the page in a way that acknowledged the problems popular culture posed for the representation of the African American folk subject, while at least partially circumventing those problems. This opposition remained a potent paradigm for the New Negro era with its concern for representing "authentically" the racial (or national) self without being imprisoned by the implicitly or explicitly racist expectations of white readers, actual or potential, or of variously accommodationist black readers.

One trend within Harlem Renaissance poetry is a continuation of the radical democratic impulse that can be traced back to Phillis Wheatley. As Countee Cullen pointed out when questioned about his affinity for Keats:

> She turns to one of my poems, and indicts me for my love of Keats, for concerning myself with names like Endymion and Lancelot and Jupiter. It is on the tip of my tongue to ask why Keats himself should have concerned himself with themes like Endymion and Hyperion.[6]

Cullen's claim about his relationship to Greek myth was that it was exactly the same as Keats', and his relationship to Keats was exactly the same as that of white Americans: attachments formed through reading and education, not through biogenetic transmission. So what, he infers even if he is too polite to ask, gives a "white" American poet any more claim on Keats than Cullen, other than some pseudo-biological notions of race and pseudo-historical ideas of Europe and Africa? Cullen's implicit question resembles Du Bois' queries to white Americans in the final chapter of *The Souls of Black Folk*: "Your country? How came it yours?"[7] In short, he asserts full cultural citizenship, contesting pseudo-biological racist notions of artistic propriety and property. In the face of the intensification and extension of Jim Crow during Cullen's youth, this assertion of a larger cultural citizenship rests on a democratic spirit that transcends nation. At the same time that Cullen stakes a claim to citizenship in the republic of letters, he does not negate his particular position as a gay black man in the Jim Crow United States in which to be an active homosexual is to commit a crime for which one could be, and often was, jailed.

Dunbar's split between high and low allows Cullen to assert his cultural citizenship while addressing his particular subjectivity as he saw it. In his poetry Cullen assumed the split between high and low proposed by Dunbar (and other expressions of turn of the century African American dualism) and then rose above it by eliminating the low—at least so far as diction and syntax goes. Again and again, one finds in Cullen's poetry the idea of a divided self, and a divided society, where such explicit categories of identity as black and white, Negro and poet, pagan and Christian, and nature and civilization coexist and yet contradict or conflict with each other.

The depiction of warring selves threatening to tear asunder the black speaker clearly recalls Du Bois' *The Souls of Black Folk*. However, the notion that this conflict is a permanent condition of the speaker without even the possibility of resolution that Du Bois holds out resembles even more closely the split posed in Dunbar's poems. Because these warring selves seem in permanent conflict with each other without any likelihood (or even desirability) of lasting victory by one side or another, they are strangely linked through the mind, soul, and body of the poet so that they become at times indistinct or doubles of each other, yet always retaining at least a trace of conflict or division. This blurring and doubling is echoed by the androgynous and racially ambiguous figures of Charles Cullen (no relation to the poet) that illustrate Countee Cullen's collections *The Black Christ and Other Poems* (1929) and *Copper Sun* (1927) and the long poem *The Ballad of a Brown Girl* (1927).

As many have observed, much of Cullen's love poetry is not clearly marked by racial signs. However, it is worth pointing out that most of Cullen's first-person love lyrics not only lack racial markers but are unmarked as to gender as well. In short, these poems, often filled with loss, confusion, regret, and/or resentment, allow space for almost any sort of romantic pairing possible. When seen within the frame of Charles Cullen's illustrations, which both foreground and collapse together categories of race and gender, these poems are far from "universal" in some abstract sense, but instead quite personal and quite specific with regard to the condition of a gay black man in the early twentieth century.

For example, Cullen's best-known poem, "Heritage," is still seen in terms of various oppositions of paganism versus Christianity, nature versus civilization, Africa versus Europe, passion versus reason, and so on, resembling the various sorts of primitivism popular among Cullen's black and white contemporaries. There was of course a long-standing dichotomy between the secular and the sacred—as in the opposition of the blues and various sorts of sacred music—in African American culture which would give this poem a particular resonance for a black audience. And, obviously, the various dichotomies of the spirit and the flesh, nature and civilization, etc. have a long history in the so-called western world in general and the United States in particular.

Nonetheless, read in these ways, it is still hard not to think that the poet is more than a little overwrought and that there is an emotional discrepancy between the apparent subject of the poem and the poem's anguished rhetoric of a latent criminal against God and society who can just barely, for the moment, repress his evil desires. As with Cullen's "Yet Do I Marvel," which poses "poet" against "black," the reader is forced to ask whether there is such a dichotomy between blackness, as it were, and Christianity, between the laws of God and those of African American nature, between a generalized passion associated with Africa and reason. Similarly, the reader of "Yet Do I Marvel" might wonder why it is so marvelous in the sense of an awful strangeness that God should "make a poet black, and bid him sing." Yet it is also clear that some genuine and powerful emotions are at work in these poems' strange oscillations between repulsion and attraction, love and self-loathing—as they are in "Tableau," "Uncle Jim," and even "The Colored Blues Singer."

One clue the reader who is familiar with the literary scene of Harlem in the 1920s receives as to how to interpret these poems is the dedication of "Heritage" to Harold Jackman. Whatever Cullen's precise relationship to Jackman, it was well known during Cullen's lifetime that sexual attraction was an important part of their friendship. One might add here that the possibility that Cullen's foster father, a Methodist minister who was the subject of much speculation about his sexuality, was gay might also provide a new view of what "heritage" might mean, particularly with respect to the dichotomy of Christianity and homosexuality.[8]

If read within a black homosexual context, "Heritage" becomes paradigmatic of many of Cullen's poems. "Heritage" begins in a mythic landscape in which there is no contradiction between the speaker's sexuality and the demands of society and of God. Then there is a fall into a historical present in which the speaker's sexuality is in conflict with the society which the speaker inhabits and the God in whom the speaker believes. Again, this conflict, the subject's sense of alienation from a sexual "mainstream," is displaced onto a discourse of a sexualized racial difference. Finally, there is a realization that there will be no resolution to this contradiction in this world and that this sexuality can be suppressed or covert, but it cannot be either erased or overtly practiced—at least as far as the poem's speaker is concerned.

Of course, this could be read within a heterosexual context. But such a reading removes the immediacy and the power of the poem. Cullen was gay. He also was a Christian. While today there may be relatively orthodox Christian denominations which no longer consider homosexuality a terrible sin, this was not the case in Cullen's lifetime. Cullen, like another Christian gay poet, W. H. Auden, was obviously extremely conflicted about the demands of his religious beliefs and those of his sexuality. Similarly Cullen was an extremely social man in many respects. Though it is perhaps unfair to claim, as a number of critics do, that Cullen was too enamored of "bourgeois" culture in any simple manner—his endorsement of the Communist Party Presidential and Vice-Presidential candidates in 1932 would seem to undercut this notion—it is clear that "society," particularly of the black community where he lived, wrote, and taught (and where his foster father was a prominent minister), was important to him. Again, it is worth making the obvious point that homosexuality was outlawed and homosexuals were frequently prosecuted for their "crimes" in the 1920s and 1930s. There is obviously a huge difference between whispered comments, however deeply believed by the whisperers, and an open declaration of homosexuality. Certainly, Cullen's career in the New York public schools, where he began teaching in 1932, would have been impossible if he had made such a declaration. In short, "Heritage" is a poem of extreme personal anguish over a very specific aspect of the poet's nature that is in a real conflict with the poet's conscience and society and cannot be approached directly, but instead utilizes the language and tropes of dualism for expression.

Even more than Cullen, Hughes, like Dunbar, embodied a dualistic split within his early poetry, formally as well as thematically. However, both sides of this split could be seen as a sort of nationalism that is at odds with the internationalism of Cullen and Dunbar—though one might see in this nationalism a sort of challenge to the United States resembling that of Dunbar. Of course, one has to qualify the notion of Hughes' nationalism a bit. After all, even among the polyglot, peripatetic, and cosmopolitan artists and intellectuals of the Harlem Renaissance, Hughes stood out. His travels as an artist, activist, and merchant sailor, his friendship with artists and intellectuals around the world (especially those of Africa and its Diaspora), and his translations of such writers as Nicolás Guillén, Federico Garcia Lorca, Jacques Roumain, and Vladimir Mayakovsky (many for the first time in the United States) were exceptional. Nonetheless, the sort of nationalist split indicated by his early adoption of Sandburg and Dunbar as his literary models persisted in his work throughout the Harlem Renaissance—and, in some important respects, beyond.

Hughes' Sandburgian poems consist of free-verse catalogs, such as "The Negro Speaks of Rivers" and "Negro," and short imagistic portraits of urban life and scenes from Hughes' travels in the Americas, Europe, and Africa, such as "Mexican Market Woman" and "Young Singer." While Hughes uses an irregular end-rhyme in these poems more often than Sandburg, his diction shares with Sandburg's a plain, almost colloquial, but not conversational character. This diction is not marked particularly as African American, but is still like that of Sandburg (and Walt Whitman) a generic "American" language posed against a "high" literary diction like that of Cullen's that is more or less British in its derivation and alleged sensibility. While not as clearly "Red" as much of his writing in the 1930s, Hughes' 1920s verse drawing on the work of Sandburg prefigures the more self-consciously "proletarian" diction and themes of Hughes' "revolutionary" poetry during the Depression. The common "American" language of Hughes' Sandburgian poems in the 1920s evolves into Hughes' working-class "American" diction of the early 1930s. Interestingly, these Sandburgian poems, especially the longer free-verse catalogs, are often vehicles for Hughes' deepest musings on the nature of African American identity and its historical, cultural, and spiritual connection to Africa.

Hughes' early African American vernacular poetry is clearly indebted to the dialect poetry of Dunbar. As in Dunbar's dialect poems, Hughes' vernacular pieces make plain their identity as speech, generally either a folk monologue or song. It is true that Hughes' vernacular poems generally stake a claim to a certain sort of authenticity that is undercut in Dunbar's work where outside claims for the peculiar verisimilitude of the dialect poetry, whether by William Dean Howells or the Dodd, Mead Publishing Company, were posed against tropes of masking, deformity, and imprisonment. However, Dunbar's stance is closer to that of Hughes than might be seen at first glance.

One way in which Hughes attempted to reclaim vernacular poetry from the limitations of minstrelsy, "coon songs," and the plantation school of dialect literature during the Harlem Renaissance was to anchor it in identifiably black "folk" and popular forms, especially the blues, gospel music, jazz, and various sorts of sacred and secular rhetoric. Sometimes, as in his famous "The Weary Blues," a work from the 1926 collection of the same name that is often taken to be the beginning of the sub-genre of "blues poetry," the black folk voice of a blues singer is framed by the slightly colloquial, but more or less "standard" English of a somewhat alienated African American intellectual. One way in which the song of the blues singer is protected from confusion with popular culture misappropriations is through the eye- and ear-witness of the speaker of the poem, guaranteeing the authenticity of the performance:

> Droning a drowsy syncopated tune,
> Rocking back and forth to a mellow croon,
>   I heard a Negro play
> Down on Lenox Avenue the other night. (*Collected* 51)

Interestingly, the speaker of the poem is both an insider and an outsider, one who has a special affinity for the singer and his music and yet is somewhat distant from the singer at the beginning of the poem. One might say that the tension set up by this sort of alienation from the folk that an implicit authorial consciousness seeks to overcome marks the entire collection. However, the speaker enters into the music and is by the end of the poem so bound up with the bluesman that the speaker is inside the singer's bedroom (and head) after the show is over:

> The singer stopped playing and went to bed
> While the Weary Blues echoed through his head.
>   (*Collected* 51)

The authenticity of the scene of the re-creation of the folk voice is guaranteed both by the speaker's original distance allowing a sort of objective account and by the speaker's final identification with the singer demonstrating a deeper understanding of the folk spirit contained in (really produced by) the music, as well as a potential if not altogether happy healing of the split consciousness of the speaker.

This authenticity is also guaranteed by the form, the rhythmic stresses, the rhyme scheme, and the tropes of the blues itself, a musical genre associated with African Americans that was, by the 1920s and the enormous growth of the recording industry, widely recognizable throughout the United States (and beyond). While the actual rhyme schemes, lineation, and patterns of rhythmic stresses of the early blues varied, Hughes interpolated an adaptation of the common AAB blues verse into the second strophe. In this variation of the blues stanza, the first line is repeated in the second line (sometimes, as in "The Weary Blues," with a slight difference or "worrying"), followed by a different, but rhyming, concluding line. Generally, there would be a slight pause or caesura in the middle of these lines. Hughes broke the lines in two at the caesura so that his typical blues poetry stanza was six lines instead of three. This adapted version of the AAB stanza became the standard for blues verse in American poetry throughout the twentieth century. Hughes, and later such poets as Sterling Brown and Waring Cuney, saw in this form a key building block for a distinctly African American lyric poetry that utilized the blues much as "high" poetry in Western Europe had adapted such song forms as the sonnet, the ballad, the rondeau, and the villanelle. In this, Hughes echoed, anticipated, and influenced the sense of much modernist poetry in the United States, that, as Ezra Pound argued in his 1934 *ABC of Reading*, "music begins to atrophy when it departs too far from the dance; that poetry begins to atrophy when it gets too far from music."[9]

Nonetheless, as in the work of Dunbar, there remains a split between authentic uses of African American folk and popular culture and minstrelized misappropriations and misreadings of black culture. In Hughes' vision, this distinction rests on a dialectical relationship between tradition and innovation. One might say that in Hughes' view innovation is one of the marks of the authentic African American popular culture. In "Negro Dancers," for example, a black dancer announces that "Me an' ma baby's / Got two mo' ways, / Two mo' ways to do de Charleston!" (*Collected* 44). It is this innovation that, both the dancer and the speaker of the poem suggest, distinguishes the true African American expressive spirit from white imitation and misappropriation. The notion of the crucial and inextricable relationship between cutting-edge black creativity and a cultural continuum reaching from the urban ghetto through the rural South to, in a more distant and attenuated manner, Africa, remained a centerpiece of Hughes' poetry for the rest of his career.

Interestingly, Hughes' second collection of poetry, *Fine Clothes to the Jew* (1927), largely finesses the question of the troubled relationship between the black artist and the folk through a composite portrait of the black working class and the floating world of rounders, grifters, prostitutes, and gamblers, of the urban African American communities. Even more than in *The Weary Blues*, Hughes negotiates the problems presented by popular-culture and high-culture representations of the black poor by embedding their stories and their voices in a wide variety of "authentic" black forms, especially the blues, but also gospel songs, ballads, street calls, church testifying, overheard conversations, and so on.

Still, the notion of a divide both within the black intellectual-artist and between the black intellectual artist and the folk remained a theme in Hughes' poetry into the 1930s. As Hughes moved more and more into the cultural and political world of the communist left with the deepening of the Great Depression, however, the divided speaker is stirred into a communion with the folk, now something more like the working class, not so much through the power of African American culture, but through a forced contact with reality, or what the communists used to like to call life itself. For example, in the final poem of the 1931 collection *Dear Lovely Death*, "Aesthete in Harlem," the long and peripatetic search of a black artist for "Life" is finally and unexpectedly realized when the "aesthete" finds "Life" "stepping on my feet" on a Harlem street (*Collected* 128). It might be added, however, that Hughes' poetry in the early 1930s remained in many respects divided into three strands: a more directly Dunbarian poetry of racial uplift primarily aimed at the black audiences he encountered on the reading tours to African American schools, churches, reading circles, and so on, that he began during this period; a less racially inflected, class-based revolutionary poetry aimed at a radical audience who read *New Masses, The Harlem Liberator, The Anvil,* and other journals of the left and the proletarian literature movement; and a more literary sort of verse aimed at readers of modern literature. Of course, these categories overlapped to a certain extent. Hughes would often slip one of his revolutionary poems into his readings before black audiences on his tours. His poetry in left journals often addressed racial and colonial oppression, placing those issues (as did the Communist Party and the Comintern) as central concerns of the national and international class struggle. Sometimes, perhaps most notably in his poetic "jazz play" *Scottsboro Limited* where he attempted to openly combine elements of African American expressive culture with the "mass chant" form of the communist workers theater movement, Hughes gave his revolutionary work a more distinctly "Negro" inflection. Still, it was not really until the Popular Front era in the second half of the 1930s that Hughes successfully integrated the different strands of his poetry.

The sense of a split, of two warring selves within a single body, is even more pronounced in Hughes' early fiction, showing a persistent concern with (and insecurity about) the fluidity of racial, sexual, and class identity. His earliest adult stories published in the late 1920s, based on his experience as a merchant sailor and much influenced by D. H. Lawrence's modernist fiction of class, gender, and sexual conflict and confusion in Britain, are full of the contradictions of an African American narrator, whose predicament is not that Africa is, to quote the 1930 poem "Afro-American Fragment," "so long, so far away," but that it is right at hand. Or rather the narrator suffers the existential dilemma of arriving in West Africa with a multinational crew of "Greeks, West Indian Negroes, Irish, Portuguese, and, Americans" and finding it "so long, so far away" and frighteningly, if often movingly present at the same time. The indigenous peoples of Africa consider him an outsider, and frequently identify him with his "white" and "brown" shipmates. Of course, the confusion that the narrator experiences is not completely unique, as his fellow sailors from the United States, black and white, attempt to reconfigure "American" racial, gender, and sexual practices for an African context as white sailors "defend the honor" of African prostitutes assaulted by fellow seamen even as the narration is suffused with an understated outrage about intersecting racism, sexual exploitation, colonial oppression, and class conflict that leaves him feeling as both insider and outsider simultaneously. One finds something of this conflict in Hughes' first novel, the coming of age story *Not Without Laughter* (1930). There the protagonist Sandy moves between the women of his radically divided family, consisting of his grandmother (the sort of folk Negro Mother figure that Hughes most famously invoked in the poem "From Mother to Son"), his mother (a loving, but somewhat dim and self-absorbed domestic worker married to a usually absent and somewhat layabout blues singer, Sandy's father Jimboy), his aunt Tempy (a stiff, middle-class "race woman" who despises the culture of the black folk), and his Aunt Harriet (a disreputable classic blues singer who nonetheless provides the money for Sandy to continue his education).

As different as the works of Hughes and Cullen appear in many respects, then, both address the questions of political and cultural citizenship and filiations posed by turn of the century writers, particularly Dunbar, adopting and adapting in their different ways the dualistic models of those writers as the United States became increasingly segregated. Cullen's work as a poet substantially decreased after the early 1930s, but his perceived stance as literary internationalist, if not always his actual poetry, remained powerful, both in the production of black poetry and in the understanding of the Harlem

Renaissance, as critics saw Cullen emblemizing one pole of the movement. These models also left a large mark on the literary output of Hughes throughout the rest of his long career as he became arguably the most widely accomplished American writer, working in poetry, short and long fiction, children's literature, drama, musical theater, autobiography, journalism, translation, and combinations of genres difficult to classify, considerably influencing the work of black writers into the twenty-first century.

Notes

1. Margaret Sperry, "Countee P. Cullen, Negro Boy Poet, Tells His Story," *Brooklyn Daily Eagle*, February 10, 1924.

2. Countee Cullen, Foreword to *Caroling Dusk: An Anthology of Verse by Negro Poets*, ed. Countee Cullen (New York: Harper and Brothers, 1927), p. xi.

3. Gilbert Osofsky, *Harlem: The Making of a Ghetto* (New York: Harper and Row, 1966), pp. 84–5.

4. Kenneth L. Kusmer, *A Ghetto Takes Shape: Black Cleveland, 1870–1930* (Urbana: University of Illinois Press, 1976), pp. 158–64.

5. Langston Hughes, *The Big Sea* (1940; New York: Thunder's Mouth Press, 1986), p. 51.

6. Countee Cullen, *My Soul's High Song: The Collected Writings of Countee Cullen* (New York: Anchor Books, 1991), p. 568.

7. W. E. B. Du Bois, *The Souls of Black Folk*, ed. David W. Blight and Robert Gooding-Williams (1903; New York: Bedford Books, 1997) p. 190.

8. George Chauncy, *Gay New York: Gender, Urban Culture, and the Makings of the Gay Male World, 1890–1940* (New York: Basic Books, 1991), pp. 264–5.

9. Ezra Pound, *The ABC of Reading* (1934; New York: New Directions, 1960), p. 14.

APRIL C.E. LANGLEY

What a Difference a "Way" Makes: Wheatley's Ways of Knowing

Now *Manto* comes, endu'd with mighty skill,
The past to explore, the future to reveal.
　　　　—Phillis Wheatley, "Niobe" ll. 37–38

The epigraph above is illustrative of early African American literature's reconfiguration of literary space into a figurative junction between African and Western ways of knowing. Wheatley, a displaced Senegalese griotte, an eighteenth-century American slave-poet laureate, and a foremother of African American literature, was born in Senegal in (approximately) 1753 and brought to Boston in 1761 via the slave ship *Phillis*, after which she was named. The sickly African girl, who arrived with little more than a cloth to cover her small shivering frame, had "in sixteen months time" attained satisfactory proficiency in the English language, Greek mythology, Greek and Roman history, English poetry, and Latin.[1] Juxtaposing the exploration of the past alongside the revelation of the future, poet Wheatley imagines herself and the seer-poet Manto as simultaneously occupying the traditions of classical Western mythology and West African praise singers. In classical Western (Roman and Greek) mythology, Manto is known primarily as seer or prophet, a priestess, and a poet (rivaling Homer). Therefore, extending Thomas Hale's definition of griot/griotte to include such functions

From *The Black Aesthetic Unbound: Theorizing the Dilemma of Eighteenth-Century African American Literature*, pp. 57–95, 170–174. © 2008 by the Ohio State University.

as "genealogist, historian, adviser, spokesperson . . . mediator, interpreter . . . witness, praise-singer . . . [and] participant in a variety of ceremonies" (57), I interpret Manto as a griotte. Notably, beyond her primary role as seer, Manto also functions as ceremonial participant and praise singer in Latona's worship, as she exhorts "the Theban maids" to pay tribute to the goddess. Further, as ceremonial participant, Manto "brings people together with [her] speech" (49), and, as praise singer, Manto "announce[s] not simply of [Latona's] qualities but also [the Thebans'] duties and responsibilities" (48). I take a similar position with regard to the poet Wheatley, whose revision of the Niobe myth, from Book VI of Ovid's *Metamorphoses*,[2] demonstrates her functioning as poet/griotte with comparable and diverse roles. Illustrative of her operating within this West African griot tradition, Wheatley endeavors (through "Niobe") to mediate, celebrate, inspire, translate, and foreshadow the national and natural distress engendered by slavery, indenture, and other oppression in an era of American independence. For, just as Manto is endowed with "eyes [that] could see what was to come," Wheatley is bequeathed a history of experiences of what had been. Manto's prophecy, like Wheatley's poetry, disseminates knowledge about the past and future even as it envisions alternative possibilities within the present historical moment.

Wheatley highlights the dilemma involved in attempting to rewrite both the spiritual and political histories upon which enslaved and nominally free African-descended people, especially African-descended women, have been constructed. The poet engages this dilemma through her multiple ways of knowing—African, American, and Afro-British American. Demonstrating her intellect and poetic genius as well as her political savvy, Wheatley creatively and purposefully interposes African and British-American experiences to reveal the shape and substance of an eighteenth-century Afro-British American aesthetic.

In "Subjection and Prophecy in Phillis Wheatley's Verse Paraphrases of Scripture," William J. Scheick argues that "Wheatley's dual exposure to theological and secular applications of Holy Writ accounts for the compatibility of her religious and her political writings . . . [a] double exposure [which] encouraged her to relate evangelical Protestantism to both Revolutionary patriotism and romance neoclassicism" (123). He maintains that "Wheatley's deliberate application of biblical matter in her verse often registers underground observations about slavery, observations that she evidently believes are supported by the Bible" (124). Scheick proposes that David became a surrogate for Wheatley because of his "ruddy skin" and ascension from servitude, that she may have gleaned knowledge about biblical passages from "popular interpretations" such as Matthew Henry's commentaries, and that in her "vicariously . . . experienced . . . reenactment[s]" (124), Wheatley evinces a "displacement of anger toward [slavery and slaveholders]" (125). These observations provide valuable insights into the poet's subversive employment of biblical paraphrase. John C. Shields adds that in "combining Christian and classical elements, Wheatley [not only] falls within a common tradition," but she also (more importantly) "casts her own practice of such syncretism into her own mode" ("Phillis Wheatley's Use of Classicism," 102). Importantly, Shields attributes this unique "third theological element . . . hierophantic solar worship" (103) to her African origins. Scholar Marsha Watson maintains that the "fusion of pagan and Christian myths in Wheatley's poetry . . . suggests something more complicated . . . Wheatley['s] attempts to rewrite the contemporaneous, received 'wisdom' about her people" (121). The scrupulous attention (of the aforementioned scholars) to the "polycultural"[3] voices in Wheatley's classic works suggests valuable considerations for interpreting "Niobe" as a paraphrase of at least one (Hagar) if not more (Eve, Mary, etc.) biblical stories.

In this chapter I will argue that Wheatley applies what might be termed a *syncretic Senegalese poetics* to her reinterpretations of two concurrently revered and despised mythologized figures of women—Niobe and Hagar. Moreover, I maintain that through Wheatley's use of Afro-British American ways—grounded in culturally specific African knowledge—she is able to travel through and unpack thousands of years of African women's history within an African frame of reference. And, in the process, she suspends time itself. By "suspend" I do not mean to suggest that Wheatley's recovery of mythological and mythologized figures denotes some static recovery of Africa and African women. Rather, I use this term to suggest at least one way in which Wheatley's use of time might be viewed from the perspective of West African measurements of historical time. Wheatley's recovery of Africa is exemplified in the tradition of the Sankofa-Bird, or bird of passage, which constantly moves forward to the future even as it continually looks behind to its past. Not only does this image of Sankofa echo themes of life and death seen throughout the poet's work, but this West African way of viewing time also alludes to the way in which the past is continually brought forward into the present and continued into the future. Further, she signifies the present condition of African-descended people who appear ghostlike to hang above, dangle, or swing backward and forward between worlds fraught with irresolvable dilemmas. In this context, time is both a transcendent and concrete measure of progression and development—numinous and temporal, fluid and liminal. Thus, when I suggest that Wheatley suspends time, I intend to point up the prophetic power of her poetry to simultaneously move beyond (by looking back to the present and forward to the future) and yet capture the present time. She captures time in this way for the valuable lessons it can teach and because such a way of presenting time permits the poet to more strikingly convey her messages and its meaning to her audiences. Importantly, Wheatley invokes parallel historical moments of "distress" from a mythic past to tackle critical concerns in the present. As poet, griotte, seer, and ancestor, Wheatley recovers mythological figures of women, refiguring a history that makes a difference for the very real women they were meant to symbolize, and—equally important—the societies that attempted to hold them and their voices hostage.

Part of Wheatley's unbinding of Afro-British American women's history from its British-American internment is done through her engagement with the dilemmas that American freedom poses for African descended peoples. Specifically, "Niobe" illustrates her intervention into a newly forming American space, a complex space compounded by multiple discourses of motherhood, gender, lineage, race, and class. To further complicate, and thereby necessarily trouble, this space, Wheatley speaks from a suspended and imagined but nonetheless real position as an American citizen. It is from this position that she depicts her own metamorphosis from victimhood to survivorhood and then to autonomous selfhood. I invoke Bassard's model of survival here as I consider "the matrix of gender and culture in which this discourse of race and racializations occurs" (33).

Suspended thus, above and safely beyond the slave ship and the Middle Passage, Wheatley attempts to unwrite one "discourse of difference" (43) while rewriting another. She engages the dilemma of unwriting herself as a black American slave, and rewriting herself as an Afro-British American citizen. As in many of her other works,[4] the black Christian Wheatley challenges racially motivated views of religious truths and the distortions of biblically based myths upon which American nationhood is established. "Niobe" represents a challenge to the paradoxes she embodies—race, gender, religion, and nation.

Consequently, to re-member "Niobe," Wheatley draws upon a very personal and particular knowledge of violence and oppression. As a young slave girl, she had survived the rupture of kinship and endured the violence of the Middle Passage firsthand. As both a slave and an Afro-British subject, Wheatley complicates American national identity and subjectivity by interrogating the extent to which this new nation[5] and its citizens could truly be considered independent. In fact, with white women accepted only marginally as citizens, and African slaves, both male and female, completely excluded from citizenship, America as a nation could not morally claim true independence. In response to this paradox, Wheatley presents an autobiographical text that speaks both to the independent and dependent aspects of eighteenth-century America. As in many of her other works, the black Christian Wheatley challenges the racially motivated view of religious truths and the distortions of biblically based myths upon which American nationhood was established.

Against such distortions of Africa as a static or impermeable space of "dark abodes"—literally and figuratively—Wheatley's invention of Africa is grounded in an understanding of Africa as a term that signifies and reconstructs as it defines.[6] Rather than assuming an essentializing or totalizing representation, Wheatley assumes, as do many eighteenth-century Afro-British Americans, that whatever is African is also Afro-British and Afro-American. As a result, Wheatley weaves out of "Niobe" an integrative and inclusive myth of early American origins, using not only Western ontologies and epistemologies but fragmented African ones as well. In the same way that traditional etiological myths recapture and recover discrete British origins, Wheatley's "Niobe" reimagines synthesized African origins. More importantly, Wheatley reinvents Africa as a necessary stage in re-membering and resituating herself within the newly imaginable independent America. Countering the delimiting and dysfunctional assumptions embedded in "interpretation[s] . . . based on western unilineal perception[s] [of] African woman as [inescapably and perpetually] oppressed from all social positions" (Kalu, "Those," 81), Wheatley reimagines motherhood, womanhood, humanity, and her own subjectivity within an African-derived context that interpolates her as an "active participant in all aspects of . . . existence" (82). This way of interpreting and relating to herself and her experiences shows Wheatley's awareness of the universal and multidimensional roles that African women play in the development of society. Scholars such as V. Y. Mudimbe and Kwame Anthony Appiah have suggested the limits of African self-invention. Mudimbe exposes the flaws inherent in systems of African-centered "models of analysis explicitly or implicitly, knowingly or unknowingly" that not only "depend on Western epistemological order" but also on the tendency of "Africanists . . . to separate the 'real' African from the westernized African . . . rely[ing] strictly on ['real' Africa]" (x–xi) as the ultimate source of African knowledge. This troubling of the very foundations upon which knowledge by and about Africans has been invented exposes underlying systems of Western-derived knowledge which effectively silences African voices. More pertinent to my own study in this book is how such theorizing about the dilemma, critical frameworks of representation and analysis, supports my argument about the need to reconnect and reorder (or in Mudimbe's terms "recolonize") the conditions under which we locate black aesthetics and meaning in eighteenth-century Afro-British American literature. Following Mudimbe, I maintain that recovering history within African frameworks derived from

"real" and "westernized" African ways of knowing not only reveals how
Africa was reinvented by these early black writers, whose texts created new
epistemological systems, but also implicates contemporary scholars (including myself) in yet another type of invention of Africa. Appiah broaches the
dilemma of the invention in Africa: "[W]hat, given all the diversity of the
precolonial histories of the peoples of Africa, and all the complexity of colonial experiences, does it mean to say that someone is African?" (25). Unlike
Mudimbe or myself in his critique of African essentialism (the invention
of a static monolithic Africa and African structures), Appiah dismisses the
viability of African structures of meaning as interpretive lenses for reading
early black literature. Nevertheless, Appiah's rejection of topologies of nativ-
ism that marginalize the diversity out of which African texts are generated
is a valid one. Moreover, Appiah's concerns about the way in which such
topologies overstate and misstate the audience to which African writing is
addressed points to the shared dilemma faced by the earliest African writers
and their modern descendants. For it is this same kind of essentialism which
displaced eighteenth-century Afro-British American writers from their
African, British, and American mournings/moorings. Ultimately, I concur
with Anthonia Kalu, who recognizes the cultural significance of the productive invention of Africa, which in turn enables rereadings like "Niobe."
Namely, I extend Kalu's "understanding [of] the complementary relationship between ancestral and Africanized western knowledge bases [that] also
facilitates a new reading of the African writer's efforts to synthesize a tran-
sitional culture" ("Traditional," 37).

Kalu's analysis applies to several other issues related to the problematic
relationship between American independence and Afro-British American
identity. Hence, Wheatley's "Niobe" can be interpreted as an attempt to
grapple with this dilemma. Thus, she uses her neoclassical myth ("Niobe")
to explore the catastrophic repercussions of colonial America's race, gender,
and class oppressions. Even more arrestingly, Wheatley exposes the powerful effects of such manifold excesses of power on the literary and physical
bodies of eighteenth-century women and slaves. Unlike analyses of power
and agency which depend upon the subverting of primarily dominant
Western ontologies and epistemologies, Wheatley's text resituates not only
African women's subjectivity, but also cultural hegemony within African-
derived contexts.

Pointing to the ways in which Wheatley's work may be seen as a recen-
tering of both African and European women, David Grimsted argues that
Wheatley's egalitarian treatment of elegies suggests "a public extension of
women's centrality in the private rituals of death" (353). He further submits
that "Niobe represented a rare attempt to give fully tragic stature to woman's

centrality in the family and in the age's rituals of mourning" (370). Grimsted argues that Wheatley's "personifications of favorable things such as Liberty . . . and Peace are made feminine, while *negative* things like Death and Power are masculine" (370). I agree with Shields, who, countering Grimsted's reading of associations of death in Wheatley's work as negative, argues that the poet's celebration of death is in fact a "reject[ion] [of] transitory life on earth and [her] long[ing] for escape through death" (*Collected Works*, 252).

Bassard's readings of Wheatley's elegies further complicate both views of death in Wheatley's work. Specifically, she argues convincingly that Wheatley expresses her own grief through the "device of having the deceased speak words of comfort to the loved ones left behind [as] a sort of self-ventriloquism" (70). Consequently, Bassard concludes that Wheatley's elegies signal her "desire to speak beyond the 'grave' of separation to those she left behind" when she was "brought from Africa to America" (70). Significantly, if Wheatley brings so much of herself to a genre designed toward literal expression of an objectified grief of another person, then the figurative representations of death in her neoclassical poetry demand equally and introspectively guided interpretations. We will want to look more closely at what gendered personifications and figurations of transitory death tell us about the poet's own view of death. At the same time, we can hardly ignore the poet's desire for either escape or resurrection.

Indeed, addressing the question of why "Wheatley returned to [the elegiac] form so often that it became her primary vehicle for poetic expression" (59), I offer the following. Perhaps such a return can be found in the poet's longer than usual rumination on what might arguably be said to be the longest elegiac expression in Wheatley's corpus. In this extended elegy, "Niobe" mourns the physical death of fourteen children, the spiritual and social death of two others as well as their mothers and fathers, and the geographical spaces they represent—Africa and the Americas. Further, it seems crucial to expand on what might be termed the quintessential moment of self-subscription for a black woman poet, Wheatley's gesturing and signifying of death, power, childbirth, spirituality, war, incest, murder, and slavery, culminating in her own engagement with a discourse of silence or silencing (depending upon one's reading or attribution of the final lines).

If, as Bassard suggests, separation from one kind of community permits an attachment to another, it might necessarily follow that such an attachment permits the creation, but not necessarily the total assimilation, of another kind of community. Thus, Wheatley mourns her African roots at the same time she is moored to European community and ways of knowing. Further, she attaches herself metaphorically to Africa in order to sustain, develop, and survive in America. Indeed, part of her survival depends on her ability to create a viable American community. She brings with her what remains of what she mourns. In the absence of what she doesn't have she creates out of what is there. If, following Bassard, we are to successfully contextualize Wheatley's poems "within the frame of cultural memory" (69), then we must be able, as Wheatley was, to expand our notion of culture. To be sure, culture for Wheatley, while it included Africa, America, and Europe, was no simple matter.

Yet, because "all fixed points are problematical" (Baker, 200), one must understand that women's centrality cannot be mediated solely through death or spiritual (re)birth. In fact, early black poetry such as Wheatley's questions the very grounds upon which such false categories as margin and center exist. That is, through its engagement with different and unknown tongues, Wheatley's poetry translates and mediates converging and diverging registers. As Niara Sudarkasa notes, "The 'public sphere' in most West African societies was not conceptualized as 'the world of men.' Rather, it was one in which both sexes were recognized as having important roles to play" (55). In Ogunyemi's terms, "the erection of borders where they did not exist before is the heretical sign of colonialism and divisiveness. . . . Rupture along gendered lines, rather than a parallel working-together, becomes the colonial heritage" (49).[7] Logically, the erection of borders is problematic whether its intent is to decenter dominant constructions or recenter those perceived at the margins. This is so because a "center-periphery model, where the periphery is totally victimized and disempowered, is not very useful" (49). Moreover, the terms under which one is located or dislocated are rarely assigned by those most at risk. As an enslaved African woman, Wheatley would not have missed the opportunity to poetically critique the unequal power relations of all types, including those between women and men. Such is suggested in Wheatley's juxtaposition of simultaneously powerful and disempowered figures in such works as "Niobe." As a Middle Passage survivor, who mourned the thousands gone (most vividly her mother and father), her work most certainly would have expressed grief and desire to speak to them as well as her own desire to transcend at times this lonely space. However, she could ill afford to retreat to such literal or figurative spaces as those imagined in her creative works for too long. Thus, in the spirit of Sankofa the African griotte sought to bring forward from each space of grief those lessons which were most valuable for her and others.

In terms of Wheatley's Christian ways of knowing, a celebration of death did not signal a disdain for life. Rather, the poet understood that suffering and sacrifice in the material world gave value to the rewards of the spiritual world. The devout Christian Wheatley would not have overlooked the significance of Jesus Christ's physical birth and earthly life; for without these events there could have been no crucifixion, death, or spiritual rebirth. More importantly, as much of Wheatley's work attests, she clearly comprehended the grave significance of The Great Commission,[8] which could only be carried out in the temporal world. To be effective, concepts such as death and spiritual rebirth must be interpreted within an integrative framework that engages the dynamic energy of men, women, and children in such realms. Brooks's *American Lazarus* provides important tools for scholars revisioning death in eighteenth-century black texts. She argues that scholars must address the ways in which writers like Wheatley were "creating from the chaos of colonization and slavery new identities, new communities, and new American literary traditions" (6). Significantly, early black writers like Wheatley had a different relationship to death than whites, one which Brooks poignantly locates in the biblical tradition of Lazarus which "encompasses both death and resurrection" (9). Hence, the "early writings [of African Americans] reflect the imposed discontinuities, cruelties, and mortalities of life under slavery and colonialism, and they demonstrate the drive to claim life from death and meaning from chaos" (9).

Indeed, Wheatley's death corpus exists in a marketplace[9] in which "whole kingdoms in [*Death's*] gloomy den are thrust / and nations mix with their primeval dust" ("To a Gentleman and Lady" ll. 7–8). While the celebration of death as a vehicle through which humanity can pass from the ephemeral to the eternal world is meant to assuage and redirect the sentiments of the bereaved in Wheatley's elegies, her own understanding of life and death is rendered with far more complexity. Thus, Wheatley's self-consciousness is revealed in texts such as "Niobe," which put Wheatley's Christian self in simultaneous dialogue with her female, African, and American selves.[10] Although "Niobe" cannot be deemed autobiographical by traditional standards, when interpreted through the matrices of African ways of knowing, Wheatley's poem transposes and redefines the limits which define autobiographical texts. Further, such revisioning by its assumption of creative agency as a literary and cultural inheritance enables us to read "Niobe" as a text that undermines the concept of nation as a stable and natural entity. Thus, "Niobe" critiques the underlying ontologies and epistemologies that construct master narratives or proof texts to establish knowledge about raced, classed, and gendered others. Rather than merely challenging hegemonic control by exposing the effects of its practices, the counterdiscursive narrative of "Niobe" destabilizes hegemonic control by exposing underlying bases that enable supposedly natural and national codes and values.

Before moving to a discussion of the different ways in which Wheatley's work can be seen to destabilize various forms of power, it is necessary to clarify how African *ways* of knowing make a *difference* in our reading of power in Wheatley's poetry. What I have been referring to as a syncretized

Senegalese poetics is a synthesis of West African modes of expression and historical transmission—Senegalese *taasu*, Nigerian *palava*, Akan Sankofa Bird, Ghanaian Bird of the Wayside—and African American theoretical models of interpretation—speaking in tongues, signifying. Moreover, no single attribute above will be wholly representative of this African-centered approach to analyzing Wheatley's work.

For example, her public performance of the mythic warring goddesses marks what might otherwise be invisible, the poet's very private "distress" at her own familial—maternal—disconnections. Carrying forward the seeds from an ancient past in her mourning/mooring of political upheavals, social chaos, and spiritual degeneration, her words reflect present crises facing Revolutionary America. Symbolic of the power of myths which are often imbedded in the histories brought forward in West African griot traditions—signified in the Sankofa and Wayside birds—the poet's words can be seen to carry more than one meaning and function, and on more than one level. I want to reiterate that what I am identifying here is a hermeneutic structure that privileges African modes of cultural expression and interpretive strategies—drawn both from culturally specific West African structures of meaning and those structures which represent a fusion of Western and African traditions.[11]

As I hope to demonstrate in my reading of "Niobe," all these elements of a syncretic Senegalese poetic—grounded in both culturally specific West African and African American ways of knowing—provide a new way of seeing Wheatley. In so doing, I argue that we are also able to view Wheatley's revisiting of "Niobe" as her most significantly personal, political, spiritual, and African work. Thus, we free previously bound views of race, class, and gender in eighteenth-century Afro-British American aesthetics. Such a liberating reading will enable us to consider the extent to which Wheatley's use of religion to veil antislavery protests was even more powerfully executed and extended through her longest poem, "Niobe." It will be useful to consider how the poet, who was so well versed in secular classical traditions—identifying with such classical mythological female figures as Niobe, Latona, Aurora, Phoebe, Mneme, and Flora—might also have had some equally important biblical figures of women in mind as she reimagined Ovid's Niobe. While there is no evidence to suggest that she modeled Niobe after such biblical women as Mary, Eve, or Hagar, we can be sure that Wheatley, as a devoutly Christian Methodist, was well acquainted with these holy women from her biblical readings.

Indeed, I agree with Shields that in both "Goliath of Gath" and "Niobe" Wheatley goes beyond mere "biblical paraphrase, a popular form of the time" (*Collected Works*, 258). However, in the case of her "Niobe" poem, it may be equally important to consider the extent to which her use of biblical paraphrase represents an extension of this popular form. In this regard, it may be useful to think of how she may have used biblical paraphrase to draw upon the allegorical associations to be had by highlighting the stories of such well-known biblical women as Eve, Mary, or Hagar. Such female figures were not typically the subjects of this popular eighteenth-century form. However, references to such figures are to be found with some regularity and predictability in various other literary forms. For example, in published religious writings from 1600 to 1790, one can find references to Hagar in discourses, sermons, and treatises addressing such issues of doctrine and canon as: God's Providence, Law and Grace (especially with regard to the Two Covenants of Old and New Testament Dispensations), denominationally and doctrinally mixed marriages, children's baptism, Psaltery primers, and even the inclusion of the apocrypha into the Anglican canon of scripture. Able to adapt and fuse the biographical form of puritan elegy to her own elegiac verses, the political form to her occasional poetry and her letters, biblical paraphrase to a heightened form of secular and sacred aesthetics not only predates and possibly informs nineteenth-century romanticism and transcendentalism, but also locates parallel black African envelopes in which to house her fused Afro-British American voices and messages.

Concurrently, Wheatley interrogates knowledge and power in order to complicate notions of race, class, and gender. She does so by rereading of histories of female empowerment and disempowerment through her revisioning of women's sacred history in the figure of Hagar. Indeed, this controversial biblical figure has generated much controversy among biblical and women studies scholars. Importantly, their work highlights the complex nature of women's relationships to one another, to patriarchal and matriarchal societal structures, to men, children, and history. For example, Phyllis Trible argues that "as one of the first females in scripture to experience use, abuse, and rejection, Hagar the Egyptian slave claims our attention. Knowledge of her has survived in bits and pieces only, from the oppressor's perspective at that, and so our task is precarious: to tell Hagar's story from the fragments that remain" (*Texts of Terror*, 9).

Savina Teubal suggests that the absence of any confirmable biblical accounting of the birth of Ishmael, which could have given a more balanced insight into the relationship between Hagar and Sarah, alongside a failure to sufficiently acknowledge the implications of these two women's surrogacy agreement as it related to matrilineal heritages of power and authority, have obscured some of the most dynamic elements of women's religious history (76).

Janet Gabler-Hover's *Dreaming Black/Writing White: The Hagar Myth in American Cultural History* is the only formal full-length study of Hagar from the perspective of literary analysis. Gabler-Hover provides critical insights into the difference between nineteenth-century white and black women writers' use of the Hagar myth. In particular, she notes that differences between black and white women writers' metaphorical use of Hagar's body result from their respectively distinct relationships to race, class, and gender. Further, she suggests that such differences provide evidence that both blacks and whites read Hagar as—if not directly then indirectly—a black woman. Gabler-Hover surmises that this conclusion is based at least in part on Hagar's Egyptian and slave heritage, but mostly on racialized stereotypes of black women's perceived freer sexuality.

A more important consideration may be what nineteenth-century women's symbolic investment in Hagar may suggest about Wheatley's own revisionary interpreting of this biblical figure of an African slave woman through "Niobe." Admittedly, Hagar was not available as an iconic image to the eighteenth-century white woman, at least not in the same way it was to the nineteenth-century women in Gabler-Hover's study. However, Wheatley's perspective as an enslaved African woman (like Hagar) may have permitted her another way of viewing and making similar symbolic use of this biblical myth. Gabler-Hover contends that nineteenth-century women used the Hagar myth to read and rewrite shifting societal values, and in terms that symbolically revealed intersecting poles of race, gender, and biblical symbolism. While we cannot know for certain, it is certainly plausible that Wheatley, as someone familiar with the Bible and the story of Hagar, might have been able to draw upon parallels between her life and this biblical character. Certainly, if black male writers of this period were able to draw on biblical characters in their narratives (for a variety of reasons) as Angelo Costanzo and other scholars have noted, then it is not so far-fetched that Wheatley, who was equally creative and intelligent, would have been able to make similar use of female characters.

Her "Goliath of Gath" poem provides ample evidence of her ability to integrate biblical myth into neoclassical epic form; that she did not similarly celebrate any female biblical characters, but rather chose to use a mythical secular goddess, and that she chose to critique negative rather than convey such essentially positive attributes of these female characters, offers a fertile site for analysis and recovery of perhaps what might be argued as the first attempt by a black woman author to render an imagined African female deity in her writing—albeit veiled. Surely, if Wheatley began her book of *Poems* by first imaging then invoking Maecenas as an African muse, and if she was well versed enough in Latin and Greek, and Roman mythology to poetically render "Niobe," she was clever enough to see the parallels between the secular and sacred worlds in which she lived and those she imagined in a mythical

Thebes. Gabler-Hover contends that "the real question is not what happens when white women 'dream' Hagar but what happens when white women who are intensely invested in the disempowerment of 'real' black women dream a black, sexualized Hagar in their own narratives of white self-empowerment" (31). Analogously, Wheatley's "Niobe" perhaps enables us to consider what happens when an enslaved black woman who is intensely invested in the empowerment of real black women dreams a black goddess.

Importantly, part of Wheatley's recapture of Africa through her syncretic Senegalese poetics in the "Niobe" poem necessitates a return to a literal and literary *Genesis*—in order to reinsert the African women's voice that was more than once removed. Centuries before Teubal, Trible, or the nineteenth-century black and white women writers they study, Wheatley responded to the call of her Afro-Christian ancestors to speak in her poetry through the vehicle of a less traditionally sacred if equally spiritual form—the Ovidian neoclassical myths of *Metamorphoses*. And, it is through the reinsertion of the voices of Niobe and Hagar that we hear again the African woman's voice. It is significant that Wheatley's voiced expressions do not suggest a deific, omniscient position from above. Rather, her poetics listens for the spaces where these voices can in fact be heard—despite historical silencing through misinterpretation. In so doing, she makes clear the difference a *way* of hearing, or not hearing, speaking or not speaking, writing or not writing, makes. In this case, previously unheard voices come to the forefront through our listening for the unknown tongues, patterns of direction and indirection, and shifting registers of discord and harmony. Most significant is that "Niobe" invites Wheatley's African ways to aural and oral *palava* with her Afro-British American ways of knowing. Wheatley's own history plays an important role in her assumption, adaptation, and reappropriation of these multiple ways of knowing.

As early as age thirteen, according to Margaret Odell's biography, she demonstrates her knowledge both of the classic texts and rudiments of a proper woman's education and an understanding of Christianity well beyond her years and social circumstances. In "To the University of Cambridge in England," Wheatley admonishes the "sons of science / [and receivers of] the blissful News from messengers from heaven / [. . . to] suppress the deadly serpent in its egg" (ll. 10–26). As self-appointed spokesperson for a society growing weary of the wastefulness of its prized youth and their diminishing reputations as young men unworthy of the privileges bestowed upon them, her poem is effectively "an exhortation"—in Muhktar Ali Isani's words—"to the boisterous students of Harvard to live a Christian life . . . put[ting] the luckier, yet less zealous Christians to shame" ("Gambia on My Soul," 65). Hence, in her advisory address to the white, wealthy, male students at this prestigious university, the young slave girl reminds them of their inherited privilege based on race, class, gender, and their equally important responsibility as Christians. Joanna Brooks poignantly argues, "Wheatley knew what the 'sons of science' were unwilling to acknowledge: that neither rational causes nor natural forces governed the events of this world" (*American Lazarus*, 5). Moreover, Wheatley's exhortation to her white brethren is meant to remind them that if they were bold enough and certainly smart enough to manipulate religion and science to justify slavery and the oppression of women, she—a mere "Ethiop" woman—would not through her silence be complicit in their actions against her and her African brothers and sisters. Instead, she exposes their feigned ignorance about one of the most blatant sins confronting their society—the removal of African people from their "dark abodes" to an even "gloomier" state of physical and spiritual enslavement.

The poet's charge to the young men to "see him, with hands outstretched upon the cross" (l. 13) is meant to signify the great earthy and heavenly debts that are owed, for neither is without costs. Ironically, both the "sublimest skies" of spiritual salvation and the "transient sweetness" of the material wealth and comforts come as a result of the blood, sweat, and tears of others.[12] To see their "redeemer," who shed his "blood" upon the cross "with hands outstretched" to his enemies and friends, those who followed, denied, and crucified him should convict or prick the hearts of the poet's enslavers. More important, her admonition to "suppress the deadly serpent in its egg" (l. 26) is meant to guide them toward salvation, as they begin to see others—including enslaved Africans—through the eyes of their redeemer. This veiled, but nonetheless powerful, antislavery protest through a reordering and recapturing of the true meaning of the spirit and the letter of the law of scripture is especially significant coming from an enslaved teenage African girl.[13] Similarly, in an often-quoted passage from "On Being Brought from Africa to America," the fifteen-year-old insists that while "some view our sable race with scornful eye / Their color is a diabolic die. / Remember, *Christians*, *Negros*, black as *Cain* / May be refin'd, and join the angelic train" (ll. 5–8), Wheatley redefines the conceptual connections and cultural contexts of blackness and Christianity and resituates the historical misrepresentation of African peoples within Christian doctrine.

One of the most vivid illustrations of her role as African griotte defined as genealogist, historian, praise singer, and warrior may be seen in her longest poem, "Niobe." In this poem Wheatley translates Ovid's classic (Western) myth of pride and vengeance into an African praise song of motherhood and community. Simultaneously, she effects a historical indictment of the inhumanity of internal and external warring through her reimagining of mythological genealogy of the figures Niobe and Latona within African,

American, and especially Afro-Christian contexts. As Holloway maintains, "Because belief in divinity and belief in the ancestors are both elements of traditional religion in Africa, the figurative presence of feminine deities (goddesses) in creative literatures by women indicates the creative relationship of this metaphor to the culture and gender of the author/artist" (*Moorings and Metaphors*, 165). While Holloway refers specifically to contemporary black American and African literature, I believe her critical views on the value of myth for revealing the recursive strategies of remembrance enhance our understanding of how an eighteenth-century black aesthetic operates in works such as "Niobe."

Further, in recovering her historical lineage through Niobe, Wheatley echoes the resounding cries of a "Hagar in the Wilderness." For Hagar, like the enslaved African Wheatley, comes to us without history and voiceless. Indeed, our first knowledge of Hagar (not unlike Wheatley) is that of one who is seemingly powerless from all perspectives. Egyptian handmaid and African slave, both Hagar and Wheatley are objects of patriarchal exchange and intragender oppression. Hagar is transferred from Pharaoh through Abram to Sarai. Wheatley is purchased by John Wheatley as a servant for his wife, Susanna. It will be rightly objected that Wheatley's experience with her tender mistress Susanna can hardly be compared to the cruelty Hagar experiences in her relationship with her mistress Sarai. The relationship between two women of unequal power—essentially rivals—is most certainly not the same as a surrogate mother/daughter relationship (albeit between a slave and her mistress). The point I am making here, though, is how Wheatley reflects on and then depicts multiple complementary and angularly related circumstances from literal experiences in the real world to mythic experiences in Niobe's world. Of equal significance is the way the poet extracts fragments from several different histories to imagine one history that tells many stories and serves many audiences.[14] Wheatley's ways—in the context of a Senegambian poetic—move beyond interpretations that suggest a one-on-one correspondence or merely parallel view of similar models of power relationships. Consequently, we need to be able to see such gendered and race-inflected models as expandable images—that is, as constituting parts of a larger single text. At the same time, such models can function interchangeably as the demands of the story change. As Bassard's poetics of recovery reveal, this African way of imagining enables us to see Wheatley's georacial unwriting "of the discourse of blackness/Africanity as a discourse of difference" (43). Such a way of imagining also enables Wheatley to rewrite this racially blackened discourse as well. Briefly, Wheatley's Senegambian poetics enable her to participate simultaneously in both an Africanist and Americanist discourse—without negating either. Crucially, as in the Senegalese women's *taasu*, Wheatley's "Niobe" is performed in the context of its expandability and portability to issues of particular concern to women, and in conjunction with matters that are central to others within the community.

Consequently, Wheatley's depiction of Niobe's distress is as much a way of talking about Wheatley's own distress over what happened to Africa's children as it is the impending doom facing America's black and white children—both the Ishmaels and the Isaacs. "Niobe" gave the black, devoutly spiritual poet yet another vehicle through which to convey her literary, cultural, political, and, most important, spiritual roles. It also permitted her to attempt to reconcile for herself (and others) what it meant to be both African and Christian. In so doing, she redefined and simultaneously complicated once sacredly held assumptions about what it meant to be both black and a slave. And she did so in ways that forever severed ties between the so-called Christian mission of saving Africans from their lives in darkness and spiritual enslavement on their continent to the light of spiritual purity and whiteness as enslaved bondsmen and women in the New World.

Quite brilliantly, Wheatley radically and symbolically repositions the enslaved African woman within the redemptive history and legacy of the fallen Eve, the outcast and enslaved Egyptian Hagar, and the venerated Mary. In this context it is possible to consider Eve, Hagar, and Mary as representative of symbolic female whiteness and blackness, with their concomitant and equally problematic class and gender assignments. Hence, Wheatley recaptures (and composes) deifying and reifying myths about blacks and women. Out of the religious texts of her Christian masters, the poet signifies on the biblically based raced and gendered narratives of oppressed peoples. While early black writers' relating of their struggles to that of Old Testament figures is well known, such associations are typically read within a context that assumes male-centered master narratives. In contrast, Wheatley, through Eve, Mary, and especially Hagar, reconsiders the religious history with regard to slavery by juxtaposing the symbology of daughters of Hagar alongside the sons of Cain and the sons and daughters of Ham.

Juxtaposing the harsh reality of her own experiences and America's impoverished, oppressed, and enslaved mothers and children alongside the American nation-building project, she exposes the means by which they are all kept in bondage. Not unlike the nation-building promises in the patriarchal covenants, the creation of a wealthy national body—through the American Revolution and slavery—would be fulfilled in the bodies of women and children. Wheatley was well aware that both the sacred and secular worlds exacted a similar level of violence on women. However, her own interpretation of Eve, Hagar, Sarai, and Mary through "Niobe" invests a certain measure of power and responsibility in women for their part in upholding patriarchal and national interests.

We can only speculate whether the image of Latona (as a woman, a mother denied) invoked the very memory of her own African mother pouring out water. Given Wheatley's knowledge of classical literature and myth, her attraction to the myth of the goddess Leto (Latona) is even more striking when one considers that Latona is the patron goddess of mothers. Leto's daughter Artemis (Phoebus) is depicted in images of classical Greek mythology as standing with bow, water jug, and bowl before her mother, who is seated. This mythic scenario in which the child stands before the seated mother with an offering bowl of water, reverses a scene of Wheatley's literal memory. Yet, even as such a narrative unwrites one story, it rewrites another—that of the child's return to the mother as well as the child's fulfillment of the retribution for her mother's suffering. West African cultural traditions such as Mammywata (goddess of water) evoke similar themes of simultaneous barrenness and fertility. My intention is not to conflate either the vastness of West African goddess traditions into one monolithic myth, or to discount the continuum of traditions and reciprocal borrowing of African and Western traditions from antiquity to modern time. Rather, my intention is to further widen the spaces within which African conceptualizations and deifications of female principals can be represented. Karla Holloway has described this kind of metaphor—of summoning ghosts—in terms of African women writers' use of goddess traditions to engage splintered knowledge. In both Western and African traditions Wheatley offers Niobe and her abundant progeny as idealized yet analyzable symbols of the natural wealth and prosperity associated with motherhood.[15]

> Seven sprightly sons the royal bed adorn,
> Seven daughters, beauteous as the rising morn;
> As when Aurora fills the ravished sight,
> And decks the orient realms with rosy light,
> From their bright eyes the living splendors play,
> Nor can beholders bear the flashing ray. (ll. 23–28)

Understanding that motherhood for displaced African women meant perpetual enslavement for their children and increased property values for their masters,[16] Wheatley's description of Niobe's children moves beyond their Ovidian use-value as producers of "sons- and daughters-in-law" (Ovid, *Metamorphoses* vi.183–84).[17] It is significant that this passage's transposition of the meaning of the relationship between children and their parents (in both Ovid's and Wheatley's time) undermines dominant ideological frames of reference for family by resituating family within an African context. Notably, Wheatley's remembering and reimagining of Niobe's children in all their splendid magnificence is also reminiscent of the way in which a young woman's beauty and fertility are emphasized in traditional African ceremonial wedding songs. Indeed, Niobe's children are more resplendent and glowing than Zeus himself, by Wheatley's embellishment of Niobe's account, suggested by the fact that Niobe's daughters, as well as her sons, number "seven," and therefore both Niobe's children, and metaphorically Africa's children, are lacking in nothing. Wheatley's description of them as perfect suggests that they, too, can potentially become gods, for it is quite clear that Niobe, an "empress with a goddess join'd" ("Niobe" 1.74), sees herself as perfect in both heavenly and earthly realms.[18]

The supernatural luminosity with which Wheatley symbolically endows Niobe's divinely descended royal children is meant to expose the sociopolitical and economic systems which underlie the construction of naturalness. Wheatley's interrogation of the natural association of intelligence with brightness, through her incorporation of the terms that imply double meaning in the concept of brightness in her reinterpretation of Niobe's children, points to ways in which light (or white) people are thought to be brighter (smarter) than Africans. If, as Thomas Jefferson contends, "in the countenances [of Africans], [there is an] immoveable veil of black stars which covers all emotions" (*Notes*, 138), such is disputed in Wheatley's representations: in the "rosy light" of Niobe's (and Africa's) daughter's dawn, or the "sprightly" and animated faces of her sons, or by staring into the "bright eyes" that reveal a "play" of "living splendors" ("Niobe" ll. 23–27). Like Wheatley's own mother, who in daily ritual obeisance "prostrated herself before the first golden beam that glanced across her native plains"[19] (Richmond, 12), Niobe is similarly overcome by the brilliance and splendor of her "blooming maid[s], and celestial boy[s]" ("Niobe" l.36).[20]

The play of colors in her imagery points to Wheatley's location at the crossroads as cultural interpreter. Implicit in Wheatley's revision of the dark and barren life of the slave child is an interrogation of both the spiritual and aesthetic devaluing of African children and, by extension, their African mothers. A similar type of alteration can be seen in Ogunyemi's twentieth-century deification of motherhood. Ogunyemi compares Chi[21] "to a woman who bears children and/or divides the largesse among them." She notes that "in Igbo comic wisdom, Chi is also conceptualized as dwelling in the sun," and "that, when one is at one's best, Chi is the sunshine within, almost turning one into a super being. To the child, the mother is the morning sun that shines on him/her specially; she is also the supreme being to be adored as a bountiful provider" (41). Both Wheatley's luminous evocation of children

and Ogunyemi's radiant magnification of their mothers point to the centrality of motherhood and childhood in African culture. Wheatley authorizes,
improvises, and mediates African and Western motherhood and in doing so
imbeds a valuable legacy and marker of African experience(s) of motherhood
in the eighteenth century both inside and outside slavery.

Although women's fertility is central to both African and Western
women's cultures, Wheatley subverts dominant Western-based discourses
that locate white women's symbolic and material value solely in procreation,
while simultaneously ascribing a dubious and exploitative value to African
women's progeny. Wheatley imagines autonomy and empowerment through
a constructed African-derived concept of motherhood rather than an essen-
tialized or natural one. Such a concept of motherhood relies upon women's
spiritual wealth as manifested in and through their children, and more
importantly, their ability to coexist in harmonious intragender relationships
that ensure the survival of their communities as a whole. Hence, Wheatley's
pronouncement that Niobe "had'st far the happier mother prov'd, / If this fair
offspring had been less belov'd" ("Niobe" ll. 31–32) can be interpreted as an
indictment of Niobe's and Latona's virulent and myopic fixation on women's
roles as supernatural propagators to the exclusion of their roles as maintain-
ers of structures that sustain and continue life in all its forms. Both Latona's
preoccupation with her royal lineage as "spouse and sister of the thund'ring
Jove" (l. 94) and Niobe's obsession with her "large progeny" (l. 79) prevent
either of them from combining and drawing upon their real rather than relative power.

What has been forgotten in slavery and colonization Wheatley attempts
to remember: the political and social agency of African women as daughters,
wives, and mothers. In her analysis of African (Igbo) gender systems, Ifi
Amadiume emphasizes the value placed on women's equal participation in
all matters of society. According to Amadiume, "Nnobi [African] women
have always been articulate and not mere objects circulated among and acted
upon by their men-folk. . . . Nnobi women made [and continue to make]
political use of their roles as daughters . . . through the control of funerals
of patrilineage members, wives and mothers . . . [and] fertility ceremonies
during marriage and childbirth" (87). Clearly, Niobe and Latona (not unlike
Wheatley's ancestors) lived in a world in which women had a similar power
in society. Indeed, it is the abuse of such power to which Wheatley alludes.
However, in demonstrating such abuse, she necessarily exposes the potential for a more positive wielding of the authority and privilege which these
women possess. Indeed, the exploitation of power is not merely limited to
Niobe and Latona, though theirs clearly represents the most extreme and
irresponsible handling of power.

Certainly, Amadiume's observations point to the participation and centrality of African women in structures that both center and decenter women's
social orders. In "Niobe," society is called into existence through the words
of Manto. As I have noted earlier, Manto, like the Sankofa bird, had the gift
of prophecy: "endu'd with mighty skill / The past to explore, the future to
reveal" (Wheatley, "Niobe" ll. 37–38). Thus, she must have foreseen what her
"mandate" (40) would set in motion. Yet, her prophetic power compels her to
instruct the women of Thebes to pay proper homage to Latona. Thus, it is the
words—Manto's words—which are the spark that ignites the flame of bad
blood. Indeed, the women of Thebes become mere pawns in what would end
in a deadly game. "The Theban maids obey / And pious tribute to the goddess
pay" (ll. 47–48). Yet, if Manto—and the Theban society that listens to her—is
representative of responsible actions in the execution of power, the same cannot be said of Niobe. As a queen of Thebes she should set the example for her
people and pay tribute to Latona as a goddess. However, her power becomes
a justification to deny proper respect to Latona. Instead, Niobe revels not only
in the sovereign authority that she and her husband, Amphion, command, but
also in her numerous issues. The history of the troubled relationship between
Latona and Niobe is said to have been exacerbated by Niobe's taunting of the
goddess, who has only two children, in comparison to Niobe's fourteen. To
be sure, the story reveals that the pride she exhibits in her children proves to
be her undoing.

Of equal importance to understanding the implications of abuses of
power in "Niobe" is what Wheatley does not include. As Shields and other
scholars have observed, the poet, who is quite thorough in all her details,
deliberately omits Ovid's prelude to "Niobe." Thus, Wheatley signifies
(through indirection) that which the Phrygian queen ignores: a history that
might have saved her. Preceding the Niobe myth is a tale about Arachne, a
young woman whose pride and arrogance in her skill at weaving result in her
metamorphosis into a spider. Not only had the young woman failed to pay
tribute, but she denied even the "suggestion of a teacher ever so great" (Ovid,
vi. l. 24) as the goddess Pallas. Instead, she engaged in a weaving contest with
Pallas, which resulted in her tragic transformation. "Now Niobe, before her
marriage, / . . . had known Arachne . . . as a girl / . . . And yet she did not /
take warning by her countrywoman's fate to give / place to the gods and speak
them reverently" (vi. ll. 148–51).

Thus, while Niobe might have heeded history, she was rather a victim
of it. Ultimately, Latona, who as goddess wields the greatest power, succumbs
to the same pride and abuse of authority as Niobe. Moreover, because her
children are used as weapons to brandish her power and exact vengeance,
Latona reproduces this corruption through her heirs. I have taken the time

to consider the significance of power because, as I argue, it is a recurring image that sustains nearly every element of Wheatley's critique in "Niobe." Thus, the confrontation of power—through its assumption, use, and subsequent abuse—can be viewed in three ways. First, there is the power of the word—through Manto's ability to affect change in society. For Afro-British Americans like Wheatley, words represent both power and the abuse of it. In a historical moment when perceptions frame reality, the naming of a people as barbaric, inhumane, irrational, pagan, or chattel grants a society permission (provides a context or rationale) to enslave, brutalize, or otherwise marginalize such people. Thus, like Theban maidens, colonial Americans rush to pay homage to their own goddess "Freedom" (Wheatley, "To the Right Honourable William, Earl of Dartmouth" ll. 8–11)—as the enslavement of others remains an unspoken history.

Second, there is the political power of the governing body—American aristocracy and British monarchy. Like Niobe's Thebes, colonial American authority resides primarily in its wealth—and ironically that wealth is upheld by the contracted (indentured) or free (slave) labor of the bodies. Like Niobe's children, such bodies are vulnerable to the attacks and violence their leaders bring upon them.

Third, there is divine power, which is manifested primarily but not only in the Christian Church. While it is potentially the most liberating power, it is also that which may be most easily and effectively abused. Indeed, the distortion and perversion of Christian values to serve political and economic demands of the developing American nation were very heavily critiqued by Afro-British American writers. In a society increasingly dependent on slave labor, religion proved a valuable tool for maintaining the status quo. Of course, it was equally utilized as a strong antislavery weapon. Ultimately, I am not arguing that "Niobe" can simply be read as an allegory with a one-to-one correspondence to Revolutionary American society—it cannot. However, I draw attention to some of the parallels as a means to grapple with what are complex threads of a dilemma facing the worlds inhabited by Afro-British America.

Hence, as we consider how power operates in both Wheatley's mythic and actual worlds, it is critical to acknowledge, as did the poet herself, that certain seemingly discrete elements of power are inextricable. Most evident is the way that divine power authorizes linguistic and political power. In order to more fully grasp the force of Wheatley's poetics—her African, British, American, and Afro-British American ways—it will be helpful to consider her particular approach to engaging the audience. Ernest Mason contends that "an aesthetic is fundamentally concerned with experience or with the act of experiencing or perceiving something . . . [with] black art in particular

... understood as an elucidated experience" (2). Thus, examining Wheatley's strategy of elucidation is critical for our recovery of an eighteenth-century black aesthetic in "Niobe." More important, such recovery enables us to articulate more clearly how Wheatley's reconnection with African ways of knowing demonstrates one such aspect of this early black aesthetic. We can get a clearer picture, for example, of how Wheatley signals the dilemma of motherhood and gender in a slaveholding society by reflecting upon another text from Ovid's *Metamorphoses*—"Biblis":

> Biblis is a warning
> that girls should never love what is forbidden
> She loved her brother, and the way she loved him
> Was not the way sisters should love their brothers.
>   (qtd. in Galinsky, 35)

Galinsky maintains that in passages such as this, Ovid's intention was to distance himself from the subject in order to depersonalize the relationship between the narrator and his narrative. In particular, Ovid wanted to "prevent the reader from recognizing in the mythological story [familiar] human experience" (Galinsky, 35). In this way, Ovid was able to insert his own authoritative narrative moral proscriptions concerning the dangers of excess and improper love, and, finally, through *Metamorphoses* to expose the complexities, potential, and enigmatic nature of humanity. Thus, Ovid's caveat concerning excess and incestuous love (in "Biblis") warrants attention not only because it is illustrative of his style (in *Metamorphoses*), which draws attention away from the myth by "drawing attention to himself" (Galinsky, 35), but also because in his warning to Biblis is echoed parallel sentiments in Wheatley's "Niobe." To wit: that a "love too vehement hastens to destroy / each blossoming maid, and each celestial boy" ("Niobe" ll. 35–36).

Yet Wheatley's (equally calculated) strategy was intentionally designed to exact the opposite reactions from her readers. Namely, she renders a critical reading of Western contexts through West African lenses in her use of the direct mode of signifying. Wheatley reads Ovidian love in such a way that it makes a statement about literal and figurative experience of the African mother's right to love her children. As a result, she chastises her audience for its lack (rather than overabundance) of universal love and its participation in depriving a child of her mother's love. Wheatley wants her readers to see in the larger-than-life goddesses (Niobe and Latona) not merely the universal condition of motherhood, but the African mother and child in eighteenth-century society. She wants to draw her audience of mostly white, male, propertied citizens, who are already as distanced from their subjects as any audience could be, closer to these women, these mothers, these Africans. Further, she wants her white, male, propertied audience to recognize and reflect upon their own mothers, sisters, wives, and female slaves, in the tragic consequences of Niobe, Latona, and their children. The subject, the imagery, the word choice, and the deeply imbedded passion with which she reimagines both Niobe and Latona is purposefully employed to beckon her reader into her imagined community of independent and, therefore, free citizens, who must collectively fight tyranny and oppression in all its manifestations. She wants them to reflect upon the high black and white infant mortality rate and the poor free and slave children bartered and separated from their mothers due to society's devaluing of them as disposable objects ("throwaways"). Yet, if the consequences for poor whites are tragic, Wheatley insists upon directing their attention to the more markedly tragic consequences for the mothers of those deemed natural slaves, consigned to perpetual servitude.

Indeed, Wheatley's strong and stunning imagery in her description of Niobe's mythical children exposes both "the ravished sight" of "the holocaust of slave raiding and trading, [in which African children] were equated with economic challenge and servitude in the colonies," and the "flashing ray" of those African children who "had [once] represented wealth and the recycling of life" (Ashcraft-Eason, 76). Niobe's children are as much Africa's children as they are America's children, "beauteous," "bright," and "ravished." "Ravished" refers to the bartered and battered condition of eighteenth-century America's black and white poverty-stricken children, as well as the precarious condition of Revolutionary America's motherhood. Because of its supposed naturalness, motherhood is equally susceptible to the kind of blindness and distance that can lead to subjective understanding. "Ravished" is a term that even in the eighteenth century is as relevant to rape as it is to racism. To "ravage" is to take away, to snatch, to leave bare, and this is what happens in slavery, in rape, and in childbirth (*OED*). In considering what happens to a mother's body before, during, and after the childbearing process, the metamorphoses that occur in both the child and the mother speak metaphorically to the "ravishment" that occurred during the eighteenth-century rape of Africa,[22] colonization, and the subsequent birth of the North American nation, with the women and Africans discarded like afterbirth.

The purportedly natural process of nationalization that I have described here represents an integral part of national myths which belies the systems of power and knowledge that Wheatley's interrogation of naturalness from the perspective of motherhood and gender uncovers and historically reconstructs. At the same time that Wheatley affects a measure of sympathy for Niobe's distress, read metaphorically as America's (and Africa's) distress, she also interrogates Niobe's willingness to sacrifice some of her children for the sake of her position, her pride, and what she feels as her natural right of ascendancy to wealth and power over this "new-sprung deity" ("Niobe" l. 64). Thus, in Niobe's devaluing of Latona's parentage, we can see Wheatley's interrogation of national identity from the perspective of lineage and class. Symbolically, Titans, who are considered lesser gods assigned to the domain of earth, and Latona, whose past troubles have placed her in a precarious class position, are linked through Niobe's perspective in order to elevate her own lineage. Niobe's attitude is thus presented as a mirror image of eighteenth-century American men who, while fighting for their own freedom against the tyranny of the British, failed to consider the human rights of displaced African slaves and devalued white women. Wheatley's depiction of the devastating war between the "haughty" Niobe and Latona underscores the dangerous presumptuousness of white, propertied males about Africans and women. Metaphorically, Niobe, who serves as both a symbol of African and white colonial motherhood, is a reminder of the shared oppression of colonial white and black women, whose freedom remains insufficiently addressed in the post-Revolutionary world. This kind of deliberate detachment from the equally valuable concerns of black people at the inception of the formation of the American nation produced a legacy of civil wars and "ills innum'rous" ("Niobe" l. 2), against which we can still hear the "woeful" cries of "Niobe[s] in distress for [their] children slain by Apollo."

In Niobe's voice, one can also hear the voices of Wheatley's African ancestors and African American descendants. Alicia Ostriker's articulation of "alternative portrait[s] of female pleasure" (165) is germane to an exploration of Wheatley's remembering of "Niobe." Specifically, in "Niobe," Wheatley creates a metaphorical African woman who, not unlike herself, is "composed of [her] parents, extended in her children, vitalized by the powers of spiritual ancestress, determined to identify with and redeem the defeated" (178). Wheatley's critique of class in her interrogation of Latona's "indignant" ("Niobe" l. 80) reaction to Niobe's attempts to subvert her superior position, and the subsequent excessive anger that triggers Latona's wrathful destruction of Niobe's children, comments ironically upon Revolutionary America's simultaneous assumption of national identity at the expense of personal and particular identities and liberty.

As Wheatley makes clear, while Niobe, Latona, and indeed America failed to imagine the freedom of others in their own conceptions of national identity, they did so with the full expectations that their own rights would be upheld. One notes the self-righteous tone with which Latona's children express their intent to defend their mother's honor. Apollo and Phoebe pledge "to punish pride, and scourge the *rebel* mind" ("Niobe" l. 104; my emphasis). Ovid's phrase "a long complaint is but delay of punishment" (Ovid, vi. l. 215) is equally harsh but much less moralistic. I emphasize *rebel* here to underscore Wheatley's use of Revolutionary rhetoric to evoke images of courageous Revolutionary American soldiers battling tyrannical British ones for their freedom. At the same time, *rebel* signifies on the scores of rebellious slaves whipped daily by their masters for insubordination—asserting their rights to freedom.

Wheatley points throughout "Niobe" to the irony of such a double standard of freedom, and the implications such arrogant and self-righteous attitudes may suggest for Christianity. For example, Latona's authority to exact vengeance on Niobe is based on her kinship to the deity "thund'ring *Jove*" ("Niobe" l. 94). Ironically, Niobe cries out to the same god for retribution of Apollo's murder of her seven sons: "Why sleeps the vengeance of immortal *Jove*?" (l. 168). Here, Wheatley interrogates the self-righteous arrogance of white American citizens who use Christianity to uphold slavery, while simultaneously invoking images of the very people they enslave—Africans and women—to exact sympathy for their own freedom from British tyranny. As Erkkila argues, the polemic of the American Revolution was couched "in the language of two primary social tropes: the family and slavery, with America figuratively represented as the natural right of the son or daughter to revolt against a tyrannical parent and the natural right of a slave to revolt against a master" (225).

Yet, if the slave had a natural right to revolt against his or her master, such is disputed by the actions of the slaveholding colonists who daily invoked their rights to scourge their slaves for such rebellion. As Erkkila suggests of both Abigail Adams and Phillis Wheatley, women and slaves used similar rhetorical strategies to voice their respective struggles for enfranchisement and freedom. The most important gift of the American Revolution "was not real or political rights, but the knowledge, the moral ground, and perhaps most of all the language and metaphors with which to 'foment' further rebellion against the constituted orders of white masculine authority in the United States" (239). While Erkkila's assertions are historically valid, women like Wheatley understood that it would take more than moral ground to free them. Slaves knew that standing on such moral ground had yet to result in their freedom. In eighteenth-century Revolutionary America, an African woman like Wheatley always had to be consciously aware of not only her African self, but also her gendered self. Thus, Wheatley's "Niobe" renders visible the historical oppression and alienation of both the African slave mother and the poor white woman that is often veiled within the masculinist rhetoric of revolution. Johanna Miller highlights the plight of the white, female, indentured servant: "If a woman serving a term of indenture became pregnant, not only did she lose her child to the legal system, but her term was extended by one year as a punishment ... such a system had the potential to hold women prisoner almost indefinitely if they became pregnant by their masters, willingly or unwillingly" (202). As an African and as a woman—consigned to what white propertied male society deemed her *rightful* place—Wheatley was doubly silenced; therefore, her poetry countered such censoring through a simultaneously direct and indirect (or doubled) type of signification. One example of Wheatley's attempt to unbind her own poetic tongue can be seen in the way she makes use of signification as a tool that highlights presence through absence. Thus, signifying facilitates the construction of particular history Wheatley wants to bring forward.

I want to return now to an earlier discussion in this chapter about Wheatley's use of African time as a way to consider the poet's engagement of historical landscapes through yet another Akan myth—the Bird of the Wayside. You may recall from the introduction that the Bird of the Wayside is the narrator in the prologue of Aidoo's play *The Dilemma of a Ghost*. "Significantly, the Bird of the Wayside, a literal translation from the Akan, referring to the unseen eye of public opinion . . . also serves as a dramatic device to engage the audience with the subject . . . and to invite it to make up its mind about the transpiring events" (Elder, 159). Wheatley's "Niobe" functions much like this "dramatic device" as the poem creates a space for her audience to trouble static views of history—African and European—by inviting them into a conversation between the mythical women characters. Much like the conversation between the two village women in Aidoo's *Dilemma*, Latona and Niobe engage in a kind of verbal warfare throughout "Niobe" that echoes the devastating action occurring in the tragic narrative scenes that depict the massacre of Niobe's children. Oddly, in many ways, the physical combat is but a backdrop—at best, exemplum—to the catastrophic dilemmas their conversations reveal. In truth, the words that pass between Niobe and Latona can hardly be considered conversations as neither woman actually listens or speaks to the other. In the spirit of Sankofa, it is the messages, lessons, and information to be passed on that are most important. For in such words are survival mechanisms and codes for reconnecting with one's community and one's self. Equally important, then, are the words that pass among the members of the Theban community.

Particularly revealing, both for what it highlights and what it obscures, is Latona's response to Niobe's call for a dialogue about their respective lineages. Essentially, what emerges from the verbal warfare between the two women is a more completely reconstructed, if problematic, history of both. Latona reminds her children of Niobe's history:

Niobe sprung from Tantalus inspires
Each Theban bosom with rebellious fires;

No reason her imperious temper quells,
But all her father in her tongue rebels.
        ("Niobe" ll. 95–98)

A comparison between Latona's and Niobe's narrative exposes the dilemma of history as yet another vehicle for silencing and misnaming—especially for African-descended people like Wheatley. We first come to know Niobe from Wheatley's description of her motherly grief and distress, a "queen, all *beautiful in woe*" (ll. 9–10; my emphasis). Next, we learn of Niobe's lineage and from a perspective very different than that of Niobe's. In Latona's version (above), Tantalus is a "rebellious," hot-tempered father whose equally unreasonable daughter inherits her father's "imperious temper" and his "tongue." This view of Niobe's history provides a striking contrast to the Phrygian queen's description of her father as: "*Tantalus* divine / He most distinguish'd by *Dodonean Jove* / To approach the tables of the gods above" (ll. 14–16). Indeed, Niobe's royal lineage is further enhanced by her "grandsire *Atlas* / . . . / and her other grandsire / . . . *Jove*" (ll. 15–21).

The context in which Latona describes Tantalus is a negative one. Her purpose is to discredit Niobe's status as equal to her own. Latona means to characterize Niobe as being from ignoble parentage to remind her own children (Apollo and Phoebe) of their high parentage and their high birth, as well as their responsibility to defend their nobility. While Latona is correct in emphasizing Tantalus's bad temper, her motives are suspect. While Niobe is correct in her celebration of her father's high position at "the tables of the gods," she provides a rather incomplete history. A more complete history follows:

> Tantalus . . . son of Zeus . . . is best known for the punishment he suffers in Hades. . . . he stands in the midst of a lake, but when he bends to drink, it dries up; a fruit-laden bough flies up when he reaches for it; and an overhanging stone threatens to crush him. . . . The punishments were inflicted for various crimes. . . . [He] betrayed [the gods'] secrets and gave ambrosia to his friends . . . offering a banquet to the gods . . . he served his dismembered son Pelops. (*Benet's Reader's Encyclopedia*, 1006)

Thus, Tantalus's history is symbolic of perpetual desire and deferral. He was consigned to an eternity of desiring the very thing that was within his reach, yet he could never obtain. Clearly, "*Tantalus* divine" ("Niobe" l. 14) had fallen. Yet, because the variant myths of Tantalus suggest a range of identities from villain to Promethean-like hero, even when the facts are more fully apprehended, only a kernel of truth remains. Far more important is what both Niobe and Latona (from Ovid to Wheatley) make of the history that remains. For Latona, Tantalus's history—after his fall—is far more valuable for what it allows her to deduce about Niobe. First, that like her father, Niobe is both unworthy and far too "haughty" to be considered equally among goddesses such as Latona. Indeed, Latona may be said to be signifying that Niobe, like Tantalus, is doomed to want what she cannot have—true status as a goddess.

Whereas Niobe describes herself as both an "empress with a goddess join'd" ("Niobe" l. 74), it is Latona, after all, who is the goddess and therefore worthy of the tribute Niobe refuses to pay. While Niobe's beauty, royalty, and large progeny, as well as her marriage to King Amphion, provide evidence of her rightful place, Latona demonstrates that Niobe's history suggests otherwise. Notably, she "inspires" rebellion and lacks control over her emotions, to such an extent as to make it impossible to reason with her. The cause of this teeming and abundant anger—which is second in its excessiveness only to her procreative powers—seems explainable only in terms of her bloodline. "All her father in her tongue rebels" ("Niobe" l. 98). This statement is doubly inflected as it suggests that Tantalus's history is that of an overreaching mortal whose punishment is an eternity looking at that which he cannot have. In addition to Latona's anger at being shunned by Niobe, her words reveal she is far more threatened by what Niobe inspires, a rebellion of Theban society. Ultimately, it is Niobe's "tongue" that most offends Latona—Niobe's words carry great power. Recall that at Niobe's command the "*Theban* dames ... / [No] longer off'rings to *Latona* pay" (ll. 83–87).

Beyond unveiling the power of history to name and unname others based on different ways of creatively interpreting facts, absences locate additional spaces of reconnection with Wheatley's African ways of knowing. The first noticeable absence is Niobe's mother. It might be argued that if, as I suggest, Wheatley's intent (at least in part) is to highlight the shared oppression of women, then the absence of both Niobe's and Latona's mothers points to the devaluing of women's history—in the missing maternal line of ancestors. More likely, Wheatley doesn't include the name of Latona's mother because it is simply unavailable. Ovid comes as close as contemporary scholars do to naming Niobe's mother. In his version, Niobe's "mother ... is a sister of the / Pleiades" (Ovid, vi. ll. 174–75). Far more perplexing, and perhaps ironic, is Wheatley's decision not to include even the limited information available. Her choice not to include the reference to the Pleiades is especially puzzling given the possibilities it offers for the young griotte's praise song to her ancestors.

Perhaps it is in such a space of absence as this that we find Wheatley's own mother—hiding in plain sight. Clearly, the poet's reference to the

Pleiades would have allowed an additional signification of brightness, ascent, and perfection. The seven sisters of the Pleiades were known for such beauty that they attracted, had affairs with, and bore children for gods ranking as high as Zeus. Certainly, such an illustrious female line of ascendancy would have further exalted the stature of Niobe's "Seven daughters, beauteous as the rising morn" (l. 24). Indeed, Wheatley's embellishment of Ovid's "seven daughters" from whom Niobe expected to "soon have sons- . . . in-law" (Ovid, vi. ll. 183–84) does just that, as it resurrects the Seven Sisters of the Pleiades in the seven daughters of Niobe. In this view of the seven daughters as recovery of Niobe's own matrilineal line, we are able to revisit the use-value of daughters to make good marriages—a focus I earlier argued is overshadowed by their internal and inherent radiance. Revisiting Niobe's seven daughters as resurrections of the Pleiades, as a recovery of Niobe's (and Wheatley's) mother, we are reminded that six of the sisters (and in some myths all seven) married well. Specifically, they each married gods, and did prove valuable producers of wealth. Indeed, if one of the Pleiades is Niobe's mother, then she (Niobe's mother) produced a daughter who in effect reproduced the Pleiades. Yet, even as we sift through multiple layers of signification to locate and recover Niobe's (and Wheatley's) mother through her daughters, we do so just in time to observe their demise. As in the African dilemma tale "[t]he end is not quite . . . an end. The adventure is finished but it is the audience that gives the conclusion. The end is an enigma to resolve" (Bascom, 2).

Thus, Wheatley offers war as a dilemma for both Theban and colonial American society to ponder. Namely, though both black and white women were at risk, the false consciousness of nationalistic claims of equality for all through American independence produced a historical divide between the Niobes and the Latonas. Rather than working together to resist and abolish their common oppression(s), both white and black women became accomplices in their own respective destruction(s).[23] Though Wheatley emphasizes "Apollo's slaying" of Niobe's children as the primary and most violent manifestation of oppression against mothers and children, she also draws attention, by apostrophe, to Latona's mandate to "wrap [Niobe's children] in the shades of death!" (l. 90).

As illustrated metaphorically by "Niobe," and supported literally by "To the Right Honourable William, Earl of Dartmouth," Wheatley inserts herself into the space of a newly independent American nation as the rightful heir to citizenship. In contrast to the self-indulgent goddesses Niobe and Latona, Wheatley offers "Freedom" as a *"Goddess* long desir'd" ("Right Honourable William, Earl of Dartmouth"l. 11), not only for an "enslav[e]d"*"America,"* but also for its enslaved *"Africans"* (ll. 15–25). In what Shields describes as "a rare autobiographical portrait" (*Collected Works,* 235) Wheatley likens her physical enslavement to the "enslave[ment] [of] the land" ("Right Honourable William, Earl of Dartmouth," 19), with her poignant depiction of the "excruciating" manner in which she was "snatch'd from *Afric's* fancy'd happy seat" (l. 25). Her poetry and her life point to the way in which the history of both whites and blacks can represent an attempt to escape from the oppression of tyranny and slavery. Wheatley refused to write and imagine herself from the position of a permanently enslaved and disenfranchised African. Rather, she wrote from the position of an American with the same rights and privileges as any other citizen. In her elegy "On the Death of General Wooster," Wheatley identifies with both her African and her American self as she "maintains that ... an American military and political victory over Britain" should necessarily mean freedom for Africans (Shields, *Collected Works*, 238). "But how, presumptuous shall *we* hope to find / Divine acceptance with th' Almighty mind / While yet (O deed Ungenerous?) *they* disgrace / And hold in bondage Afric's blameless race?" ("Death of General Wooster" ll. 26–30; my emphasis). Wheatley radically saw her struggle for freedom from slavery (and less directly patriarchy) as synonymous with that of white America's struggle for independence from Britain.

Wheatley's poetry refigures and resituates Africans at the crossroads between slavery and independence in the American Revolutionary landscape. Her works reveal through their reinterpretation and improvisation complementary spaces of freedom and independence. Seen thus, an eighteenth-century Afro-British American aesthetic emerges and with it a model for an interrogation not only of its temporal, but also of the spatial boundaries of freedom and enslavement. Clearly, Wheatley's revisionary designations of freedom and independence as that which ignored the enslaved, indentured, and nominally free existence of the peoples it claimed to represent demands a more radical contemporary interrogation.

Wheatley imagined herself as a natural and equal member of the soon-to-be independent community of free Americans. For, although Wheatley may legally have been a slave, much of her work points to her affinity for liberty. "Niobe" in particular suggests a conception of herself as a part of the newly independent American nation. Shields contends that "so complete was her absorption in the struggle for freedom [both in this world and the next], that [it] governed her conception of poetry" (*Collected Works*, 230). Dissatisfied with a "world which allow[ed] slavery to remain legitimate," Wheatley "buil[t] in her poems another, acceptable world" (xxix).

Thus, in "Niobe" Wheatley envisions a world in which African women, like her, inhabit the space of the independent American citizens rather than the enslaved objects. Moreover, Wheatley recuperates the lineage of "the [beautiful] Phrygian queen" (Emily Watts, 10) as that of potent gods, rather than that of Ovid's usurping, undeserving, and overreaching mortals. Niobe is, after all, "the wealthy heir to Tantalus divine" ("Niobe" l. 14), son of Zeus, the ruler of the gods. Of equal importance, especially to an eighteenth-century British audience, is the image of slavery and freedom that the term *Phrygian* invokes. Wheatley was certainly aware of the import of the term's well-known iconic value, especially during this historical moment. In particular, "during the eighteenth-century, the Phrygian cap evolved into a symbol of freedom, held aloft a Liberty pole during the American Revolution" (*OED*).

Further, the fact that "Phrygian" and "queen" are linked in this poem suggests Wheatley's awareness of the complex and yet common association of the dual imagery that women and enslaved Africans suggest for the white American males who would no longer be enslaved under British tyranny. Erkkila's analysis of the poet's manipulation of gendered and racial associations of the Revolutionary period invites us to direct critical attention to the unmistakable links between the figure of "Niobe" and "'Britannia Mutilated' . . . [in which] Britain appears as a naked female figure, enchained, amputated, and deprived of her former power by aggressive colonial policies of king and Parliament" (226). In fact, the black slave poet's coupling of the seemingly unrelated terms—"Phrygian" and "queen"—point to the paradox of the parallel injustices endured by both the white American citizen and the enslaved African. It is the latter term that Wheatley means to emphasize—as her use of "Phrygian" signifies on its double meaning. It serves as both an image of liberty denied by the British and liberty attained by America. However, Wheatley is all too aware of the "Phrygian" cap of freedom that continues to elude the enslaved African woman. To her credit Wheatley fully understands the implications of her use of such inconsistent terms of reference—both in the mythic tale of Niobe and the real history of the British colonies—the enslaved black and the nominally free white woman. Tragically, sovereign ascension is inextricably and perpetually contingent on the maintenance and upholding of the legacy of slavery by both king and queen.

As for the Phrygian cap which symbolized both British subjection and American entitlement, for the enslaved black woman it represented an identifiable marking (or branding) and constant reminder of her immutable difference. For, even if she attained freedom, and in so doing the Phrygian cap, it would always be worn as a symbolic reminder of her former status as a slave and her current status as at the bottom of the chain of being. Moreover, unlike the emancipated Roman slaves whose freedom this cap signified, the formerly enslaved African's descendants remained slaves as a condition of their birth to a slave mother. There is little doubt that Wheatley's poetic preoccupation with slavery and freedom—as demonstrated in her linking of the images of woman and liberty—clearly identifies the Revolutionary strain in her poetry.

Notably, in "To a Gentleman of the Navy" Wheatley laments the "Phrygian hero" Paris's "set[ting] the world in arms" over Helen's "resistless charms" (ll. 10–15). Far more interesting, and related to the poet's rendering of "Niobe" is the conversation—the call and response that ensues during "The Answer [By the Gentleman of the Navy]" and "Phillis's Reply to the Answer." One cannot miss the classical Greek allusions to Phoebus and Apollo echoed in "The Answer," "Niobe," and throughout many of her other works. For example, given Wheatley's knowledge of Greek, Latin, and the neoclassical tradition, as signified by this brilliant and original translation of Ovid's texts, her choice of subjects is deliberately complex in order to draw critical white propertied males' attention to undervalued, dehumanized, eighteenth-century black humanity—certainly a new twist on traditional eighteenth-century poetic forms of indirection and Afro-poetic signification.

It is literally Wheatley's objection, as much as it is metaphorically Niobe's, that "Coeus' offspring is obeyed / while to [her] goddesship no tribute's paid" (ll. 67–68). Clearly, the Revolutionary voice of the slave poet Wheatley is as much a "rebel against an established order" (Emily Watts, 38), as the mythical heroine Niobe. As Ostriker notes, "Niobe could rail despairingly against the gods in a way that Wheatley, who is elsewhere demurely Christian and patriotic, could not" (214). Hence, Wheatley's poem is about "women and power" (214), and the "natural" right of all mothers to maintain and sustain their progeny, despite dominant Western assumptions of ownership. More importantly, "Niobe" is a remembering of African and American subjectivity in terms which are restated by African voices in an attempt to neutralize the devastating effects of slavery and racism. Wheatley's historical encoding of African worldviews and her synthesizing of African and Western ways of knowing in both the form and content of her poetry point to ways in which early Afro-British American writers struggle for self-definition and determination in the literal and figurative landscapes of the world they inhabit, rather than the worlds that attempt to capture them.

Wheatley's creation of such a setting through her arrangement of color and light to emphasize physical beauty and fertility echoes the biblical renderings of Eve and Hagar. Like Wheatley's biblical foremothers, the mythical women she captures in "Niobe" express a similar lament at the suffering as well as their pride in God's gift, their progeny. As dangerously heretical as Wheatley's analogy between perceived "pagan" goddesses and the mother of the Lord, Jesus Christ, seems, her use of "Niobe" to expose the horrific consequences of an ethnic other, nearly her mirror image, as it applies to social conditions, is a far more dangerous proposition. Thus, images such as Niobe must be far more cautiously presented, as they might dangerously threaten to empower, if only metaphysically and spiritually, African women, and indict white Christian patriarchal and matriarchal power. Thus, "Niobe" becomes a bridge through which the devoutly Christian poet can simultaneously invoke and recuperate the fallen and bruised African woman. Unlike her white and black literary descendants, with the exception of the nineteenth-century author Pauline Hopkins who wrote about Hagar, Wheatley projects the black woman's desire for freedom, respect, and power onto a racially ambiguous figure—Niobe, the Phrygian queen. In so doing, she captures "Niobe" as a vessel through which she can regain a legacy of empowerment. Wheatley—through "Niobe"—traces a reconnected line of descendants through Eve and Hagar to the venerated Mary. The movement from illegitimate outcast to authorized and sanctioned citizen is enabled by means of a symbolic passing through multivalent gendered states.

What I am suggesting here is what is unique about Wheatley's subtle rendering of the Hagar myth is the way in which she uses the neoclassical and secular to get at this idea of the "fallen" and certainly outcast and exiled woman. Thus, the pious Christian slave-poet figures Niobe as representative of both African and European womanhood in order to render scathing critiques of race, class, and gender. In particular, she signifies upon the divisiveness that separates actual white and black women in America—through the figures of Latona and Niobe. Latona and Niobe signify both black and white women who are similarly oppressed on the basis of gender and whose children are similarly vulnerable. Wheatley underscores such risks of superficial pride and assumed superiority based on relative power, in her depiction of the consequences that arise in the parallel lives of mythological goddesses. Latona, as a representative of the history of exile, in her story that precedes the Niobe myth, of the homeless, landless mother wandering in the wilderness without water or food, while the wicked and prideful "Niobe" wallows sinfully in her abundant fertility, echoes the Virgin Mary, who wanders looking for a place to give birth to her son Jesus. Further, early black writers like Wheatley—using popular scriptural allusions and Revolutionary language—reverse the gender symbology of the "fall" of mankind. However, between Eve and Mary there remains Hagar to be recovered and it is in the neoclassical myth that Wheatley recovers through repetition the exiled mother who is parched and ejected perhaps from humanity, but not from God.

Wheatley's revelatory arrangement and paradoxical juxtaposition of the "distress" experienced through the dark and barren life of a mother and child alongside Niobe's celebration of such brightness highlights the "fall from grace" which results in the spiritual devolution of the position of motherhood. Certainly, the differently cast versions of banishment which are equally oppressive to Eve, Hagar, and Mary are worth considering. Eve, not unlike the enslaved African woman, bears the responsibility, through childbirth, of the enslavement and "fall" of her posterity. The legal mandate that the child shall follow the condition of the mother cannot only be seen to be useful in a socioeconomic and political structure of a society that depends upon the institution of slavery for its prosperity and growth, but such a mandate can also be seen to advance the biblical *Patriarchal Narratives* which promulgate the edification of the Christian God's Kingdom through the legacy of the patriarchs, such as Abraham. Hagar's perceived helplessness and oppressed situation as a slave who was at the mercy of a mistress and a master, and who is punished for what little bit of "haughtiness" or pride she is bold enough to demonstrate in her ability to procreate, are linked (through "Niobe") to Eve's own sins of pride.

Cain, the son of Eve—the woman who was the instigator of the action which leads to the banishment of mankind from the Garden of Eden—who kills his brother Abel, is linked to the history of enslaved Africans.[24] Enslaved Africans, who like Cain are "tillers of the ground," "fugitives and vagabonds," are said to bear the mark of Cain, manifested in their "blackness" which is a sign of their sin and one of several significant biblical justifications for their enslavement in perpetuity. Similarly, Ishmael, the "son of the bondwoman" Hagar, the "wild man; [whose] hand [would] be against every man; and every man's hand against him" (Genesis 16:12–13), had also been represented as the historical marker of illegitimacy, and therefore questionable inheritance, at the same time that he is the "lad" out of whom God "made a nation" because "he was [Abraham's] seed" (Genesis 21:13) and because God responded to the cries of Hagar. Even the most revered of all, Mary, the mother of Jesus, not only experiences homelessness during her most crucial hours, but she also risks, if only fleetingly, societal rebuke for what is initially perceived as a sin of sexual indiscretion. "Espoused to Joseph," meaning not yet married, she is "with child." And, despite the fact that her pregnancy occurs "before they came together" (Matthew 1:18) or perhaps because of this circumstance, Joseph doubts her chastity. "Being a just man, and not willing to make her a publick example, was minded to put her away privily" (Matthew 1:19). Mary experiences additional suffering as a new mother, as she, her husband, and her child must "flee into Egypt" to save her young child's life. As in the narratives of Hagar and Eve, the Lord intervenes and fulfills promises and covenants made to the patriarchs.[25]

Once again these images of motherhood (and parallel barrenness) ring strikingly familiar for an eighteenth-century woman well aware of both the significance and dangers of childbirth. Though of course at the time Wheatley wrote "Niobe," she was not yet a mother or a wife, but a young girl, her elegies to women and children are testimony to her consciousness of this type of woman's suffering. Later in life she would lose one child in infancy and die in childbirth with another. Alongside Wheatley's linking of the enslaved eighteenth-century African within a Hagarian circle of spiritual and physical "distress" associated with motherhood is the young poet's celebration of God's divine intervention as significantly signaled in the following passage:

> What! shall a Titanness be deified,
> To whom the spacious earth a couch denied?
> Nor heaven, nor earth, nor sea received your queen,
> Til pitying Delos took the wand'rer in.
> Round me what a large progeny is spread?
> No frowns of fortune has my soul to dread.
> What if indignant she decrease my train?
> More than Latona's number will remain. (ll. 75–82)

In this passage Niobe's indictment and harsh mockery of Latona must be reckoned with and balanced against Wheatley's equally revelatory pointing to the self-righteousness with which Latona orders and receives the pledge of her two children, Apollo and Phoebe, "to punish pride, and scourge the rebel mind" (l. 104). Latona aims to murder all of Niobe's children and she intends to use her children as the instruments of murder. Thus, both women become implicated in the horrific slaughter. Equally important to look at is the way Wheatley's imagery remains focused on parental anguish or "distress." Niobe's mythical children, like Eve's and Hagar's, occupy unstable positions on earth—despite God's favor in heaven.

Such is echoed in the lives of the sacred mothers of Christianity and Islam respectively, Sarai[26] and Hagar. It is interesting to note that in the biblical narrative of Hagar and Sarai both women have been at some level, at one time or another, "sacrificed" for Abraham. First, in Genesis 12, Abram asks Sarai to pose as his sister so that the Egyptian kings will not kill him—a situation that, as biblical scholars have argued, puts Sarai in a precarious position. She is taken to be a single woman and brought into the harem of the Egyptian king. Before God's intervention, Sarai, not unlike Hagar, becomes bondservant or "slave" to the dominant male authority. Notably, the exception is that Hagar (as scholars have pointed out) endures a further level of oppression and subjection as bondservant to the woman Sarai. This increased level of violence enacted upon one woman by another is brought forth in "Niobe." As I noted earlier, Niobe's reminder to the other Theban women of the unfortunate circumstances under which Latona gave birth to her twins draws attention to their class differences.

In the Ovidian version of Latona's displacement, to which Niobe refers, the relationship between slavery, women's oppression, and religion is more vividly punctuated. "Stirred by / the later [Niobe's fate], they tell / . . . [of one] whom the queen of heaven once shut / out from all the world / . . . [who] / brought forth her [divine] twin babes / . . . weary / of her long struggle, / [and] faint by reason of /sun's heat and parched with thirst; / [her] hungry children had drained her breast dry of / milk" (Ovid, vi. ll. 315–43). This history of a mother with breasts milked dry, parched with heat who is denied even a cool drink of water, a mother who is denied even a place to rest her tired body, a mother who is cursed and abused, echoes the historical oppression and alienation of both the African slave mother and the economically and socially oppressed white woman.

In Niobe's voice one can also hear the voices of Wheatley's African ancestors and African American descendants. Consequently, when Wheatley reaches outside of the mythological realm of neoclassical Ovidian myth, the political rhetoric of the Revolution, and the sacred writings of the Word, she reaches inside to unlock her own pain and distress. In this revelation Wheatley highlights the presence of that which appears invisible—an awareness of the absence of the African child's father and mother as equally heart-wrenching.

Wheatley was not unaware that while white Revolutionary fathers were highly and heroically visible, white and black mothers and daughters and black fathers and sons were rendered invisible. In the same way that Wheatley unearths women's historical oppression through her reference to Latona's history, the young African woman Christian poet's repetition of the *distress* of the "fallen woman—Eve," the "outcast Egyptian bondswoman—Hagar," and "the Virgin Birth of the Christian Savior Jesus, through Mary"—she indirectly signifies on the displacement of African fathers with one Western and Christian Father, who is problematically constructed as a god in support of a white patriarchal structure, which sanctions those fathers who embrace some sons and deny others, even as he sacrifices his own son, Jesus Christ, for all of Ishmael and Isaac's sons and Eve, Hagar, and Mary's daughters. Wheatley remembers African and American subjectivity in terms that redefine and celebrate a more "authentic" women's Afro-Christian spiritual self. In so doing, she poses critical questions that remain to be answered as we explore the complex relationship between religion, slavery, gender, and race.[27]

Notes

1. See Margaret Odell's biography on Wheatley and John Wheatley's letter (dated November 14, 1772) to the publisher of *Poems on Various Subjects Religious and Moral.* http://docsouth.unc.edu/neh/wheatley/wheatley.html#wheat9. Accessed July 9, 2007.

2. All references to Ovid's text, unless otherwise noted, will be the translation in the Loeb Edition. See Ovid, *Metamorphoses Books I–VIII*, ed. G. P. Goold, trans. Frank Justus Miller (Cambridge: Harvard University Press, 1999).

3. Michael Gomez uses this term to refer to "related yet distinguishable life-styles" (9) that differentiate between mere "synthesis of . . . European and African cultural forms" and the actual lifestyles African Americans maintained in the face of "culture[s] of coercion and . . . volition" (10). Thus, polycultural refers to both "forms of expression [and] the intent and meaning behind the slave's participation" (10).

4. E.g., "On Being Brought from Africa to America," "To the University of Cambridge, in New England," and "To the Right Honorable William, Earl of Dartmouth."

5. "Nation" refers to a group of persons related by common language, descent (or origin) and history, country, as well as "a particular class, kind, or race of persons" (OED s.v.). Between the late seventeenth and eighteenth centuries, the community of colonial subject gradually metamorphosed from a group of displaced English men and women with a common language and history into a race of white, male, proper-tied rational humans with a natural right to independence and ascendancy over those who were of other nations (race and gender). The evolution of the term by which colonists described themselves, from "Christian" to "free" to "white," illustrates this metamorphosis (Reich, 124).

6. My conceptualization of this term parallels Paul Gilroy's invention of "Africa" within the "rhizomorphic, fractal structure of the transcultural, interna-tional formation" (4) he calls the Black Atlantic.

7. See Glenn Hendler's work in the area of nineteenth-century sentimentality, gender, and the public sphere for additional insights into this phenomenon (see Public Sentiments: Structures of Feeling in Nineteenth-Century American Literature [Chapel Hill: University of North Carolina Press, 2001]).

8. The Great Commission commands Christians to "go ye therefore, and teach all nations . . . to observe all things whatsoever I have commanded you" (Matthew 28:19–20a). The understanding that Wheatley, as a devout Christian, could not have missed was "and lo, I am with you always, even unto the end of the world" (Matthew 28:20b). This passage clearly links the Christian ethereal with the transient world. Finally, the word "life" (Greek: zoe; Hebrew: nephesh) in John 10:10 denotes that "abundant living" is promised both on earth and in heaven.

9. I describe Wheatley's work as a kind of marketplace because its synthe-sization of diverse Western and African ways of knowing creates a space of positive creative exchange and dialogue. Further, the role of the marketplace for African women as a center for cultural, commercial, and personal exchanges signifies on a feminized market space that does not exclude, but rather supports the entire community in West African cultures. According to Ogunyemi, "the marketplace [is] the site where . . . [many] purveyors thrive, each [with] a niche. The market combines, into one gigantic whole, what, in the Western world, has been com-partmentalized and masculinized [or feminized] under capitalism into the depart-mental store, the bookstore, the grocery store, the hairdressing salon . . ." (African Wo/Man Palava, 49).

10. David Grimsted argues that "death is tied imagistically to slavery. To die in Christ is to be 'from bondage freed,' though death himself 'reigns tyrant o'er this mortal shore,' exercises his 'dire dominion,' and represents 'all destroying Power,' which vainly tries to 'chain us to hell, and bar the gates of light.' Wheatley addressed the 'grim monarch' in terms that should have touched the human slave drivers: 'Dost though go on incessant to destroy, / Our griefs to double, and lay waste our joy?'" ("Anglo-American Racism and Phillis Wheatley's . . . ," 357).

11. As a result, I will not find it necessary, for example, to identify Wheatley's employment of a bird trope. Nor will I make any claims about Wheatley's specific geographic origins on the continent of Africa. I have selected Senegal as a focal point of departure for African aesthetic influence in her work because much of the historical evidence presented thus far suggests it is reasonable to do so.

12. See Luke 14:27–29 (King James Version): "And whosoever doth not bear his cross, and come after me, cannot be my disciple / For which of you, intending to build a tower, sitteth not down first, and counteth the cost, whether he have sufficient to finish it? / Lest haply, after he hath laid the foundation, and is not able to finish it, all that behold it begin to mock him."

13. See Antonio T. Bly, "Wheatley's 'To the University of Cambridge, in New-England,'" *Explicator* 55, no. 4 (Summer 1997): 205–9, for a less gendered reading of Wheatley's tactical employment of such religious themes to subvert dominant negative racial subscriptions and assert her own race pride.

14. Likewise, as critics we attempt to recover Wheatley from the fragmented remains of African, Western, and Afro-Western cultural and historical remains.

15. I am deeply indebted to Lucy Hayden's work (following John Shields), one of the first and still few scholars to suggest that Wheatley was "possibly drawing subliminally on the story-telling tradition of her African past when she wrote 'Goliath of Gath' as well as when she faced the challenge of recreating Ovid's passionate story of Niobe" (436). Necessarily, she acknowledges Shields's contribution—thinking along these lines—as I do here and elsewhere in this book. Importantly, however, she turns to Wheatley's Christian traditions for answers to the critical question she poses: "But why Book VI of The Metamorphoses and not another possibly one of those translated by Pope?" (436). See "Classical Tidings from the Afric Muse: Phillis Wheatley's Use of Mythology," *CLA* 34, no. 4 (June 1992): 432–47.

16. As of the Virginia Act of 1658, children followed the condition of their mother, thereby "demean[ing] the black mother because of her race and set[ting] her apart from white women" (Ashcraft-Eason, 70). This represents one of colonial America's earliest and most critical links between the naturalness of motherhood and the naturalness of slavery.

17. George Sandys's translation of the description of Niobe's children strikes an interpretive balance between Wheatley and Ovid: "Seven beauteous daughters, and as many boyes. All these by marriage to be multiply'd." See Sandys's *Ovid's Metamorphoses Englished.*

18. "Seven" is "used symbolically, often denoting completion or perfection" (*OED* s.v.). Niobe's children and Zeus are both the children of Titans. Zeus is the son of Chronos and Niobe is the daughter of Tantalus (Smith, *Dictionary of Classical Reference in English Poetry*, 39–167). Niobe's and Latona's relative positions to divinity have to do with Zeus's usurping of his father's throne.

19. Like Bassard, I, too, "read Wheatley's memory of her mother's morning libations as [what Holloway terms] a '(cultural) mooring' that initiates a series of African American female '(spiritual) metaphors'" (37 passim). See also Holloway (passim). The version of Wheatley's memory I cite here (from Richmond) is actually an embellishment by her biographer. The embellished version appears on the page after this original version: "One circumstance alone, it might have been said, she remembered; and that was, her mother's custom of pouring out water before the sun at rising." See B. B. Thatcher, *Memoir of Phillis Wheatley, a Native African and Slave*, 2nd ed. (Boston: Geo. W. Light, 1837), 2.

20. Robert Ferguson's elaboration of the significance of "metaphors of light" to "early republican problems of perception" is instructive. His work suggests yet another perspective from which discrete elements of eighteenth-century black aesthetics can be interpreted. If "to see is to know in eighteenth-century thought" and if sight—in its American Enlightenment context—is constructed within a "secular frame of reference" (28), then Wheatley's appropriation of the conventional use of metaphor of light creates a subtle but radical upheaval. Specifically, the black female poet dares to affirm her physical powers of observation alongside her mental and spiritual ones. Rising above the "sons of science," Wheatley ascends through her use of metaphors of light to "clarify" and redefine that which is simultaneously known and unknown—motherhood and nation. In so doing, she subtly and symbolically unveils and exposes the dilemma of a nation blinded and enslaved by its own view of freedom. As I elaborate on a bit more fully later, Wheatley's relationship to sight, seeing, and associated metaphors also links her to West African traditions of Sankofa and the Wayside Bird.

21. "Chi," according to Ogunyemi's interpretation, is "the quidditas inside the human body, the part that cannot be detected but that we know is there. It is essence, innateness, instincts, genetics, luck, endowment, destiny, empowerment; it is the caretaker and giver installed within" (36). She also points to the centrality of motherhood in the myth of Osun, who is the mother of Esu, the intermediary between the divine and human realm and one of the most important Yoruban deities.

22. Boubacar Barry notes that between 1681 and 1810 an estimated 304,330 to 500,000 slaves were exported from the Senegambia region alone. *Senegambia and the Atlantic Slave Trade* (Cambridge: Cambridge University Press, 1998), 61–80.

23. Wheatley, not unlike her contemporary Abigail Adams, is concerned about improved conditions for women in the newly imagined postcolonial society. More importantly, though, the poet understands that "all men [and women] would be tyrants if they could" (Adams qtd. in Adeola James, *In Their Own Voices*, 68).

24. Recent works such as David Goldenberg's *The Curse of Ham: Race and Slavery in Early Judaism, Christianity, and Islam* (Princeton, NJ: Princeton University Press, 2003), and Newell G. Bringhurst and Darron T. Smith's *Black and Mormon* (Urbana: University of Illinois Press, 2004) offer important insights on this topic. Of course, Werner Sollors's numerous works on ethnicity and mixed-race literature and culture and Winthrop Jordan's *White over Black* remain key texts for further study on this tradition.

25. Comparisons as well between Isaac and Ishmael were well known during this period with many eighteenth-century religious texts using Sarah and Hagar as examples of the "Two Covenants" Law and Grace, respectively.

26. The alternate spelling of Sarah's earlier name as Sarai is meant to signify on the drastically different biblical metamorphoses (cultural and spiritual conversions) that these two women experience. More important, the Genesis narratives of name changing have important implications for reading national and natural identity in Wheatley. Specifically, from Genesis 16 to 17, there is a significant renaming of both Sarai and Abram. Abram becomes "Abraham, father of many nations" and Sarai becomes "Sarah, mother of many nations." Three chapters later after the promised birth of their son Isaac, the child through whom the covenant with God and lineage of the nation of Israel will be fulfilled, Hagar experiences a metamorphosis without name change. Sarah's complete transformation to natural versus stepmother sparks a monstrous transformation for Hagar, whose movement

from bondswoman of the house of Abraham, and mother of a son of Abraham who is heir to his household and inheritor of a proud lineage, becomes "Hagar the Egyptian" outcast mother to Ishmael the wild man, who would become the ruler of an "other" kind of nation.

27. I conclude with a reference to displaced African fathers to signify the critical attention that remains to be paid to the multiple codings and balanced rendering of "gender" in Wheatley's works.

Contributors

HAROLD BLOOM is Sterling Professor of the Humanities at Yale University. He is the author of 30 books, including *Shelley's Mythmaking, The Visionary Company, Blake's Apocalypse, Yeats, A Map of Misreading, Kabbalah and Criticism, Agon: Toward a Theory of Revisionism, The American Religion, The Western Canon,* and *Omens of Millennium: The Gnosis of Angels, Dreams, and Resurrection. The Anxiety of Influence* sets forth Professor Bloom's provocative theory of the literary relationships between the great writers and their predecessors. His most recent books include *Shakespeare: The Invention of the Human,* a 1998 National Book Award finalist, *How to Read and Why, Genius: A Mosaic of One Hundred Exemplary Creative Minds, Hamlet: Poem Unlimited, Where Shall Wisdom Be Found?,* and *Jesus and Yahweh: The Names Divine.* In 1999, Professor Bloom received the prestigious American Academy of Arts and Letters Gold Medal for Criticism. He has also received the International Prize of Catalonia, the Alfonso Reyes Prize of Mexico, and the Hans Christian Andersen Bicentennial Prize of Denmark.

PONTHEOLLA T. WILLIAMS was at the time of publishing her book on Robert Hayden teaching in the humanities division at Morris College. From 1984 to 1986 she was a presidential appointee serving in the adult literacy division at the U.S. Department of Education.

B.J. BOLDEN is associate professor of English at Chicago State University and also the director of the Gwendolyn Brooks Center for Black Literature and Creative Writing. Besides her work on Brooks, she has published essays on Diana Chang, Edgar Allan Poe, Lucille Clifton, Haki Madhubuti, Sonia Sanchez, and Ntozake Shange.

WOLFGANG KARRER is a professor of American literature at Osnabruck, Germany.

JAMES SMETHURST teaches English at the W.E.B. Du Bois Department of Afro-American studies at the University of Massachusetts in Amherst. In 1999 he published *The New Red Negro: The Literary Left and African-American Poetry* and in 2003 published as co-author *Left of the Color Line: Race, Radicalism, and Twentieth-Century Literature of the United States*.

CAROLINE GEBHARD is associate professor of English at Tuskegee University. She has written about nineteenth-century American women writers; her current project is a book on Paul Laurence Dunbar.

FRANCES SMITH FOSTER teaches English and women's studies at Emory University. She is a contributing editor—with Henry Louis Gates, Jr. and Nellie Y. McKay—to *The Norton Anthology of African American Literature*.

KEITH D. LEONARD is assistant professor of literature at American University. He has contributed to *African American Review* and *The Oxford Companion to African American Literature*.

PAULA BERNAT BENNETT taught at Southern Illinois University in Carbondale. She has also written on Emily Dickinson. Her most recent project is co-editing a volume of essays on nineteenth-century American poetry.

EMILY BERNARD teaches English and ethnic studies at the University of Vermont. She has edited two books: *Remember Me to Harlem: The Letters of Langston Hughes and Carl Van Vechten* (2001) and *Some of My Best Friends: Writers on Interracial Friendship* (2004). Bernard is the recipient of fellowships from the Ford Foundation and the National Endowment for the Humanities.

LENA AHLIN is associated with the English department at Lund University in Stockholm.

APRIL C.E. LANGLEY is associate professor of English at the University of Missouri in Columbia.

Bibliography

WORKS BY THE POETS

Gwendolyn Brooks

Blacks. Chicago: Third World Press, 1991.

Report from Part One. Detroit: Broadside Press, 1972.

Selected Poems. New York: Harper Perrenial, 2006.

Sterling A. Brown

The Collected Poems of Sterling A. Brown. Evanston, Ill: Triquarterly Books, 1980.

Harper, Michael S., ed. *The Collected Poems of Sterling A. Brown*. Evanston, Ill: Another Chicago Press, 1989.

Countee Cullen

Caroling Dusk: An Anthology of Verse by Black Poets of the Twenties. Secaucus, N.J.: Carol Publishing Group, 1993.

On Thee I Stand: An Anthology of the Best Poems of Countee Cullen. New York: Harper & Row, 1966.

Paul Laurence Dunbar

Howells, W.D., ed. *The Complete Poems of Paul Laurence Dunbar, With an Introduction to "Lyrics of Lowly Life."* New York: Dodd, Mead & Co., 1967.

Langston Hughes

Selected Poems. New York: Vintage, 1974.

Rampersad, Arnold and David Roessel, eds. *The Collected Poems of Langston Hughes.* New York: A.A. Knopf; distributed by Random House, 1984.

Roessel, David, ed. *Langston Hughes: Poems.* New York: Knopf, 1999.

James Weldon Johnson

Wilson, Sondra Kathryn, ed. *Saint Peter Relates an Incident: Selected Poems.* New York: Penguin Books, 1993.

Claude McKay

Dewey, John and Max Eastman, eds. *Selected Poems of Claude McKay.* New York: Bookman Associates, 1993.

Cooper, Wayne F., ed. *The Passion of Claude McKay: Selected Poetry and Prose.* New York: Schoken Books, 1973.

Melvin Beaunorus Tolson

Nelson, Raymond, ed. *"Harlem Gallery" and Other Poems of Melvin B. Tolson.* Charlottesville: University Press of Virginia, 1999.

Jean Toomer

Jones, Robert B. and Margery Toomer Latimer, eds. *The Collected Poems of Jean Toomer.* Chapel Hill, N.C.: University of North Carolina Press, 1988.

Phillis Wheatley

Poems of Phillis Wheatley: A Native African and a Slave. Bedford, Mass.: Applewood Books, 1995.

Mason, Julian D., Jr., ed. *The Poems of Phillis Wheatley*, rev. and enl. ed. Chapel Hill: N.C.: University of North Carolina Press, 1989.

WORKS ABOUT THE POETS

Ahlin, Lena. *The "New Negro" in the Old World: Culture and Performance in James Weldon Johnson, Jessie Fauset, and Nella Larsen.* Stockholm: Department of English, Centre for Languages and Literature, Lund University, 2006.

Alexander, Elizabeth. *The Black Interior: Essays.* Saint Paul, Minn.: Graywolf, 2004.

Baker, Houston A. *A Many-Colored Coat of Dreams: The Poetry of Countee Cullen.* Detroit: Broadside Press, 1974.

Benson, Bryan Joseph and Mabel Mayle Dillard. *Jean Toomer.* Boston: Twayne Publishers, 1980.

Benston, Kimberly. *Performing Blackness: Enactments of African American Modernism.* New York: Routledge, 2000.

Bolden, B. J. *Urban Rage In Bronzeville: Social Commentary in the Poetry of Gwendolyn Brooks, 1945–1960.* Chicago: Third World Press, 1999.

Bontemps, Anna. *The Harlem Renaissance Remembered.* New York: Dodd, Mead, 1972.

Brawley, Benjamin Griffith. *Paul Laurence Dunbar: A Poet of His People.* Port Washington, N.Y.: Kennikat Press, 1967.

Brooks, Joanna. *American Lazarus: Religion and the Rise of African American and Native American Literatures.* New York: Oxford University Press, 2003.

Brunner, Edward. *Cold War Poetry.* Urbana: University of Illinois Press, 2001.

Bryant, Jacqueline, ed. *Gwendolyn Brooks' Maud Martha: A Critical Collection.* Chicago: Third World Press, 2002.

Burr, Zofia. *Of Women, Poetry, and Power: Strategies of Address in Dickinson. Miles, Brooks, Lorde, and Angelou.* Urbana and Chicago: University of Illinois Press, 2002.

Cooper, Wayne F. *Claude McKay: Rebel Sojourner in the Harlem Renaissance: A Biography.* Baton Rouge: Louisiana State University Press, 1996, 1987.

Cunningham, Virginia. *Paul Laurence Dunbar and His Song.* New York: Dodd, Mead, 1947.

Dorsey, David F. "Countee Cullen's Use of Mythology." *College Language Association Journal* 13, 1970: pp.68–77.

Douglass, Frederick. *Narrative of the Life of Douglass, an American Slave Written by Himself.* Boston: Anti-Slavery Office, 1845. http://docsouth.unc/neh/douglass/menu.html.

Dowling, Robert M. *Slumming in New York: From the Waterfront to Mythic Harlem.* Urbana and Chicago: University of Illinois Press, 2007.

Egar, Emmanuel E. *The Poetics of Rage: Wole Soyinka, Jean Toomer, and Claude McKay.* Lanham, Md.: University Press of America, Inc., 2005.

Faber, Genevieve and Michel Feith, eds. *Jean Toomer and the Harlem Renaissance.* New Brunswick, N.J.: Rutgers University Press, 2001.

Farnsworth, Robert M. *Melvin B. Tolson, 1898–1966: Plain Talk and Poetic Prophecy.* Columbia: University of Missouri Press, 1984.

Ferguson, Blanche E. *Countee Cullen and the Negro Renaissance.* New York: Dodd, Mead, 1966.

Flasch, Joy. *Melvin B. Tolson.* New York: Twayne, 1972.

Fleming, Robert E. *James Weldon Johnson.* Boston: Twayne, 1987.

Ford, Karen Jackson. *Split-Gut Song: Jean Toomer and the Politics of Modernity.* Tuscaloosa: The University of Alabama Press, 2005.

Gabbin, Joanne V., ed. *The Furious Flowering of African American Poetry.* Charlottesville, Va.: University of Virginia Press, 1999.

———. *Sterling Brown: Building the Black Aesthetic Tradition.* Westport, Conn.: Greenwood Press, 1985.

Gayle, Addison, Jr. *Oak and Ivy: A Biography of Paul Laurence Dunbar.* Garden City: Doubleday, 1971.

Gayles, Gloria Wade, ed. *Conversations with Gwendolyn Brooks.* Jackson: The University Press of Mississippi, 2003.

Gibson, Donald B. *Modern Black Poets: A Collection of Critical Essays.* Englewood Cliffs, N.J.: Prentice-Hall, 1973.

Glaysher, Frederick, ed. *Collected Poems: Robert Hayden.* New York and London: Liveright Publishing Corporation, 1996.

Goldstein, Laurence, and Robert Chrisman, eds. *Robert Hayden: Essays on the Poetry.* Ann Arbor: University of Michigan Press, 2001.

Guterl, Matthew Pratt. *The Color of Race in America, 1900–1940.* Cambridge: Harvard University Press, 2001.

Harris, Sharon M. *Executing Race: Early American Women's Narratives of Race, Society, and the Law.* Columbus: The Ohio State University Press, 2005.

Hatcher, John. *From the Auroral Darkness: The Life and Poetry of Robert Hayden.* Oxford: George Ronald, 1984.

Houston, A. Baker, Jr. *A Many-Colored Coat of Dreams: The Poetry of Countee Cullen.* Detroit: Broadside Press, 1974.

Hudson, Theodore R. *From LeRoi Jones to Amiri Baraka: The Literary Works.* Durham, N.C.: Duke University Press, 1973.

Huggins, Nathan Irvin. *Harlem Renaissance.* London, Oxford, and New York: Oxford University Press, 1971.

Hutchinson, George. *The Cambridge to the Harlem Renaissance.* Cambridge: Cambridge University Press, 2007.

Jackson, Blyden and Louis D. Rubin, Jr. *Black Poetry in America.* Baton Rouge: Louisiana State University Press, 1974.

Jones, Robert B. *Jean Toomer and the Prison-House of Thought: A Phenomenology of the Spirit.* Amherst: The University of Massachusetts Press, 1993.

Kaplan, Sidney. *The Black Presence in the Era of the American Revolution, 1770–1800.* Greenwich, Conn.: New York Graphic Society, 1973.

Kerman, Cynthia Earl. *The Lives of Jean Toomer: A Hunger for Wholeness.* Baton Rouge: Louisiana State University Press, 1987.

Langley, April C. E. *The Black Aesthetic Unbound: Theorizing the Dilemma of Eighteenth-Century African American Literature.* Columbus: The Ohio State University Press, 2008.

Lasky, Kathryn. *A Voice of Her Own: The Story of Phillis Wheatley, Slave Poet.* Cambridge, Mass.: Candlewick Press, 2003.

Lee, Valerie. *Granny Midwives & Black Women Writers.* New York: Routledge, 1996.

Leonard, Keith D. *Fettered Genius: The African American Bardic Poet from Slavery to Civil Rights.* Charlottesville and London: University of Virginia Press, 2006.

Locke, Alain. *Four Negro Poets*. New York: A. & C. Boni, 1925.

Martin, Jay, ed. *A Singer in the Dawn: Reinterpretations of Paul Laurence Dunbar*. New York: Dodd, Mead, 1972.

Mason, Julian D., Jr. *The Poems of Phillis Wheatley*. Chapel Hill and London: The University of North Carolina Press, 1989.

McCaskill, Barbara and Caroline Gebhard, eds. *Post-Bellum, Pre-Harlem: African American Literature and Culture, 1877–1919*. New York and London: New York University Press, 2006.

McKay, Nellie Y. *Jean Toomer, Artist: A Study of his Literary Life and Work, 1894–1936*. New York: Simon & Schuster, 1984.

Melhem, D. H. *Gwendolyn Brooks: Poetry and the Heroic Voice*. Lexington: The University Press of Kentucky, 1987.

Metcalf, E. W., Jr. *Paul Laurence Dunbar: A Bibliography*. Metuchen, N.J.: Scarecrow Press, 1975.

Mootry, Maria K. and Gary Smith, eds. *In A Life Distilled: Gwendolyn Brooks, Her Poetry and Fiction*. Urbana: University of Illinois Press, 1987.

Nielson, Aldon Lynn, ed. *Reading Race in American Poetry*. Urbana: University of Illinois Press, 2000.

Nordloh, David J. *Paul Laurence Dunbar*. Boston: Twayne Publishers, 1979.

North, Michael. *The Dialect of Modernism: Race, Language, and Twentieth-Century Literature*. New York: Oxford University Press, 1994.

Price, Kenneth M. and Lawrence J. Oliver, eds. *Critical Essays on James Weldon Johnson*. New York and London: G. K. Hall; Prentice-Hall International, 1997.

Ramesh, Kotto Sree and Kandula Nirupa Rani. *Claude McKay: The Literary Identity from Jamaica to Harlem and Beyond*. Jefferson, N.C.: McFarland & Company, Inc., 2006.

Rampersad, Arnold. *The Life of Langston Hughes: Vol. I: I, Too, Sing America*. New York: Oxford University Press, 1986.

Redding, J. Saunders. *To Make a Poet Black*. Chapel Hill: University of North Carolina Press, 1939.

Redmond, Eugene B. *Drumvoices: The Mission of Afro-American Poetry*. Garden City: Anchor/Doubleday, 1976.

Robinson, William H., ed. *Critical Essays on Phillis Wheatley*. Boston: G. K. Hall, 1981.

Sanders, Mark A. *Afro-Modernist Aesthetics and the Poetry of Sterling A. Brown*. Athens, Ga.: University of Georgia Press, 1999.

Shields, John C., ed. *The Collected Works of Phillis Wheatley*. New York: Oxford University Press, 1988.

Smitherman, Geneva. *Talkin' That Talk: Language, Culture and Education in African America*. London: Routledge, 2000.

Thompson, Robert Farris. *Flash of the Spirit: African and AfroAmerican Art and Philosophy*. New York: Random House, 1983.

Tidwell, John Edgar and Cheryl R. Ragar, eds. *Montage of a Dream: The Art and Life of Langston Hughes*. Columbia: University of Missouri Press, 2007.

Tillery, Tyrone. *Claude McKay: A Black Poet's Struggle for Identity*. Amherst: University of Massachusetts Press, 1992.

Tracy, Steven C., ed. *A Historical Guide to Langston Hughes*. New York: Oxford University Press, 2004.

———. *Langston Hughes and the Blues*. Urbana: University of Illinois Press, 1988.

Trotman, C. James, Arnold Rampersad, and Emery Wimbish, Jr., eds. *Langston Hughes: The Man, His Art, and His Continuing Influence*. New York and London: Garland Publishing, Inc., 1995.

Wagner, Jean. *Black Poets of the United States from Paul Laurence Dunbar to Langston Hughes*, trans. by Kenneth Douglas. Urbana, Chicago and London: University of Illinois Press, 1973.

Watts, Jerry Gafio. *Amiri Baraka: The Politics and Art of a Black Intellectual*. New York and London: New York University Press, 2001.

Wideman, John Edgar. "Frame and Dialect: The Evolution of the Black Voice in American Literature." *American Poetry Review* 5, no. 5 (1976): 34–37.

Winston, James. *A Fierce Hatred of Injustice: Claude McKay's Jamaica and His Poetry of Rebellion*. London and New York: Verso, 2000.

Woodson, Jon. *To Make a New Race: Gurdjieff, Toomer and the Harlem Renaissance*. Jackson: University Press of Mississippi, 1999.

Acknowledgments

Pontheolla T. Williams, "The Apprenticeship: *Heart-Shape in the Dust* (1940). From *Robert Hayden: A Critical Analysis of His Poetry.* Copyright 1987 by the Board of Trustees of the University of Illinois. Used with permission of the University of Illinois Press.

B.J. Bolden, "The 1940s: A Milieu for Integrationist Poetics." From *Urban Rage in Bronzeville,* copyright 1999 by B.J. Bolden, reprinted by permission of Third World Press Inc., Chicago, Illinois.

Wolfgang Karrer, "Black Modernism? The Early Poetry of Jean Toomer and Claude McKay." From *Jean Toomer and the Harlem Renaissance,* Fabre, Genevieve and Feith, Michel, eds. Copyright © 2001 by Rutgers University. Reprinted by permission of Rutgers University Press.

James Smethurst, "The Adventures of a Social Poet: Langston Hughes from the Popular Front to Black Power." From *A Historical Guide to Langston Hughes.* © 2004 by Oxford University Press. Reprinted with permission.

Caroline Gebhard, "Inventing a 'Negro Literature': Race, Dialect, and Gender in the Early Work of Paul Laurence Dunbar, James Weldon Johnson, and Alice Dunbar-Nelson." From *Post-Bellum, Pre-Harlem: African American Literature and Culture, 1877–1919.* © 2006 by New York University Press. Reprinted with permission.

Frances Smith Foster, "Creative Collaboration: As African American as Sweet Potato Pie." From *Post-Bellum, Pre-Harlem: African American Lit-*

erature and Culture, 1877–1919. © 2006 by New York University Press. Reprinted with permission.

Keith D. Leonard, "'Bid the Gifted Negro Soar': The Origins of the African American Bardic Tradition." From *Fettered Genius: The African American Bardic Poet from Slavery to Civil Rights,* pp. 19–49. © 2005 The University of Virginia Press.

Paula Bernat Bennett, "Rewriting Dunbar: Realism, Black Women Poets, and the Genteel." From *Post-Bellum, Pre-Harlem: African American Literature and Culture, 1877–1919.* © 2006 by New York University Press. Reprinted with permission.

Lena Ahlin, "The Harlem Renaissance: Depicting the 'New Negro.'" From *The 'New Negro' in the Old World: Culture and Performance in James Weldon Johnson, Jessie Fauset, and Nella Larsen.* © 2006 by Lena Ahlin. Reprinted with permission.

Emily Bernard, "A Familiar Strangeness: The Spectre of Whiteness in the Harlem Renaissance and the Black Arts Movement." From *New Thoughts on the Black Arts Movement,* Collins, Lisa Gail and Crawford, Margo Natalie, eds. Copyright © 2006 by Rutgers University. Reprinted by permission of Rutgers University Press.

James Smethurst, "Lyric Stars: Countee Cullen and Langston Hughes." From *The Cambridge Companion to the Harlem Renaissance.* © 2007 by Cambridge University Press. Reprinted with the permission of Cambridge University Press.

April C.E. Langley, "What a Difference a 'Way' Makes: Wheatley's Ways of Knowing." From *The Black Aesthetic Unbound: Theorizing the Dilemma of Eighteenth-Century African American Literature.* © 2008 by the Ohio State University.

Index

Characters in literary works are indexed by first name (if any), followed by the name of the work in parentheses

DATE DUE
